Sons and Adversaries

Sons and Adversaries

Women in William Blake and D. H. Lawrence

Margaret Storch

The University of Tennessee Press
Knoxville

First Edition.

The paper in this book meets the minimum requirements of the American National Standard for Permanence of Paper for Printed Library Materials. ♾ The binding materials have been chosen for strength and durability.

Library of Congress Cataloging in Publication Data

Storch, Margaret, 1941–
Sons and adversaries : women in William Blake and D.H. Lawrence / Margaret Storch.—1st ed.
p. cm.
Includes bibliographical references.
ISBN 0-87049-656-5 (cloth: alk. paper)
1. Lawrence, D. H. (David Herbert), 1885–1930—Characters—Women. 2. Blake, William, 1757–1827—Characters—Women. 3. Masculinity (Psychology) in literature. 4. Maternal deprivation in literature. 5. Mothers and sons in literature. 6. Psychoanalysis and literature. 7. Women in literature. I. Title.
PR6023.A93Z9244 1990
820.9'352042—dc20 90-31101 CIP

For Rudi
and
For Vanessa and Nicholas

Contents

Illustrations

Preface

Although parallels between Blake and Lawrence have often been noted, no full-length study of this affinity has been published. They are indeed similar in their creative spirit and in their ideals for individual life. Here I focus upon their treatment of women and upon accompanying images of masculinity and themes of male bonding; response to women and to male identity is, I believe, the central issue for each man. These two artists stir powerful reactions in many people because they are in close touch with the sources of love and hate in all of us. I suggest that the emotional patterns emerging from their works have far-reaching cultural importance.

The theoretical basis of my study is object-relations psychoanalysis, specifically, the ideas of Melanie Klein. Although Klein was working within the Freudian school, she advanced certain parts of Freud's theory significantly, notably in opening up our understanding of the early phases of life and in throwing light upon the deepest, most permanent layers of the psyche. Klein envisages human development in terms of a dynamic drama of conflicts surrounding internalized fantasy objects that we never truly outgrow. Since she explores the foundations of human nature, her views can be especially revealing when used to investigate works of art. Neither Blake nor Lawrence has previously been studied extensively in the light of Kleinian psychoanalysis.

My reading of Blake here had its inception in two papers published in the early eighties. In "Blake and Women: 'Nature's Cruel Holiness'" (1981),[1] I argue that despite Blake's conscious sympathy for women's social disabilities, his work is informed by an antipathy towards women that reveals itself in split images of menacing women; defensive fantasies of enclosing wombs; phallic female forms; and the notion of men as primary beings who give birth to women, their ***emanations***, only to reabsorb them in the perfected state of redemption. In "The 'Spectrous Fiend' Cast Out: Blake's Crisis at Felpham" (1983), I took these perceptions further in examining Blake's oedipal conflicts, his projection of an ideal father, and his presentation of the bond of brotherhood forged in blood and phallic strength.[2]

Although psychoanalytic theory has sometimes been applied to Blake, this has usually been with the assumption that Blake himself was an actual and deliberate precursor of modern psychoanalysis. Few commentators have confronted the existence of unconscious material within Blake himself. Thus, Daniel Majdiak and Brian Wilkie in "Blake and Freud: Poetry and Depth Psychology,"[3] suggest that Blake arrived independently at Freud's major theories but differed from Freud in his belief that in the oedipal situation the father, and not the son alone, experiences jealousy. Diana Hume George's *Blake and Freud* (1980),[4] is the first full-length study of Blake to relate psychoanalytic theory to his work. Again, George does not deal with Blake's unconscious fantasies but asserts that he anticipated some important parts of Freud's theory and revised Freud in certain problematic areas. George is acute and discerning in her comments on psychoanalytic patterns in Blake's earlier poems, giving an illuminating defense of both Freud's and Blake's view of women. I cannot, however, agree with her that Blake's feelings about women were predominantly positive.

It is probably true that Blake, like other Romantic poets, notably Wordsworth, was aware of the workings of the unconscious in a way that begins to resemble modern psychoanalysis. However, there is a difference in kind between an analyst's formulation of theory and the revelation of the motifs of the inner self that we find in art. As I suggested in my earlier papers, Blake has an urgent emotional involvement with his themes and dramatic enactments: his perceptions about human nature are ultimately perceptions about himself.

Brenda Webster's *Blake's Prophetic Psychology*, published in 1983,[5] was a landmark in Blake studies, presenting for the first time a comprehensive Freudian psychoanalytic study[6] of Blake's work. In her book, and in a later paper, "Blake, Women, and Sexuality,"[7] Webster gives a wide-ranging and coherent view of psychic patterns fundamental to Blake's poetry and visual art. She finds that Blake was "psychosexually involved in his work to the highest degree"[8] and that he demands Freudian interpretation because many of the psychic paradigms central to Freud are present in his work. She believes that he had a strong sense of guilty aggression towards sexuality and parent figures; that fantasy and defense form much of the texture and coherence of his later works; and that in his plea for freedom from repression, he was driven by a compulsion that shows him to be quite *unliberated*. In "Blake, Women and Sexuality," she notes that Blake characteristically deals with oedipal dreams and adolescent emotional states, and that his male figures are incapable of mature love.[9]

Webster and I both find in Blake a deep animosity towards women, linked with a feeling of maternal deprivation, against which he defends himself by idealized masculinity and male bonding. I am indebted to her thorough and detailed analysis of Blake's poetry and visual art for many illuminating insights and connections. My own contribution is to apply Kleinian theory to the study of Blake – a theory that gives us an especially fine-honed method for investigating ambivalent or conflicting feelings related to the mother figure.

Lawrence has, from the beginning, more readily attracted psychoanalytic comment than has Blake, largely on account of his partial self-analysis in *Sons and Lovers* and his polemical theorizing in both *Fantasia of the Unconscious* and *Psychoanalysis and the Unconscious*. Earlier psychoanalytic studies, notably Daniel Weiss's *Oedipus in Nottingham*,[10] were essentially Freudian. I suggest, most particularly in my discussion of the supposedly classically Freudian text *Sons and Lovers*, that Kleinian theory, with its capacity to probe the most fundamental layers of the psyche, reveals to us deeper elements in Lawrence's emotional life.

A number of more recent critics have applied post-Freudian theory to Lawrence. Marguerite Beede Howe in *The Art of the Self in D.H. Lawrence*[11] draws eclectically upon the work of psychoanalysts of several schools, including Erikson, Jung, and Laing. Existential anxieties, Howe suggests, are at the heart of Lawrence's work; thus, he develops his own "psychology of the ego," in that in each of his novels he attempts to create a self that can withstand the demands of reality. She notes that "escape from the mother appears as a theme in nearly every Lawrence novel."[12] Using object-relations theory, I show in depth what lies behind this relationship with the engulfing mother, and the son's feelings of masculine inadequacy.

In *D.H. Lawrence and the Devouring Mother: The Search for a Patriarchal Ideal of Leadership*,[13] Judith Ruderman gives a fine study of Lawrence's ideal of masculine leadership, locating its source in a fear of maternal destructiveness emanating from the preoedipal phase of development. She and I concur in finding a necessary connection between Lawrence's exaggeration of male power and his fear of the female, a connection that is also noted and compellingly examined by Cornelia Nixon in her nonpsychoanalytic study, *Lawrence's Leadership Politics and the Turn Against Women*.[14] Ruderman and I differ markedly, however, in our fundamental methods. Her notion of the "devouring mother" is a global one, derived from Freud, Erikson, and Jung. For me, the specifics of Kleinian theory offer a more subtle and exact tool for critical interpretation. Klein's concept of splitting; of the defenses that the child constructs in order to withstand the threat of annihilation; of the feminine position; and of the child's inversion of aggression all make clear to us the significance of dominant themes within Lawrence. Furthermore, Klein's placing of the oedipal phase at an earlier stage of development than Freud assigns to it reveals a special association between infantile aggression, fear of independence, erotic attachment, and assumption of gender role.

Daniel Dervin, in *A "Strange Sapience": The Creative Imagination of D.H. Lawrence*,[15] applies to Lawrence the insights of object-relations psychoanalysis, especially those of Winnicott and Balint. While his use of theory is learned and perceptive, Dervin tends to focus upon Lawrence's life and personal development. My interest, rather, is Lawrence's writing, since creative art is the most genuine and accurate reflection of the inner psyche. In Blake and Lawrence, I find manifestations of private motifs that, in establishing a link between two major artistic figures, also contribute to our understanding of representations of women and men in modern society.

Acknowledgments

I am grateful to David Fedo, Barbara Paul-Emile and Aileen Ward for their unfailing support and encouragement throughout the time I have been working on this project. I am also indebted to Gillian Gill for reading parts of the manuscript, and for many discussions in which I benefited from her acute insights and her knowledge of feminist psychoanalytic theory. Martin Green has also generously shared ideas and made valuable suggestions. My colleagues Dennis Flynn and Alicia Nitecki have read parts of the manuscript and made very helpful comments.

I would like to express my gratitude to the staff of the Solomon Baker Library, Bentley College, for their expertise and resourcefulness, with special thanks to Lindsey Carpenter; and also to the staff of the Wessell Library, Tufts University, for their courteous assistance. I am most thankful to Mary Daly, Ruth Gural, and Mary Jellis for their gracious help in preparing the manuscript. I also express my appreciation to Carol Orr, Lee Sioles, and Jean Slattery of the University of Tennessee Press for their support, and for being such pleasant people to work with.

I am grateful to David Erdman for his vast and wise Blake scholarship. For permission to quote from the works of D.H. Lawrence, I thank the estate of Mrs. Frieda Lawrence Ravagli, and Laurence Pollinger, Ltd.; the Cambridge University Press; and Viking Penguin, Inc. I also wish to thank Otto Weininger for allowing me to reprint in part of chapter 5 material already published in *The Journal of the Melanie Klein Society*, and Dennis Jackson for allowing me to reprint in chapter 3 material already published in *The D.H. Lawrence Review*. For permission to reproduce illustrations by William Blake, I am grateful to the Trustees of the British Museum; the

Trustees of the British Library; the Houghton Library, Harvard University; and the Museum of Fine Arts, Boston.

My greatest debt is to my husband, Rudolf Storch, the most discerning and honest reader I know, for many invaluable discussions of my central ideas and for suggestions about parts of the manuscript, as well as for his moral and practical support. The book is dedicated to him, and also to our daughter, Vanessa, and our son, Nicholas, in the hope that as adults they will live in a world in which women and men understand each other better.

Key to References

KEY TO BLAKE REFERENCES

All quotations from Blake's poetry and prose are taken from *The Complete Poetry and Prose of William Blake*, edited by David V. Erdman, newly revised edition. Page references to this edition are given at the beginning of each citation, preceded by an E. The titles of works cited are abbreviated as follows:

A	*America, a Prophecy*
Bol	*The Book of Los*
Eu	*Europe*
FZ	*Vala* or *The Four Zoas*
J	*Jerusalem*
M	*Milton*
Th	*The Book of Thel*
T	*Tiriel*
U	*The [First] Book of Urizen*
VDA	*Visions of the Daughters of Albion*

References are ususally to a plate number, followed by a line number or numbers, e.g., E176–77; *J*30, 25–40 means *Jerusalem* plate 30, lines 25 to 40, found on pages 176 to 177 of the Erdman newly revised edition. *The Four Zoas*, originally known as *Vala*, was not engraved but exists only in manuscript; therefore in the case of this work references are made not to plate numbers but to pages in the *Vala* manuscript, as given in the Erdman text. Thus E354; *FZ*VII, 79, 3–6 means Night the Seventh of *The Four Zoas*, lines 3 to 6 of page 79 of the *Vala* manuscript, found on page 354 of Erdman.

KEY TO LAWRENCE REFERENCES

Bibliographical information about editions of the works of Lawrence to which reference is made is given on pages 211–12. The titles of works cited are abbreviated as follows:

CFN	*A Collier's Friday Night*
FU	*Fantasia of the Unconscious*
PS	*The Plumed Serpent*
PsyU	*Psychoanalysis and the Unconscious*
R	*The Rainbow*
StM	*St. Mawr*
SL	*Sons and Lovers*
WL	*Women in Love*
WP	*The White Peacock*

Sons and Adversaries

CHAPTER 1

Introduction

William Blake and D. H. Lawrence are close to the center of the modern radical imagination. They both speak for an ideal—of the integrity of the individual and of the unity of instinct and thought—that gains ready recognition among those who are bent on nurturing humanistic values in our increasingly mechanized and abstracting society. Lawrence, in his lifetime, always seemed to be a spokesman, however idiosyncratic or controversial, for the freeing of the individual from cant and conformity. Blake's importance was not fully recognized until the twentieth century. In the sixties, he was enthusiastically acclaimed as a major artistic voice: here, it seemed, ready-formed and awaiting interpretation, was a body of art containing all the essential elements of a vision of integrated personal wholeness in a free social setting, an image of an ideal future produced in the past.

Both men were formed by the English dissenting tradition, an important source for the radical social and political ideas of the nineteenth and twentieth centuries. How revealing then are the emotional responses towards women of these two male artists who apparently represent the essential spirit of individual liberation? The radical dissenting imagination was committed at the rational, surface level to improving the condition of both sexes but was actually fired by deeper psychological needs that produced reform in the image of men alone, not perceiving the imperfect situation of women.

Both Blake and Lawrence are strikingly ambivalent in their treatment of women. On the one hand, each is unusually sensitive to the feminine experience. Blake, in the early paintings *The Penance of Jane Shore* and *A*

Breach in the City Wall, interpreted historical events in the light of female response. In his *Visions of the Daughters of Albion*, he presents a critique of the debased and exploited position of women in the 1790s, recognizing that it is a facet of capitalism, class division, and religious oppression. Lawrence, initially as a result of his unusual closeness to his mother, represents women's feelings and responses with sympathetic insight, for instance, the personal growth and work experience of Alvina in *The Lost Girl* and the depiction of mothers struggling with poverty in *The White Peacock*, "Odour of Chrysanthemums," and *Sons and Lovers*. Through women activists in his own Midlands society and then through his wife, Frieda, he was in contact with the most advanced views of his day regarding the situation of women. Because he realized that the needs of the women of his generation were a paramount social issue, he made *The Rainbow* the story of a woman moving towards the right to her own history and freedom from biological servility.

The keen sensitivity to women shown by Blake and Lawrence is only a part of the total pattern of feelings surrounding women manifested in the work of each artist. Each also has a powerful antipathy towards women, readily recognized in Lawrence, especially since the publication of Kate Millett's *Sexual Politics*,[1] but not so often perceived in Blake. Lawrence's natural sympathy for and identification with women is at variance with his urgent statement of the need for the total submission of women to male phallic power. The dichotomy is often found within the same work, where the creation of a strong independent woman, such as Ursula Brangwen in *Women in Love*, Lou Carrington in *St. Mawr*, or Kate Leslie in *The Plumed Serpent*, is matched all the more readily by a superior male force: the tough resistance of Birkin, the ideal of unassailable maleness symbolized by St. Mawr, and the total masculine assurance and independence of Don Cipriano. In Blake, too, there is a contradiction between his sympathetic view of women at the sociological level and the emotional animosity that lies behind his characterizations of women in most of his major poetry. In his symbolic world, the prevailing tone is one of masculine activity. Women, as emanations, are subservient to men since they have no true existence except in the divided state of the male psyche; they are customarily associated with fluidity and vagueness, while Blake attaches moral value to "the definite." Furthermore, in both Blake and Lawrence, we find strong male relationships opposing the tendency to be drawn into the female orbit: the powerful sense of "brotherhood" and the illustrations of homosexual fellatio in Blake's *Milton* correspond to the ideal brotherhood of *The Plumed Serpent* and the repeated close male relationships in Lawrence: Birkin–Gerard, Aaron–Lilly, Don Ramon–Don Cipriano.

The two men show a similar pattern of development in their depictions of women and of heroic masculinity. The sympathetic critique of women's social position comes early in their respective careers, followed by images of animosity towards women in middle or later phases of life. This progression in Lawrence has been extensively documented.[2] In Blake studies, the phenomenon has been less thoroughly examined.[3] Yet in several important respects, Blake reveals close parallels with Lawrence.

Lawrence's changed attitude towards women is usually attributed to social and political causes. Hilary Simpson relates his increasing antifeminism to his contact with the women's suffrage movement and to a deepening of feeling against women on the part of men in general, during and immediately following the First World War, in reaction to a perception of women's enhanced social power.[4] Cornelia Nixon studies, in depth, the writings Lawrence was working on during and after 1915, the period when he "turned against" women. She attributes his dramatically changed outlook to intense personal pressure brought on by the war and by the banning of *The Rainbow*,[5] but she believes that the most significant cause of his antifeminism and of the right-wing political views that he also began to manifest at this time, was his denial of his latent homosexuality.[6]

Likewise, Sandra M. Gilbert and Susan Gubar, in their major study of the condition of women and women writers in the twentieth century, *No Man's Land*, attribute a new form of male hostility towards women to anxiety caused by changes in women's social position in the modern world.[7]

Blake, too, was in contact with strong feminist opinion in his early artistic career. He was acquainted with Mary Wollstonecraft and other prominent radicals in the 1780s and early 1790s when he belonged to the circle of Joseph Johnson, the left-wing bookseller.[8] *Visions of the Daughters of Albion* and other works reflect views of marriage and of the exploitation of women, if not of women's true social equality with men, which would have been acceptable to Wollstonecraft and to William Godwin.[9] The hostile images of women that appear in the epics from the early 1790s on may, perhaps, be associated with a male reaction against an apparent new threat posed by increasing female power, as Gilbert and Gubar suggest was the case in the late nineteenth and early twentieth centuries.[10]

Sociohistorical explanations of changes in male attitudes are convincing and necessary. Are they, however, enough? Can external events or experiences actually transform a person's point of view, unless they appeal to elements deep within the personality that have hitherto been hidden? If new themes and modes of expression emerged in Blake and Lawrence at specific moments in their lives, was it not because external circumstances laid bare a self previously concealed but implicit in an earlier creative phase? Indeed, as the following chapters suggest, in both of these artists, animosity and ambivalence towards women are apparent, although not explicit, in their work from the very beginning.

The conflicts and contradictions in the attitudes towards women of both Blake and Lawrence are an essential part of the complexity of their art and must be accepted as contradictions. It is an oversimplification to attempt to smooth away the paradoxes. A true ambivalence exists in each; furthermore, it is a reflection of an ambivalence towards women that has particular features in modern society and may be universal. In many societies, women are loved and hated, adored and feared. The care and nurturing of mothers is essential to early human development, but the infant, in order to attain independent personhood, must struggle against the loving maternal ties. The struggle is all the more acute for boys, who because of their sex difference are drawn more closely to the mother and must then forge an individual self in the image of a sex distinct from that of the mother.

In *The Reproduction of Mothering*, Nancy Chodorow investigates how a female psychology of life is formed and, by implication, how a male psychology is formed and is distinct from it. She shows how boys in the modern family, from early industrial times, are likely to form a particularly close emotional bond with the mother, since authority within the home has shifted from father to mother. Because the father is more remote emotionally and is often not present as a stable model, boys have difficulty achieving masculinity and frequently need to idealize and fantasize it.[11]

Heinz Kohut gives a psychoanalytic explanation of the role that fantasy may play in male development, which complements Chodorow's. He states that a child who has a weak, absent, or depreciated parent of the same sex—preventing strong gender development—will tend to create and maintain a "grandiose" sense of self. Behind this "grandiose self" lies the deeper imago of the "dangerous, powerful rival-parent," for boys the mother.[12]

Kohut's description seems to correspond to elements in the affective pattern of both Blake and Lawrence. Their ambivalence towards women is accompanied by a struggle on the part of each with paternal authority,[13] which is resolved in an image of powerful masculine supremacy, apparent, for instance, in Blake's *Milton* and Lawrence's *The Plumed Serpent*. For both men, the bitterness at dependence upon women remains, but animosity against the father is transformed into a sense of triumphant maleness.

The impetus against this "dangerous and powerful" mother who threatens to overshadow the grandiose idealized male is sharply focused in the notion of the "Female Will" that we find in both writers. The term is used by Blake to denote the presence and effect of abstract thinking in society, culminating in the Enlightenment, all of which he believes is a great evil. He links cold and destructive abstraction with women's dominance of men. Los, in chapter 2 of *Jerusalem*, bemoans this condition as he addresses the Sons of Albion:

> What may Man be? who can tell! But what may Woman be?
> To have power over Man from Cradle to corruptible Grave.
> There is a Throne in every Man, it is the Throne of God
> This Woman has claimd as her own & Man is no more!
> Albion is the Tabernacle of Vala & her Temple
> And not the Tabernacle & Temple of the Most High
> O Albion why wilt thou Create a Female Will?
> To hide the most evident God in a hidden covert, even
> In the shadows of a Woman & a secluded Holy Place. . . .
> Is this the Female Will O ye lovely Daughters of Albion. To
> Converse concerning Weight & Distance in the Wilds of Newton & Locke.
> (E176–77; *J*30, 25–40)

Lawrence also criticizes the effects of arid rationalization in his society and considers that women, or mothers, are the source of it. The child, instead of living from the dark unconscious lower centers of the body, is subjected to idealism, an exaggerated form of parental love, of which the strongest and most perverse form is an overbearing and sentimentalized mother love, leading in adult life to "sex in the head" and a loss of contact with the primary self. As Blake considers that a power stemming from women is responsible for the rationalist aberrations of Enlightenment society, so Lawrence gives us his version of the Female Will when he locates, in an arid intellectualism set in motion by female possessiveness, the evils of war and amoral technology in the early twentieth century:

> The poor modern brat, shoved horribly into life by an effort of will, and shoved up towards manhood by every appliance that can be applied to it, especially the appliance of the maternal will, is really too pathetic to contemplate. The only thing that prevents us wringing our hands is the remembrance that the little devil will grow up and beget other similar little devils of his own, to invent more aeroplanes and hospitals and germ-killers and food-substitutes and poison-gases. The problem of the future is a question of the strongest poison gas. Which is certainly a very sure way out of our vicious circle.
>
> (*FU*, 143–4)

This association of female influences with abstract empiricism on the part of both writers is difficult to align with historical actuality. It is also problematic in that it seems to go against most of the popular and familiar interpretations of culture, according to which the realm of reason and abstract thought is seen as masculine, while the general view of femininity is that it is emotional and irrational. Romanticism has been feared because of its fluidity and absorption in nature, but Blake seems to be alone in ascribing a female tone to the Enlightenment. When we turn to the twentieth century and the modernist period, we find that Lawrence has an affinity with male writers of his time who held distinctly masculinist aesthetic views.[14] Although certain strains within modernism, such as a tendency to avoid definition and to lapse into unconsciousness, seem traditionally "feminine," some modernists, notably Pound and the Imagists, deliberately eschew the vague and effeminate in order to forge an art of clear and concrete forms.[15] In his own denigration of female-induced idealism and in his art of concrete sensuousness,[16] Lawrence can be associated with this movement.

The male experience of the female as cold and rationalizing is a repetition in the adult sphere of the fundamental pain and fear experienced by the infant at the loss of close sensory contact with the mother. The emptiness and aridity he feels threaten to annihilate him, and he must therefore project them away from himself and into the body of the mother. The condition to which Blake and Lawrence give expression is one that is common to humanity: the loss of direct sensuous contact with the mother for a more abstract state of being is a painful experience, even though it also marks a triumph of independence and selfhood. But this male distrust of the nonphysical is extreme. By a mechanism of inversion, resentment for the aggressive mother is transformed into the feeling that it is she who is insubstantial and abstract, while the male assumes the role of tough creative reformer, defending the realm of vivid and highly defined substantiality against decay and disintegration. The mother is banished from the world of solid forms because she threatens to banish her son from this state. Furthermore, the negation and insubstantiality that the male associates with women are projections of castration fear, whereby the female parent dominates the male parent and prevents the son's identification with masculinity. The vagueness and mistiness that veil women in Blake and the idealism that surrounds them in Lawrence conceal the son's fear of the absence of maleness.

My investigation of these themes is illuminated by the work of the object-relations school of psychoanalysis associated with Melanie Klein and Donald Winnicott, which focuses upon the fundamental relationship between mother and infant at a prelinguistic, almost biological, level. The intricacies of the dualistic relationship between mother and child have been set forth in detail by Melanie Klein, and have a particular bearing on the conflicts surrounding women in Blake and Lawrence, and indeed in modern society as a whole. Both Blake and Lawrence have been discussed in terms of Freudian theory, an approach that is appropriate to the triadic oedipal themes present in their work. In the final version of *Sons and Lovers*, Lawrence applies a knowledge of Freud—partly learned from Frieda—in his analysis of his own emotional life;[17] Blake presents us with several versions of the oedipal situation, most obviously the rebellious son's struggles against the father.[18] However, Melanie Klein's theories of pre-oedipal developments and her refinements of classical Freudianism give a special insight into the very ambivalence towards women with which we are concerned. In her account of the emergence of an independent ego from the parental symbiosis of earliest infancy, Melanie Klein defines several stages through which the child passes, and several mechanisms that are adopted to protect the self. The poles between which the child moves are total omnipotence in union with a nurturing mother and the terror of total annihilation, or loss of the mother. The fundamental situation giving rise to anxiety is the mother's withdrawal of nurturance and the infant's own overwhelming feelings of aggression against its mother in a state of frustrated desire. The principal defensive device is "splitting," whereby, when anger and destructiveness threaten to destroy the ego—for example, when the mother withholds food from the infant—the child in fantasy will split the mother or, at an earlier phase of object-relations development, the breast, into a good part and a bad part.[19] The infant attempts to assimilate or introject the idealized good part, while he projects the hateful bad part so that it may not harm the ideal good object.[20] Thence a fantasy image develops of a good mother and a bad mother, each an aspect of the actual mother. The infant's perception of the nurturing good mother is modified by an accompanying experience of the bad mother, who sometimes withdraws her comfort and nurture, leaving the child in a state of painful loss. The child's mental world, thus constructed, remains as the foundation of adult patterns of emotion: intense love conflicts with powerful impulses of hatred and destructiveness, as a result of which both love and hate are colored by guilt.

This notion of the mother split into a good and a bad part corresponds to conflicting images of women in many cultures,[21] and also to some of the ambivalence in Blake and Lawrence; in Blake, we note benign female figures such as Ololon and Jerusalem set against the menacing Tirzah–Enion–Vala who causes the atrophy of man's mind and senses and wreaks sadistic violence upon him. In Lawrence, we find harmonious and empathic portrayals of women together with powerfully menacing women whom he attempts to subjugate in an overbearing or sadistic manner, as in *Women in Love* and *The Plumed Serpent*.

Object-relations psychology is especially appropriate for inquiries into art since it links creativity with guilt and the urge to make reparation. Klein notes two major phases, or configurations, of anxieties and defenses in early development. The first of these is the paranoid-schizoid position, during which the infant is not yet capable of recognizing whole objects, and directs powerful hatred and aggression against parts of the mother's body as a result of frustration and envy. This is followed by the depressive position, when the child recognizes and relates to the mother. He then feels guilt and wishes to restore and preserve the good object through mourning and reparation.[22] It is at this stage that the ability to form symbols develops,[23] together with the urge and capacity to create.[24]

Klein differs from classical Freudianism in that she places the beginning of the oedipal phase considerably earlier than does Freud: at the period of development when the child is becoming aware of its individual existence and of its parents as separate beings.[25] If the threatening mother imago at this stage overpowers the son's experience of the father, then the son will have difficulties in forming his male identity and will, indeed, experience a sense of emptiness and castration fear, leading him to link the female with abstraction and aridity. Klein also notes a "feminine position" as a phase of development in boys, meaning an envy of the mother's womb and of her capacity to bear children.[26] This envy of the womb may have effects of two kinds relevant to the development of male artists: it gives rise to destructive fantasies against the mother's body for which castration is feared as punishment, and it causes the male to tend to overvalue both intellectualism and masculinity in compensation for the lack of a womb and the capacity for biological creativity. As Klein says: "The amalgamation of the desire for a child with the epistemophilic impulse enables a boy to effect a displacement on to the intellectual plane; his sense of being at a disadvantage is then concealed and over-compensated by the superiority he deduces from his possession of a penis, which is also acknowledged by girls."[27]

These general elements in the infant-mother relationship are probably universal but will be particularly intense and all-encompassing at some periods in the history of certain societies. Object-relations psychoanalysis gained ascendancy in the 1940s when there was renewed emphasis upon the family and the position of the mother in the home.[28] It is likely that the mother-child relationship also took on special value in the later decades of the eighteenth century when the pattern of the nuclear family and a new ethos of the family were emerging.[29] The rise of industrialism wrought changes upon family life that made the relationship between women and children more intense and all-encompassing than it had been in earlier phases of society.[30] As the work place became increasingly distinct from the home, women were more exclusively identified with the home and domestic values and, consequently, with the more personal and intimate areas of life.

Blake and Lawrence were born almost one hundred and thirty years apart, Blake in London in 1757, and Lawrence in Eastwood, Nottinghamshire, in 1885. Even so, there are similarities in the background of each that bind them together and make them valuable exemplars of certain kinds of social experiences as well as powerful spokespersons for particular responses to their social situations. Both grew up in the British dissenting tradition, and both lived at a time when rapid economic developments were having a far-reaching effect upon the fabric of social life: Blake during the first phase of the industrial revolution, Lawrence when a more advanced stage of industrialism at the end of the nineteenth century brought about further erosion of traditional forms. Each man was distinguished for being, in his own lifetime, an outstanding critic of the effects of these economic changes upon the individual and society.

Compared to our copious biographical information about Lawrence, what we know about Blake's life, particularly his early life, is fragmentary and unreliable.[31] We do know that his father was a hosier with his own modest business, who probably experimented with membership in several religious groups, mainly of the dissenting type, although there is some evidence that he was buried in the Church of England.[32] William Blake divorced himself early from organized Christianity, although he had a strong personal faith. As a young man, he was probably for a time a member of the Swedenborgian church, and later in his career, in his defense of John Hunt, showed a strong sympathy for Methodism. The pattern of religious loyalties of both Blake and his father seems erratic but has a unifying element: a passionate commitment to faith and a sympathy for religious groups who invited persecution or isolation from the majority.

Lawrence, too, grew up in a family with a strong dissenting background and an exceptionally lively and positive commitment to religious faith.[33] His father was a coal miner in Eastwood and his mother a woman of better education and higher social class than her husband. Her father was an engineer who became a dockyards foreman; he was an enthusiastic Wesleyan preacher and may also have been associated with the foundation of the Salvation Army.[34] Although Lawrence as an adult repudiated Christianity, the moral seriousness of his critique of society always reflected his dissenting orientation.[35]

As sons of dissenting families, Blake and Lawrence were heirs to a particularly strong emotional bond with women. The more centralized emotional function of women within the family in modern industrial society was predated by developments in the nonconformist family, the dissenting ethos itself having helped to prepare the way for the economic and social values of industrialism. The new sex roles in the family had been established within puritan culture a considerable time before they became widespread throughout society. In the puritan or dissenting ethos, woman did indeed have a more valued status, but her authority extended over a limited terrain. In the seventeenth century, the family came to be recognized as a self-contained sphere of personal life, where the husband was a reflection of God's authority, and the wife, his helpmate, held a subordinate place in the structure. As Eli Zaretsky notes, "The emergence of personal life encouraged a sense of self-assertion and individual uniqueness among men while assigning women to the newly discovered worlds of childhood, emotional sensibility, and compassion, all contained within women's 'sphere,' the family."[36] In the puritan tradition, the stress upon inner experience and personal relations was particularly great; therefore, as the mother became the center of the home, her emotional hold over her children was powerful. The biological bonds between mother and child were tightened as a result of cultural complexities. In a religious household, the mother was the principal means of transmitting religious values which, in the puritan tradition, were of two strong and conflicting types: the strictness of the moral code and spiritual elevation. E.P. Thompson refers to a "Sabbath emotionalism" set against the harshness and self-discipline of the working weekday, encouraging a fiercely repressed and sublimated emotional life.[37] Blake's isolated childhood memories reflect such a dichotomy. His early biographers relate that he was angrily punished by both his mother and his father for claiming to have had visionary experiences.[38] He makes his adult criticism of political and social oppression as one who stands back appalled at what he rationally observes, but who also understands in his own being the restrictions and moral injunctions. Lawrence's portrait of the mother in *The White Peacock* and *Sons and Lovers* as a high-minded puritanical woman, firmly in control of the home and her children's emotions, reflects the reality of family life, while Lawrence's intense responses to nature and personal relations display the psychological consequences of those early bonds.

A further quality that the two men share is that each righteously feels himself to be a reformer who stands apart from the majority. For both of them, this was exacerbated by an actual personal battle against persecution, Blake's against Schofield's accusation of treason, and Lawrence's against the repeated suspicion that he was a German spy during the First World War. The ability to stand alone as a terrible prophet guided by the burning light of faith and conscience has a source in the spirit of the Old Testament, sanctioned by puritanism.

Both Blake and Lawrence grew up in a social setting that, in combination with their personal qualities, is particularly likely to produce a radical thinker. In English society, the dissenting background itself automatically sets up a mental perspective critical of the establishment. Each man was exposed through circumstances to other strata of society, Blake through his apprenticeship to an engraver and early acquaintance with the world of artists, Lawrence through the conflicting social backgrounds of his parents. Each man was also, by reason of extraordinary talent, drawn early into a world of values distinct from those he had inherited. Furthermore, each lived at a period of history when the social structure of his own childhood was being eroded around him. Blake saw the integrity of the life of a self-employed artisan such as his father (a life Blake tried to repeat himself with bitter consequences) destroyed by the factory system. Lawrence, as he tells us in detail in *Women in Love, Lady Chatterley's Lover*, and in the 1926 essay "Nottingham and the Mining Countryside," saw the relative cohesiveness of the personal and working lives of his father's contemporaries fragmented during a new development in industrial economic management that led in the direction of automation. These circumstances, in combination with the highest powers of critical insight and sensitivity in each man, prepared the ground for two especially acute radical thinkers. Yet these two social critics and advocates for a transformation of personal life display distinct elements of animosity towards women. They illustrate within the radical imagination an ambivalence that helps to account for a lack of acknowledgment of the needs of women as free individuals even in the more enlightened reaches of modern society.

In noting a kinship between Blake and Lawrence, we should consider the later artist's response to the work of his predecessor. Lawrence knew well Blake's earlier poetry, including *The Marriage of Heaven and Hell*, and also his visual art. There is no clear evidence that he had read the epics extensively and, indeed, since Keynes's edition of Blake's writings was not published until 1921, it is perhaps unlikely that he had read them systematically.[39] The essential point is that the two men share a striking affinity in creative spirit and personal values,[40] which springs from fundamental temperament rather than from one's "influence" upon the other.

In his various comments on Blake, Lawrence reveals his notorious, irascible inconsistency. He sometimes speaks disparagingly of him, as in his essay on Poe and in a letter to Frederick Carter written in January 1924.[41] In "Introduction to These Paintings," his preface to the 1929 Mandrake Press edition of his own paintings, however, he singles out Blake as the sole English painter since the Renaissance who does not feel horror at bodily experience: "There is the exception of Blake. Blake is the only painter of imaginative pictures, apart from landscape, that England has produced. And unfortunately there is so little Blake, and even in that little the symbolism is often artificially imposed. Nevertheless, Blake paints with real intuitional awareness and solid instinctive feeling. He dares handle the human body, even if he sometimes makes it a mere ideograph."[42] The correspondence between the ideals of the two artists, Blake's global, undivided human nature and Lawrence's "intuitional awareness," is manifest.

This passage also makes clear that what Lawrence felt uneasy about in Blake was his emblematic or "allegorical" quality, which was sometimes problematic for Blake himself.[43] An apparent polarity between the two artists is that Lawrence's most desirable state of experience is the "dark consciousness," in fact an unconscious, beyond rational knowing, whereas Blake adheres always to the sharp *outline* of the imagination's control and awareness. However, Blake's wish for total consciousness is fraught with anxiety as each moment of consciousness dissolves into another.[44]

We can probably assume, on the testimony of people who knew him well, that Lawrence's continuing attitude towards Blake was positive. Aldous Huxley's character Rampion in *Point Counter Point*, based upon Lawrence, comments in chapter 9 that Blake was "the last civilized man," by which he means that Blake completely harmonized "Reason, feeling, instinct, the life of the body."[45] In addition, Jessie Chambers agreed with Emile Delavenay that Blake had been an important influence upon Lawrence's ideas.[46]

Blake's and Lawrence's accounts of cultural history do not match in every respect, but they agree in the fundamental perception that there has been a gradual loss of a healthy union of mind and body, stemming from philosophical and religious causes. In Lawrence's terms, this has led to the breakdown of the "organic" and "instinctual" life and, in Blake's, to the notion of the "cavern'd Man," perceiving the world through the chinks of his woefully diminished senses while he suffers the tragic division of his intellect and instincts. In both Blake and Lawrence, there is an acute focus upon "the body" that is the result of each man's tormented personal revolt against his puritan heritage.

In "Introduction to these Paintings," Lawrence gives his own account of a fundamental Blakean notion when he refers to his society's lost capacity to be in living contact with the material world, a capacity almost regained, momentarily, by Cézanne when he painted his apples: "But our world is a wide tomb full of ghosts, replicas. We are all spectres, we have not been able to touch even so much as an apple. Spectres we are to one another. Spectres you are to me, spectre I am to you. Shadow you are even to yourself. And by shadow I mean idea, concept, the abstracted reality, the ego. We are not solid. We don't live in the flesh. Our instincts and intuitions are dead, we live wound round with the winding-sheet of abstraction."[47] Lawrence's description would be acceptable to Blake as an account of fragmented modern man. For both, it is also the reflection of a sense of emptiness grounded upon threatened masculinity, castration fear, and the mother who overpowers the father.

Lawrence's 1915 essays collectively entitled "The Crown" are a key statement of the fundamentally new philosophy he adopted at this time, a philosophy in which the forces of darkness are recognized as an essential element in existence. The terms in which he expressed this concept are analogous to Blake's doctrine of the contraries as he presents it in *The Marriage of Heaven and Hell*: "Without Contraries is no progression. Attraction and Repulsion, Reason and Energy, Love and Hate, are necessary to Human existence" (E34).[48] In "The Crown," Lawrence represents the life-giving conflict between opposing principles by the stable equilibrium of the lion and the unicorn locked in combat, which distinctly resembles Blake's tiger/lamb fusion of opposites.[49] In both artists, this is a difficult and obscure concept; each adheres to the necessity for a faculty—energy in Blake, darkness and dissolution in Lawrence—that flouts conventional views of virtue.

Lawrence uses the same image, now adding the oppositional motif of the tiger and the kangaroo, in *Kangaroo*, a novel that marks an important stage in his agonized withdrawal from society and his submission to myths of leadership and masculine supremacy. The reference occurs in the chapter entitled "Kangaroo" on the occasion of the first meeting between the protagonist, Richard Lovat Somers, and Ben Cooley, known as Kangaroo, the head of an elitist, antidemocratic organization. Kangaroo, an enigmatic, androgynous figure, puts forward his notion of how society should be organized. As if to acknowledge the Blakean context of his ideas, he quotes the first two lines of Blake's "Tyger," and explains to Somers that the tiger, a force of energy, is one of the twin supports of the world: "The tiger stands on one side of the shield, and the unicorn on the other, and they don't fight for the crown at all. They keep it up between them. The pillars of the world! The tiger and the kangaroo!"[50] The emotional dynamic of his sociopolitical belief is explained in an interchange earlier in the discussion. The men refer to the figure of a woman who had been described in a book by a social reformer whom they despised. She unmistakably recalls Gertrude Morel and other women Lawrence had treated sympathetically in his earlier fiction: "the poor elderly woman in a battered black bonnet and a shawl, going out with sixpence ha'-penny to buy a shillingsworth of necessaries for the home" (124). To complete the parallel, Kangaroo comments, "No doubt her husband drank. If he did, who can wonder." The men laugh scornfully at her and the pleasure she takes in her misery, and express the wish to "shove her out of the house—or out of the world." She is the debased mother who, with her powerful frailty and demand for virtue and, significantly for Blake as well as for Lawrence, her demand for *pity*, encroaches upon male independence. When she has been banished from the world that men will now dominate, Kangaroo puts himself forward as the leader of the new political movement. He is a father figure who has also taken into himself the qualities of the female parent: "Man needs a quiet, gentle father who uses his authority in the name of living life" (126). References are made to Kangaroo's consoling Abraham-like bosom and nurturing presence: "His presence was so warm. You felt you were cuddled cosily, like a child, on his breast, in the soft glow of his heart, and that your feet were nestling on his ample, beautiful 'tummy'" (132). Later in the novel, his female qualities predominate, and his demand for love becomes destructive.[51] At this first meeting between Somers and Kangaroo, however, the strong and nurturing father has definite contours.

For both Blake and Lawrence, these two sets of principles are a manifestation of opposing realities. The cataclysmic espousal of the forbidden—Blake's inversion of good and evil and Lawrence's embrace of the dark powers—emanates from the need to crush the emotional demands of female-dominated social laws. The anxiety and instability that surround the psychological condition are reflected in the notion of contrary states held in tension.

Lawrence's sense of his affinity with Blake, with Blake's artistic stance, and with his feelings towards women are illustrated in Jessie Chambers's account of Lawrence's earliest recorded reference to Blake. She describes the occasion as one marked by heightened personal emotion, crystallized in a bunch of snowdrops that Lawrence brought her and asked her to fasten, not in her coat, but close to her face, which she "somehow felt to be a rare compliment." As they continued on their walk, she tells us:

> He talked to me in his rapt way about Blake, telling me what a wonderful man he was, quite poor, who taught himself everything he knew; how he made pictures and wrote poems that were interdependent, and did the printing and engraving himself, in fact producing the book entirely by his own hands. He told me that Blake's wife was a poor girl whom he taught to read, and also to print and engrave, and what a marvelous helpmate she was to him. For a little time we lived with Blake and his wife.[52]

What is reflected in Lawrence's account of Blake to Jessie is an admiration for the earlier artist and his method of working, together with an unexpectedly strong emphasis upon the pattern of his relationship with his wife, Catherine Blake, itself part of his method of working: the ideal is the male artist supported and assisted by an eager, subservient helpmate. In the young woman's account, the episode is imbued with feelings of romantic courtship, leading to the assumption that for both of them the Blakes' relationship was an ideal projection of their potential roles. It was a role that Lawrence later and deliberately fled from, choosing what he then saw as the personal freedom offered by Frieda over Jessie's restricting presence. However, that choice and the possible interpretations of Lawrence's relationship with Jessie are fraught with contradictions. Lawrence's statement about Blake makes it apparent that the role of the creative artist as dominant male had a strong appeal for him. Other episodes in his relationship with Jessie reinforce the impression that he wished to mold a woman intellectually supportive of his needs: he forbade her to read *Wuthering Heights* because it might "upset" her[53] and recommended to her father that he should not allow her to go to college where "They grind them all through the same mill."[54] This autocratic behavior is belied by contrasting strains in his writing and some of his later actions, yet it defines his view of his artistic role as a powerful male. No less is true of Blake–Los bearing witness to his true vision through all social vicissitudes and wielding his active masculine tools of creation, the hammer and the mace, while women passively weave and weep into their veils.

Beyond Lawrence's sympathetic allusions to Blake, there are recurrent themes in the work of the two artists that reflect their fundamental affinity. Both Blake and Lawrence denounced most vehemently the effects of abstract thinking upon society and individual experience. In Lawrence, this is exemplified in the extract quoted from "Introduction to These Paintings" and in the repeated denunciation of the "mechanical" principle in society, as opposed to the "organic." The very structure of Blake's myth of the fall and of the distinctions between the Zoas and, in turn, their Emanations is a cry of regret at the separation of the senses and instincts. The theme is dramatically crystallized in two important figures: Blake's Urizen, the cold, detached personification of dry Reason; and Lawrence's Gerald Crich, the young industrialist in *Women in Love*, who brings the destructive influence of his mechanical theories to the lives and souls of the miners who work for the family firm and who, on account of his own spiritual aridity, cannot forge a deep and lasting relationship with a woman. The resemblance between these two figures, each bearing the weight of the artist's commitment and conviction, has been noted.[55] There is even similarity in the texture of images that surround them. The snowbound mountains in which Gerald dies resemble Urizen's prison described in Night the Seventh of *The Four Zoas*:

> Why shouldst thou sit cold grovelling demon of woe
> In tortures of dire coldness now a Lake of waters deep

Sweeps over thee freezing to solid still thou sitst closd up
In that transparent rock as if in joy of thy bright prison.
(E354; *FZ*VII, 79, 3–6)

The resemblance goes further. Although the values of Gerald and Urizen are despised, each is loved by his creator. Birkin wishes to forge a brotherhood with Gerald and is deeply saddened when the possibility of this bond is removed by Gerald's death. In Blake, there are moments of loving reconciliation with the very Urizen who is the hated oppressive father: at the end of Night the Seventh of *The Four Zoas*, Los perceives Urizen as a helpless infant; and in plate 45 of *Milton*, Urizen, an enfeebled old man, kneels before the protective Milton, the ideal poetic father (see figure 4). For the men who created them, Gerald and Urizen are a projection of the atrophy of male powers and male identity brought about by the failure of the father. Again, this literally icy abstraction is linked with castration fears and with the fantasy of the mother's destruction of sensuous reality.

While vehemently detesting abstraction, the two artists paradoxically show an inclination to express ideas abstractly. Blake, in attacking "systems," himself creates an elaborate system whose minutely wrought details codify experience:

And the Four Points are thus beheld in Great Eternity
West, the Circumference: South, the Zenith: North,
The Nadir: East, the Center, unapproachable for ever.
These are the four Faces towards the Four Worlds of Humanity
In every Man. (E156; *J*12, 54–58)

This is matched by Lawrence's "system" of the four centers of being that he expounds in *Fantasia of the Unconscious* and *Psychoanalysis and the Unconscious*. Like Blake, he uses the human body as his model and reference point. In some of his middle and later novels, for instance, in parts of *Women in Love, Aaron's Rod*, and *The Plumed Serpent*, Lawrence becomes a "novelist of ideas"; his richly sensuous style gives way to a tractlike exposition of philosophies from the mouth of a figure representative of the author, notably Birkin. The two men seize upon abstraction and its effects as a great evil partly because each, in fact, fears his own tendency to abstraction; the shadow of insubstantiality and impotence lurks alongside their vigorous grasp of sensory concreteness.

In their call for the restoration of bodily awareness, Blake and Lawrence are both making a reasoned and perceptive critique of a society damaged by repressive moral attitudes, and of science divorced from human warmth. Yet part of the passion in the plea of each man comes from his personal involvement in the very tendencies being condemned. Alongside their inclination to fall into abstraction, we might remark that their stress upon sexuality is in part an overemphasis occasioned by puritanical elements in their personalities. Some of the need to assert sensual warmth springs from a tenuous grasp of masculinity. Despite Lawrence's mission of liberation, the sexual episodes in his novels do not often create a feeling of eroticism. In *Sons and Lovers*, Paul's sexual experiences with both Miriam and Clara take him to a mystical level beyond physical contact with the individual women, as both of the women realize:

> He lifted his head, and looked into her eyes. They were dark and shining and strange, life wild at the source staring into his life, stranger to him, yet meeting him; and he put his face down on her throat, afraid. What was she? A strong, strange, wild life, that breathed with his in the darkness through this hour. It was all so much bigger than themselves that he was hushed. They had met, and included in their meeting the thrust of the manifold grass stems, the cry of the peewit, the wheel of the stars. (353)

Here sexual union is most truly a union with the fundamental forces of nature that reflects the mother-infant bond rather than an erotic encounter. In the later novels, with the qualified exception of *Lady Chatterley's Lover*, the interest in the sexual relationship is more likely to be concerned with power and social roles than with eroticism; for example, the essential function of the sexual encounters of Kate and Cipriano in *The Plumed Serpent* is to establish the fact of male supremacy.

A major thematic interest uniting Blake and Lawrence is the body, sexuality, and the essential nature of Man and Woman. As Michael G. Ballin says, "There is a sense in which the categories Male and Female constitute the whole of reality for Lawrence and Blake."[56] Each concerns himself extensively with fundamental relationships between men and women, and with definitions of elemental male and female nature. Their dramatic situations enact pure experience, shorn of the restrictions of particular place and time, even though, especially in Lawrence's case, the actualities of place and time can be evoked with astonishing immediacy. His treatment of the marriage of Will and Anna displays his notion of the basic condition of the erotic relationship, in which man is submerged in the overwhelming power of woman. Again and again, in *The Plumed Serpent*, in *Lady Chatterley's Lover*, as well as in essays and in the *Fantasia of the Unconscious*, Lawrence shows an urgent preoccupation with defining the masculine and the feminine, urgent because his sense of his own identity is passionately involved in it. Similarly, the action of Blake's epics reveals with piercing clarity a view of the essence of human nature. There are two intertwined topics in Blake: the spiritual disintegration of humanity, and the forces within the family complex that produce aggression and cruelty. Whether as parent, child, or consort, the characteristic behavior of males and females is the dominant interest. The separation of the Zoas and their Emanations, the aberrations of each while in the separated condition, and the joyful restoration of harmony with the reunion of the female Emanations and various male forms at the end of the three epics are a major focus of emotional intensity.

Each man's recommendations for social reform center upon the body and upon the acceptance of physical human nature. The repression of sexual feelings, Lawrence believes, is a major cause of social ills. He often attacks the superficiality and dishonesty of sexual relations in his own society, for instance, in *St. Mawr*, as a mark of contemporary degeneracy. Blake, too, denounces the conventional social forces that promote fear of sexuality and calls for freedom and spontaneity of erotic relations, perhaps even more extremely than Lawrence.

The terms in which they analyze sexual dishonesty are very similar. Each focuses his attack upon the puritan element in society that has forced sex into secretive repression. Masturbation, that wastes away the vitality of young people, is emblematic of this condition. In "Pornography and Obscenity," Lawrence states that the guardians of society expect young people to masturbate in private instead of having sexual intercourse, and says "But in masturbation there is nothing but loss. There is no reciprocity. There is merely the spending away of a certain force, and no return. The body remains, in a sense, a corpse, after the act of self-abuse. There is no change, only deadening. There is what we call dead loss."[57] Sex, he says earlier in the same essay, "warms us, stimulates us like sunshine on a grey day." The same contrast between the glow of sunshine and the deadness of sensual repression is found in Blake's "Ah! Sunflower": "Where the Youth pined away with desire, / And the pale Virgin shrouded in snow" (*E25*). In *Visions of the Daughters of Albion*, Blake describes a couple engaged in "the self enjoyings of self denial" whom Lawrence would have recognized as the victims of the "grey" puritan guardians:

> The moment of desire! the moment of desire! the virgin
> That pines for man; shall awaken her womb to enormous joys
> In the secret shadows of her chamber; the youth shut up from
> The lustful joy. shall forget to generate. & create an amorous image
> In the shadows of his curtains and in the folds of his silent pillow.
> (E50; *VDA*, 7, 3–7)

While we must applaud the liberating influence upon attitudes to sexuality these two dauntless critics have had, we may note that it was often for the sake of male freedom that they wished to reform society:

> Till they refuse liberty to the male; and not like Beulah
> Where every Female delights to give her maiden to her husband
> The Female searches sea & land for gratification to the Male Genius.
> (E223; *J3*; 69, 14–7)[58]

Each man displays a strong need to feel dominant in his masculinity. In Blake, the fundamental figures in the action of the epics are masculine. Albion, the original human being, "contains" the action of the epics. In the redemptive sequence at the end of *Jerusalem*, the sexes "vanish" and are restored to an original male form, within which the female is encompassed. The female Emanations have no existence except as aspects of the male and are threatening when they try to take on any role except one of subservience:

> How then can I ever again be united as Man with Man
> While thou my Emanation refusest my Fibres of dominion.
> When Souls mingle & join thro all the Fibres of Brotherhood
> Can there be any secret joy on Earth greater than this. (E246; *J88*, 12–15)

While some critics have argued that Blake's use of male figures in conveying his vision is purely metaphorical,[59] we cannot overlook the dominance repeatedly given to the males, and the aggressive force seen in any female who takes positive action. In Blake's poem *Milton*, we can observe most fully the importance of the strong masculine role for Blake and, in this, his parallels with Lawrence. There is a crucial moment of self-realization for Blake in *Milton* when the spirit of Los, the creative artist and reformer of society who is the earthly form of the Zoa Urthona, descends to him and becomes one with him:

> And Los behind me stood; a terrible flaming Sun: just close
> Behind my back; I turned round in terror, and behold.
> Los stood in that fierce glowing fire . . .
> . . . he kissed me and wishd me health.
> And I became One Man with him arising in my strength:
> Twas too late now to recede. Los had enterd into my soul:
> His terrors now posses'd me whole! I arose in fury & strength.
> (E116–7; M22, 6–14)

This episode of male union bringing with it an access of supreme energy, together with some illustrations suggestive of homoeroticism that accompany the poem (plates 45 and 47; See figures 4 and 3), lead to the conclusion that the experience of solidarity with males is essential to Blake's personal esteem and creative purpose.

The Lawrencean work that is closest to *Milton* in this respect is *The Plumed Serpent*. Here, the supreme ideal is one of a masculine brotherhood, found in the movement of Quetzalcoatl, a neo-conservative group that sweeps through Mexico, attacking the repressions of the modern industrialized state and of the church, with the aim of restoring a mystical sense of nature. At the center of the movement are two men, Don Ramon, the new Quetzalcoatl, and Don Cipriano, known as Huitzilopochtli, between whom is the male bond that Lawrence sought to establish in other novels, never so strongly as here. It is clear that in this society male relationships are more vital than heterosexual ones. Kate Leslie, the figure of an independent, liberated Western woman, is gradually brought to accept the supremacy of that relationship and of males through her marriage to Don Cipriano. This strong woman is made to submit to a sex relationship identical to that idealized in *Lady Chatterley's Lover*, in which she must give up her aggressive and "phallic" need for her own orgasmic satisfaction, the "beak-like friction of Aphrodite of the foam": "Her strange, seething feminine will and desire subsided in her and swept away, leaving her soft and powerfully potent, like the hot springs of water that gushed up so noiseless, so soft, yet so powerful, with a sort of secret potency."[60] An early poem by Lawrence, "Virgin Youth," makes apparent some of the reasons behind this urgent need to "belong" to a company of men. The poet speaks sadly of his inability to penetrate a woman, and addresses his "lonely" erect penis:

> Thou dark one, thou proud, curved beauty! I
> Would worship thee, letting my buttocks prance.
> But the hosts of men with one voice deny
> Me the chance.
>
> They have taken the gates from the hinges
> And built up the way.[61]

The young man feels excluded from the world of male sexual prowess, which leads to his later need to dominate women as an aggressive male and to feel that he is at last accepted among other strong males.

One further insistent theme that unites Blake and Lawrence is their denial of the emotion of pity. In Blake, this resistance to pity is well-known. Beginning with "The Human Abstract," he refers to pity as a feeling that feeds upon a negative state and therefore keeps it in being. In *The Book of Urizen*, this is more explicit. Los's feeling of pity for Urizen brings about the divided state in which the "globe of life blood trembling" takes form, thus giving birth to woman, a creature distasteful above all because of her association with pity:

> Wonder, awe, fear, astonishment,
> Petrify the eternal myriads;
> At the first female form now separate
>
> They call'd her Pity, and fled (E78; *U*18, 13–19, 1)

It is at this very moment that the Woof of Science is woven, and thus begins the reign of an abstract system of knowledge.

In Lawrence too, pity has connotations that are both female and negative.[62] Gudrun's feeling of pity for Gerald as *Women in Love* approaches its climax of death is a culmination of her Pietà-like power over him. Earlier in the novel, after the death of his father, Gerald found peace and consolation with Gudrun in the elemental relationship of infant nestling at the mother's breast: "And she, she was the great bath of life, he worshipped her. Mother and substance of all life she was. And he, child and man, received of her and was made whole" (344). At this stage, Gudrun's feelings about the relationship are not sharply clarified: "But an ache like nausea was upon her: a nausea of him" (348). At the end of the novel, it is clear that she despises him for his infantile dependence upon her: "'Ah, I don't want to torture you,' she said pityingly, as if she were comforting a child. The impertinence made his veins go cold, he was insensible. She held her arms round his neck, in a triumph of pity. And her pity for him was as cold as stone, its deepest motive was hate of him, and fear of his power over her, which she must always counterfoil" (443). The scene centers upon a fundamental conflict of the sexes: he has power over her, associated with his mechanical will that wants to assert itself over all forms of life. Her power over him is ultimately stronger and has its source in the pity that Lawrence despises because it signifies man's fundamental need of woman. There is a close parallel with Blake: Gerald, "the god of the machine" who is so much the victim of pity, has through cold Urizenic rationality lost contact with his real feelings; womanly pity is born in *The Book of Urizen* simultaneously with mystery and abstraction. Dread abstraction itself is a manifestation of the male's fear of castration by the overwhelming mother. The father, the image of masculinity, therefore exists as a projection of insubstantiality. The conflicting feelings surrounding pity spring from a wish for protective union with the mother together with angry rejection of the prephallic dependence that would bring.

The way in which each man deals with pity bespeaks a profound antagonism towards women, who are seen as destructive of men's strength and purpose as they triumph over them in pity. Blake and Lawrence attack what, in its positive aspects, is usually regarded as one of the most valuable qualities associated with women, the healing and sustaining power of sympathy. They vehemently deny the loving support of women because in their dependence upon them they fear losing themselves entirely as males. More fundamentally, they oppose pity and interpersonal sympathy because these are attributes of the "good mother" whom they have not internalized. Resistance and antipathy remain.

CHAPTER 2

Patterns of Maternal Loss in Early Blake: The *Songs*

Certain early works of Blake and Lawrence reveal concerns and patterns of feeling that are fundamental to the two artists and yet do not emerge so sharply later. For Blake, this body of work includes the *Songs of Innocence and Experience*, together with drafts of these in the Notebook, and the satiric work *An Island on the Moon*. The *Songs* are among his major creations, although different in imaginative tone from his later mature work. Lawrence's first novel, *The White Peacock*, while not regarded as one of his most successful *oeuvres*, presents with particular clarity the nature of his basic emotional state regarding women. Greater artistic assurance tends to mask the raw state of the feelings. It is likely that an artist's early work will reflect the most urgent concerns of the psyche.

Blake's *Songs* and related poems, together with Lawrence's *The White Peacock*, reveal strong aggression stemming from infantile experience. The early oedipal phase is associated with both the oral and anal phases of development. The "bad" mother is seen as a persecutory agent who, the child fears, will annihilate him; at the same time, in fantasy, he attacks and destroys her with oral, urethral, and anal sadism. Brenda Webster in *Blake's Prophetic Psychology* (9–30) has shown how powerful is the presence of anal sadism in Blake's earlier works. In both the *Songs* and *The White Peacock*, we note recurrent images of helpless children suffering at the hands of cruel parents, and also images of lost children. These are a reflection not so much of direct cruelty on the part of the parents as of the child's inversion of his own unbearable aggression against them.

The great achievement of the first phase of Blake's work is to give a special and unprecedented meaning to the experience of childhood.[1] When we consider that he was writing in a pre-Wordsworthian age, the freshness of his vision of childhood is breathtaking. His response to industrialization and to inhumane, institutionalized religion, while subtle and multifaceted, has always been crystallized in the popular imagination in the figure of a vulnerable child, joyful and eager for love, whose hopes are soon to be cut down by cruelty and repression.

In her book, Brenda Webster suggests that this child is a "clean" child who springs from the need to repress feelings of hostility towards the parents (24–30). While one must recognize strong psychological tensions within these images, one acknowledges first of all the precision of Blake's social insight and its startling originality, sharpened by his personal experience. This image of threatened innocence had a ready and powerful appeal both to Blake's contemporaries and to succeeding generations of readers. It is a personal metaphor with universal dimensions.[2]

At what point are we justified in moving from an acknowledgment of Blake's perceptive and effective social statements to an investigation of the psychological pressures that lie beneath them? When we find insistent and repeated thematic patterns in an artist, it is reasonable to assume that they arise from unconscious sources in the intense psychic struggles of infancy that are never fully resolved in adult life. In Blake, these fantasy paradigms are especially powerful and vivid. The recurrent motifs in the *Songs* and, indeed, throughout his work, refer to relationships between parents and children and to the conflict and pain that surround them. These themes were particularly urgent for Blake and his contemporaries, and for succeeding generations up to the present time, because family bonds have taken on a new intensity since the inception of industrialism. His configurations of family emotions echo feelings about authority vested in a paternalistic religion and state.

The characteristic child in early Blake stands for what is beautiful, innocent, and vulnerable in human experience. At the same time, this child sometimes risks appearing sentimentalized or cloyingly sweet:

He became a little child:
I a child & thou a lamb,
We are called by his name.
  Little Lamb God bless thee.
  Little Lamb God bless thee. (E9)

The quality of exaggerated goodness comes from "idealization," whereby the child, terrified at the destructive impulses that have made the parents or himself disintegrate, creates an image of extreme virtue in order to preserve the goodness that threatens to be annihilated.[3] The child has the unreal innocence imposed upon children by an overpowering religious authority, based on a benign view of God that masks the vindictive divinity who will pounce on any straying from the constrained path of righteousness. It is an injunction for childhood behavior that represses children's spontaneity.

A recurrent motif throughout Blake's earlier works, repeated with more complexity in the epics, is that of the family group, child and parents, torn by conflict or resentment. Tiriel's account of childhood gives an explicit description:

> The child springs from the womb. the father stands ready to form
> The infant head while the mother idle plays with her dog on her couch
> The young bosom is cold for lack of mothers nourishment & milk
> Is cut off from the weeping mouth with difficulty and pain
> The little lids are lifted & the little nostrils opend
> The father forms a whip to rouze the sluggish senses to act
> And scourges off all youthful fancies from the newborn man. (E285; *T* 8, 12–18)

In this deliberate and relatively detached description, the fundamental harshness is the mother's terrible coldness and active refusal to nourish the child, an emotional context that makes possible the father's moral cruelty. Here and elsewhere, the most extreme cruelty is assigned to the mother; and therefore, the strongest anger is directed against her.

A further version of the troubled family constellation is the *Notebook* draft of "Infant Sorrow," of which only the first two stanzas appear in *Songs of Experience*. Again, as in the *Tiriel* extract, the father imposes moral restraints upon the infant. The mother's rejection of the child is less explicit but is reflected in a lack of tenderness in the child's relation to the breast:

> My mother groand! My father wept.
> Into the dangerous world I leapt:
> Helpless, naked, piping loud;
> Like a fiend hid in a cloud.
>
> Struggling in my fathers hands:
> Striving against my swadling bands:
> Bound and weary I thought best
> To sulk upon my mothers breast. (E28)

What is manifest here is the infant's terrifying vulnerability, as well as the distance and coldness of the parents. Melanie Klein refers to the child's fear of annihilation occasioned by a sense of overwhelming persecution from the "bad" parent.[4] Emblematically, this child sulks (rather than "sucks") upon the persecutory breast of the bad mother, the final source of all pain and anger.[5] The child's guilty aggression is embedded in the word "fiend." In that aggressive child "hid in a cloud," we have a reflection of an image that Blake gives us several times: a male figure associated with mistiness, like the white-clad father-God of "The Little Boy Found" or the numinous "Father hovering upon the wind" of "With happiness stretchd across the hills," the poem transcribed in an 1802 letter to Thomas Butts (E721). In "Infant Sorrow," despite the association of restrictive authority with the father, the child through identification with the weak father figure experiences the abstracting and negative influences of the persecuting mother, later to be defined as the Female Will. The mother's castrating power is experienced as emptiness and sensory remoteness. The child assuages the longing for maternal consolation in a fantasy of omnipotence. At the practical level, he employs duplicity, learning to smile or to repress anger and become the unnaturally all-virtuous child of Innocence.

Our understanding of the child's anger and its content are enhanced by studying the seven additional stanzas of "Infant Sorrow" that appear in the Notebook but were omitted from the final engraved version in *Songs of Experience*. These stanzas are heavily revised, suggesting that the emotions underlying them are urgent and complex. The boy grows until he is able to move independently, apparently at ground level:

> And I grew day after day
> Till upon the ground I stray
> And I grew night after night
> Seeking only for delight

On the ground he finds beautiful enticing blossoms, commonly symbolic of erotic desire. A priest, who is a father figure backed by the authority of a repressively virtuous society, prevents him from plucking the blossoms:

> But a priest with holy look
> In his hand a holy book
> Pronouncd curses on his head
> Who the fruit or blossoms shed (E797)

The boy must watch the father-priest embrace the myrtle blossoms "Like a serpent in the night," whereupon "I smote him and his gore / Staind the roots my mirtle bore." This obvious oedipal pattern dramatizes the jealous son acting out his aggression in parricide. Webster comments that Blake here distorts the oedipal situation in his characteristic way, casting the father as a "rapist-thief who takes what rightly belongs to the son" (149).

Another entry in the Notebook, a fragment found on page 111, gives us further information about the emotions that surround the child's relationship with the parents:

> To a lovely mirtle bound
> Blossoms showring all around
> O how sick & weary I
> Underneath my mirtle lie

Blake erased the first two lines and added two others at the end:

> Like to dung upon the ground
> Underneath my mirtle bound (E797)

In the "Infant Sorrow" stanzas in the Notebook, the child simply followed through his desires. In this additional fragment an element of guilt has entered in, guilt both at the parricide fantasy and at the desire to participate in the parents' eroticism. The boy suffers as he lies bound beneath the myrtle, transferring his anger against the father into pain that he himself feels. Since he lies "like to dung" and "upon the ground," we see that he is filled with a lowly shame and a sense of being the despicable filth of his own anal aggression. These are the layers of feeling that lie behind the sulking expression of the baby fiend in the version of "Infant Sorrow" that actually appeared in *Songs of Experience*.

Of special interest is the notion of being bound to a myrtle tree. It is common in Blake to find the image either of both parents or of the father alone binding a child in a very cruel manner. The motif springs from the child's transference of aggression to the parents, and at the same time from his sense of being trapped in frustrated anger. The state of being bound to, or beneath, a myrtle tree signifies frustrated awareness of the parents' own sexuality, an inescapable source of pain and desire. The union of the parents can be symbolized by a tree, reflecting the strength and indivisibility of the parental couple.[6] The specific use of the myrtle reflects special concerns of Blake. The Greeks held this flowering shrub sacred to Venus and also associated it with male heroism. The tree beneath which the boy is guiltily bound is related to unattainable erotic desire and also beautiful male heroism, again bespeaking a wish for identification with a strong father.

The link between a tree and the primal guilt that springs from erotic envy of the parental couple is a continuing motif in later works. In Night the Eighth of *The Four Zoas* we find one of the major references to the Tree of Mystery:

> Urizen heard the Voice & saw the Shadow. underneath
> His woven darkness & in laws & deceitful religions
> Beginning at the tree of Mystery circling its root
> She spread herself thro all the branches in the power of Orc
> A shapeless & indefinite cloud in tears of sorrow incessant
> (E375; *FZ* VIII, 171–75)

Despite further layers of complexity, the situation of "Infant Sorrow" remains. Orc, the phallic son, possesses the mother in oedipal fantasy. His guilt and the transitory nature of his triumph are manifest: Urizen, the authoritarian father, strengthens his oppressive laws, while the weeping and indefinite Shadowy Female engulfs the masculine strength of both father and son.

The *Songs* are filled with images of lost childhood delight, pictured as pastoral pleasure or joy in nature which have been taken away by dark forces or punishing parental figures, for instance in the Notebook version of "Infant Sorrow." Another example is "The Garden of Love," where again the child has been deprived of libidinal freedom by a black-garbed priest-father who binds or imprisons his desires:

> And I saw it was filled with graves,
> And tomb-stones where flowers should be:
> And Priests in black gowns, were walking their rounds,
> And binding with briars, my joys & desires. (E26)

Diana Hume George sees "The Garden of Love" as Blake's premonition of Freud's description of the triadic oedipal situation (104–6). It can be considered also as an expression of the pain of libidinal loss and of bitter oedipal conflicts. Melanie Klein places the onset of the oedipal phase at an earlier stage of development than does Freud. She believes that it may develop as early as the first year of life, before the child has necessarily made a sharp distinction between the two parent figures. The process of weaning precipitates the child's sense of separate existence, and of the mother as a whole object.[7] He becomes aware of the mother's relationship with the father and is intensely envious of the sensual pleasure from which he is excluded. Since the young child at this stage is still full of oral and anal impulses, early oedipal tendencies will be expressed according to aggression, guilt, and anxiety of an oral-anal type.[8]

The early relationship with the mother's body therefore remains strong in the oedipal phase. Her breast is still a source of intense pleasure, and the child imagines her full of gratifying riches. Aggression against both father and mother is filled with guilt and destructiveness. This we see displayed in the *Songs* and other early works of Blake. The poems are filled with images of envy and guilt surrounding a desire for sensuous possession: the fruit of the "Poison Tree" that kills the thieving foe; the "dark secret love" eating away at the crimson joy at the heart of the sick rose; the "fruit of Deceit, / Ruddy and sweet to eat." Conflicting feelings against the mother underlie the deepest aggression against the authoritarian father, whom Blake will always forgive more readily than the mother.

As we have noted, some of the *Songs of Innocence* genuinely recall in images of nature the blissful state of earliest infancy. These lyrics have a miraculous spontaneity in their evocation of delight in primordial existence. *Laughing Song*, for instance, summons up pure oral delight:

> When the meadows laugh with lively green
> And the grasshopper laughs in the merry scene,
> When Mary and Susan and Emily,
> With their sweet round mouths sing Ha, Ha, He. (E11)

Rarely again was Blake to express this joy in nature, so fresh and original in his early work. In the epics, the mother's body is closed about with "nature's cruel holiness," making it rigid and remote. Occasionally, in fleeting references to Beulah, the early joyful contact is reestablished, notably at the beginning of the second book of *Milton* where a description of the Beulah state, characterized by "the beloved infant in his mothers bosom round incircled / With arms of love & pity & sweet compassion" (E129; *M*30, 11–12) leads into a passage describing the delights of birds and of dancing flowers:

they wake
The Honeysuckle sleeping on the Oak: the flaunting beauty
Revels along upon the wind; the White-thorn lovely May
Opens her many lovely eyes: listening the Rose still sleeps
None dare to wake her. soon she bursts her crimson curtaind bed
And comes forth in the majesty of beauty . . . (E131; *M*31, 53–58)

This rapturous interlude is leading in the direction of the hard-won redemptive effect of *Milton*, but at this moment in the poem soon vanishes into a more dark and tormented state. The guilt and anger that condition the tone of the *Songs of Experience* mark aggression against that mother for whom undivided love is henceforth impossible.

We note that in some of these early poems the figure of the father is dominant as a rival and lawgiver for the son. Yet aggression against the father is embedded in aggression against the depriving mother and envy of the sensuous closeness of the two parents. As well as hating the dark authoritarian father, the son identifies with the presence of the father. In the last two lines of the Notebook draft of *Infant Sorrow*—

But the time of youth is fled
And grey hairs are on my head (E797)

—the son becomes the father, and recognizes that he shares the father's enfeebled state, as a fellow victim of the dominant mother.

A revealing family constellation is found in the Cynic's "Song" from *An Island in the Moon*, a satire marked by witty, if juvenile, scatological humor. It was written in 1784 during the period when Blake was also working on drafts of the *Songs of Innocence*. Early versions of some of those songs, for instance, "Holy Thursday," appear within it, and some of the motifs of Blake's works of this period, often in a debased and dismissive form, are to be found in it. In the Cynic's "Song," a male figure called "old corruption" copulates with a similarly impersonal female figure called "flesh" and begets a child.[9] Neither "name" is capitalized. "Old corruption" feeds the child with his own milk:

He calld him Surgery & fed
The babe with his own milk
For flesh & he could neer agree
She would not let him suck

The child resents this maternal deprivation, and in maturity seeks his revenge:

And this he always kept in mind
And formd a crooked knife
And ran about with bloody hands
To seek his mothers life

And as he ran to seek his mother
He met with a dead woman
He fell in love & married her
A deed which is not common (E454–55)

The relationships are a tangled web of sadism and aggression. In the first stanza quoted, the child is fed with milk from the father, telling us that the father is more nurturing than the mother, but also hinting at a phallic mother whose breast appears to the child to be a penis. While that renders her threatening, the male organ retains a good and positive quality. The syntax of that stanza is obscure, yet suggests an identity of "he," the male parent, and "he," the son: the harsh mother withdraws the breast from both. The son's pursuit of the mother is a quest both to satisfy his desires and to wreak violence upon her. Since she is surely the dead woman, in his fantasy he accomplishes both, without enjoying the delight of living flesh. This union produces another child of whom "old corruption" takes possession in great glee. He ties him down in order to perform cruel surgical experiments on him:

With that he tied poor scurvy down
& stopt up all its vents

And when the child began to swell
He shouted out aloud
Ive found the dropsy out & soon
Shall do the world more good

He took up fever by the neck
And cut out all its spots
And thro the holes which he had made
He first discoverd guts (E455)

The cutting, dissecting, and dismembering matches the quality of sadism that the child feels in the early phase of the oedipus complex when there is a strong wish to "destroy the libidinal object by biting, devouring and cutting it."[10] This sequence dramatizes infantile rage against the rejecting mother; fear of the father alongside identification with him; and acute anxiety springing from fantasies of cutting and attacking the good object, which at the end of the poem has been dissected to extinction. To defend the self from guilt and fear, the cruelty is projected onto the parent figures.

It is notable that in the Cynic's "Song," the two parent figures are unnamed and are referred to in a most impersonal way. "Flesh" is the ever-present element of nature, featureless and yet all-enveloping; to refer to the father as "old corruption" reflects a censorious attitude toward him, or towards his deeds. Since there is a merging of father and son in the poem, father, or son, is defined by a sense of guilt surrounding his desire for the mother. The lack of naming in the poem comes from the son's wish to deny totally all bonds with the parent figures, so that they are reduced to the final elements that cannot be denied, the mother's flesh and guilty male desire.

A prevalent image in the *Songs* is that of children suffering in some way at the hands of their parents: they may be lost, or treated with cruelty, or physically bound. The indifference of parents to childhood anguish is typified in "The Chimney Sweeper" of *Songs of Experience*:

> A little black thing among the snow:
> Crying weep, weep, in notes of woe!
> Where are thy father & mother? say?
> They are both gone up to the church to pray. (E22)

Here and elsewhere, the parents are closely associated with the forces of repression within society:

> And because I am happy, & dance & sing,
> They think they have done me no injury:
> And are gone to praise God & his Priest & King
> Who make up a heaven of our misery. (E23)

This black-robed priest is a father figure who within his own family imposed the puritanical harshness of the larger society. In "The Garden of Love," the child's libidinal joy has been changed to deathly despair by this same figure.

The fantasy of loss and pain inflicted upon children is not a simple expression of direct pain and loss but may also be an inversion of the child's own anger and aggression. Melanie Klein shows how from birth the mother's body is the total object of joy and desire for the infant and in fantasy contains all riches. Absolute bliss is transformed into absolute destructive fury when the infant loses the mother's nurturing attentions, even to a slight degree. The child's own feelings of anger and destructiveness against the mother are so overwhelming that a mechanism for dealing with them is necessary. Guilt and fear are transformed into an image of a mother or a parental couple who are themselves cruel and threatening. This suggests a source for the various types of parental failure or callousness in the *Songs of Innocence and Experience*, or the drafts in the Notebook, as well as for parts of *An Island in the Moon*. Sometimes reference is made to a mother figure, sometimes to a father, and often to a couple who are not necessarily distinct in their cruelty. Melanie Klein tells us that the mother, or initially her breast, is the original object, while the father is first experienced as a part of the mother. Later the parental couple can be seen as a combined person, particularly in envious fantasies.

Klein states that she often found among children in analysis fantasies of being lost or turned out of the home. These she interpreted as manifestations of the children's anxieties about unconscious aggression or about harm they had actually done.[11] The children experienced guilt for angry feelings towards their parents and also towards siblings, which were so powerful that they felt unable to contain them. In order to protect themselves from annihilation, they projected these feelings into images of violence outside of themselves and directed against them.

There are several poems that deal specifically with the theme of being lost: "The Little Boy Lost" and "The Little Boy Found" of the *Songs of Innocence*, and "A Little Boy Lost," "The Little Girl Lost," "The Little Girl Found," and "A Little Girl Lost" of the *Songs of Experience*. In addition, in the *Songs* and other early works as a whole, there are numerous references to abandoned or neglected children,[12] for example, in "Holy Thursday" from the *Songs of Experience:*

> Is this a holy thing to see,
> In a rich and fruitful land,
> Babes reduced to misery,
> Fed with cold and usurous hand? (E19)

and "The Chimney Sweeper" from *Songs of Innocence*:

When my mother died I was very young,
And my father sold me while yet my tongue,
Could scarcely cry weep weep weep weep. (E10)

These groups of poems are marked by imagery of desolation, as shown in "Holy Thursday," from *Songs of Experience*:

And their sun does never shine.
And their fields are bleak & bare.
And their ways are fill'd with thorns.
It is eternal winter there. (E19)

and in "The Little Boy Lost":

The night was dark no father was there
The child was wet with dew.
The mire was deep, & the child did weep
And away the vapour flew. (E11)

The landscapes of bleakness and loneliness associated with children reflect the terrifying emptiness and pain of the world that the infant creates for itself through aggression against the bad mother, whereby the mother's body becomes a place of terror, full of vengeful objects.[13]

The parents who are the projection of the child's aggression are presented in one of two ways. Sometimes they are deliberately hostile or callous, like the parents of "The Chimney Sweeper" of *Experience* who are "both gone up to the church to pray" (E22). Sometimes they themselves are subjected to suffering. The parents of Lyca, the "Little Girl Found" of *Experience*, wander in anguish while she herself is tended in a cave by the wild creatures:

All the night in woe,
Lyca's parents go:
Over vallies deep,
While the desarts weep.

Tired and woe-begone,
Hoarse with making moan:
Arm in arm seven days,
They trac'd the desart ways. (E21)

This shows the child's wish to punish the parents by inflicting pain upon them. The figure of a parent wandering in sorrow recurs throughout Blake's works. It is found in *Tiriel*, but the most striking version of the motif is in the image of Enion in *The Four Zoas* wretchedly following her scornful children:

> And then they wanderd far away she sought for them in vain
> In weeping blindness stumbling she followd them oer rocks & mountains
> Rehumanizing from the Spectre in pangs of maternal love
> Ingrate they wanderd scorning her drawing her Spectrous Life
> Repelling her away & away by a dread repulsive power
> Into Non Entity revolving round in dark despair. (E304; *FZ* I, 214–19)

Of the parental couple, it is the mother, as the prime object, against whom the most sustained hostility is directed, and she is, therefore, in the figure of Enion, subjected to total withdrawal of love and the wish to destroy. In his later works, Blake is able to forgive the father more completely than the mother. Urizen is loved and idealized as well as hated, whereas women are seen as benevolent only in subjection to men. The original condition that colors future emotional response is powerfully presented in a stark motif in "The Crystal Cabinet," a poem from the Pickering Manuscript:

> A weeping Babe upon the wild
> And Weeping Woman pale reclind
> And in the outward air again
> I filld with woes the passing Wind. (E489)

The child and the mother, who is a transformation of the seductive, imprisoning woman found earlier in the poem, are eternally separate and sorrowful. The desolate baby converts its destructive fury against the rejecting mother into punishment of her, and into the bleakness of the landscape.

The groups of poems that specifically deal with lost children, the "Little Boy Lost" and the "Little Girl Lost," seem to be linked mainly by title, having apparently quite different subject matter. However, the later versions can often be seen as Blake's deconstruction of the earlier, revealing some of the layers of feeling that lie beneath the apparently intact surface. A case in point is the pair "The Little Boy Lost" and "The Little Boy Found" from the *Innocence* poems. The father is a remote figure never physically present until he appears in white in "The Little Boy Found" as a godlike presence. In the first poem, the boy is lost because his father walks too quickly and will not answer him. The child stumbles weeping through mud and darkness to find the vanishing desired figure, led only by a "vapour" that flies ahead. In the second poem, still weeping, he is following what has become a "wand'ring light." God, apparently always at hand to take care of the abandoned boy, comes to him: "but God ever nigh, / Appeard like his father in white" (E11), and takes him by the hand back to his mother.[14] The boy's mother belongs in the category of suffering parent condemned by the child to grieve in isolation as a punishment for rejection of her baby:

> Who in sorrow pale, thro' the lonely dale
> Her little boy weeping sought. (E11)

The pair of poems can be read as an early version of the powerful mother's castrating and abstracting effects upon the boy through her destruction of the strong father. The child suffers the anxiety of annihilation as he pursues the intangible father figure. Significantly, the father will not *speak* to him, that is he will not impart to him male empowerment.[15] The God who appears to him in the second poem is not the strong father that he requires but an embodiment of social authority that imposes taboos upon libidinal desire. Like the vapor of the first poem, this being in *white* represents the empty state of the boy's castration fear; and in his exaggerated goodness, he reveals that he is an "idealized" figure, formed out of the boy's desperate anxiety to preserve the good object.[16] He is another version of the black-gowned priest, like him, imposing cruel restrictions upon the child; but since in this poem he is idealized, he is not here a manifest object of hatred. The mother, in the punished state of sorrowfully seeking her child in the "lonely dale," is the original source of anguish to which both boy and father must return.

The poem entitled "A Little Boy Lost" in the *Songs of Experience* bears no surface resemblance to the earlier poems, but gives us an explanation of some of the elements in that material. The poem opens with the boy justifying his view that it is reasonable to be self-centered and to love oneself:

> Nought loves another as itself
> Nor venerates another so.
> Nor is it possible to Thought
> A greater than itself to know. (E28)

For this desecration of "our most holy Mystery," the priest strips, binds, and burns him on the altar.[17] At the heart of the irony of Experience is the bland social assumption that the priest and his acts are virtuous: "And all admir'd his Priestly care." However, this irony is contained in the merging of the boundaries between priest and parents. The parents are assigned the dual role of suffering, "weeping" parents and cruel parents. The syntax suggests that the parents enter into or themselves perpetrate the act of punishment:

> And standing on the altar high,
> Lo what a fiend is here! said he:
> One who sets reason up for judge
> Of our most holy Mystery.
>
> The weeping child could not be heard.
> The weeping parents wept in vain:
> They strip'd him to his little shirt.
> And bound him in an iron chain. (E29)

They are the most obvious subject of the verb "strip'd,"[18] especially since elsewhere parents directly carry out such acts. Here, Blake manifests two levels of aggression against the parental couple; he has formulated his own fury against them by making them suffer and also, in a more intense form, by showing the child in his "little shirt" as a helpless victim at the mercy of cruel parent figures. The use of burning as a punishment is infantile aggression inverted into masochism: in the later, more highly wrought versions of this motif in the epics, we find that it is accompanied by images of fire and blood. All is associated with the "mystery" and "holiness" of the parents' sexuality, desired by, but denied to, the boy. The initial statement, "Nought loves another as itself" becomes an assertion of self-preservation: the context of what it means to satisfy one's own longings cannot be uttered, but it is the ultimate act of the self to maintain this conviction.

The pair of poems, "The Little Girl Lost" and "The Little Girl Found" were originally included in the *Songs of Innocence*, but subsequently transferred to *Experience*. They introduce us into a world that is, for the child, far more benign than that of the lost boy. The girl, Lyca, wanders away, led by the song of wild birds, into a remote region where she is tended by a lion and a lioness as parental substitutes.[19] From this point on, throughout both poems, she *sleeps* peacefully, whereas the parents, in searching for their lost daughter, undergo unusual anguish, particularly pronounced for the mother:

> Pale thro' pathless ways
> The fancied image strays,
> Famish'd, weeping, weak
> With hollow piteous shriek
>
> Rising from unrest,
> The trembling woman prest,
> With feet of weary woe;
> She could no further go. (E21)

Blake submits the parents to extreme suffering, and furthermore replaces them with a superior set of parents, a regal lion and a nurturing lioness. Lyca has been conveyed away from the threatening parental world into one where fundamental and libidinous desires are stripped of their threatening aspect. She is here preserved from the onslaught of her own destructive feelings, which are projected into wild creatures, now tamed:

> Leopards, tygers play,
> Round her as she lay;
> While the lion old,
> Bow'd his mane of gold. (E21)

The illustration to the first poem provides a surprising counterpoint. We see, not the forlorn parents but a young couple embracing who, as David Erdman says in his commentary in *The Illuminated Blake*, represent the youthful pair, Ona and her lover, from "A Little Girl Lost" (76). Underlying the apparent situation of the lost child and suffering parents is a fantasy of sexual fulfillment. This appears to be the son's fantasy of oedipal fulfillment with the mother, seen as his peer because she has been removed from the hold of repressive law.

The grief of Lyca's actual parents ceases when, in "The Little Girl Found," they encounter the lion pair. The damaged and punished real parents are subsumed into the idealized parents, who have been created to protect the threatened good object upon which the child depends. At the moment of meeting, the lion father's regal nature is made manifest:

> And wondering behold,
> A spirit arm'd in gold.

On his head a crown
On his shoulders down,
Flow'd his golden hair. (E22)

This "vision" resembles a figure found later in a poem transcribed in a letter from Felpham "To my Friend Butts I write / My first Vision of Light" (E712–13). There, Blake refers to the uplifting experience of being embraced by a golden figure who appears to him out of the sunlight. The figure also resembles Los emerging from the sun in *Milton* and in the poem "With happiness stretchd across the hills" (E720). This idealized father possesses the masculine strength to which the son aspires.

The sleeping child is protected from conflict. As a female child, she is the desired mother, preserved in her sleeping limbo state between aggression and idealization. Her sleep is symbolic of death, a death that is the result, not of aggression, but of unattainable wishes.[20] There is a curious balance between the emotional state of the girl and her mother, expressed at the time when she is first lost, that suggests an emotional identity between them:

If her heart does ake,
Then let Lyca wake;
If my mother sleep,
Lyca shall not weep. (E20)

The later poem in the *Songs of Experience*, "A Little Girl Lost," enacts a fantasy of oedipal fulfillment. The girl, Ona, and her youthful lover enjoy sensual delight in a blissful garden setting. Ona then approaches her father, a dim numinous figure clad in white and backed by oppressive social authority. His look immediately withers the joyful freedom of the young couple, changing it to "trembling fear" and "dismal care" (E30). George interprets the poem as a girl's oedipal fantasy with the father, which is destroyed by the imposition of the strictures of the superego (108–11). One may, however, regard it as the boy's fantasy of oedipal fulfillment with the mother, which is shattered by an awareness of the father's presence. The final malaise—

O the trembling fear!
O the dismal care!
That shakes the blossoms of my hoary hair (E30)

– refers to the young man who has imbibed the father's laws and therefore become grey-haired, as well as unhappy and fearful. It also refers to the father himself who, as a lover, the boy wishes to be. The boy must sadly identify with an enfeebled father, again the misty, white-clad father of "The Little Boy Lost," who cannot pass on to him masculine strength. The poem is concerned not so much with society's restriction of the female libido as with what this does to the male. It is often true in Blake that the denial of erotic freedom to women is regrettable principally because it curtails the erotic freedom of men.

A central episode for studying the tensions of the parent-child relationship is the birth of Enitharmon, followed by the birth of Orc, in *The Book of Urizen*. In her parturition from the male, Los, Enitharmon has a relationship of dependency to him and is an object of horror as a "separate" female. She appears as a pale shadow and instantly becomes an object of Pity to the "eternal" males. The "good" mother, who is an object of desire as a source of nurturance and sensuous satisfaction, has become virtually unattainable. Her own "shadowy" qualities merge with those of the woof of science that Urizen now weaves. The hazy mystery of what is forbidden, the incestuous desire for the remote parent figures, is the cloud within which it is concealed. Here, through the strength of male resentment and fear at the woman and the sensuous power she exerts, she is reduced to a weak, dependent creature; and her paramount female quality, the gentle and nurturing pity which man, or the male child, intensely needs, is taken from her and transformed into an object of scorn. What Blake knows cannot be possessed and controlled must be thus regarded. The links between previous themes and the birth of Orc are clear: the birth of the child brings anguish to both parents, a reflection of the anguish they, in fact, cause him.

One of the most positive female figures of the earlier poems is the nurse, found in both *Innocence* and *Experience*. She evinces a particular strength of benevolence because she is a mother substitute, not a member of the enclosed family circle. She can therefore offer libidinal delight and a hope of liberation from the family's emotional strictures.[21] As a *nurse,* she reflects the positive nurturing qualities of the "good" mother and is in tune with the genuinely pastoral qualities of childhood joy in *Songs of Innocence*:

When the voices of children are heard on the green
And laughing is heard on the hill,

My heart is at rest within my breast
And every thing else is still (E15)

She has knowledge of a further sphere of life dominated by the "dews of night" but allows the children to prolong the time they spend playing in this benign realm, on the green hill of the kind maternal breast. The "mists of night" dimly suggest guilt at the erotic jealousy that is associated with fears of castration and abstraction.

In the "Nurse's Song" of *Experience*, darkness and disturbance are imminent. She speaks with a balanced maturity, aware in her wisdom of the tragedies of life that await the children, because she knows them directly from her own youth. However, she is able to contain her sense of tragedy, and her chief objective is to protect the children, here and in the *Innocence* poem, from what must eventually destroy their short-lived bliss. For all this, the nurse herself begins to be associated with the dark aspect of life. Her nauseous memory of her own youth, beset presumably by repressions both social and sexual, is extended to the children. In the final lines, what begins as a sympathetic warning to the children ends as a statement whose bitterness the nurse herself feels:

Your spring & your day, are wasted in play
And your winter and night in disguise. (E23)

The word "waste" directed toward "spring" and "day" destroys the validity of these most precious positive moments, while "disguise" refers to the smiling duplicity with which the baby fiend of "Infant Sorrow" has learned to face the agonies of relationships. In the two nurse poems, we have the kernel of the split between the good mother and the bad mother. From the sheltered but necessarily fragile joy of *Innocence*, we move to the moment where the joy is about to evaporate in the "dews of night," associated with guilt and frustrated desire. We begin to be aware that this incipient anguish has its source in the nurse, the good nurturing mother in the process of being transformed into the bad mother, with her coldness and prohibitions. The child is on the edge of losing the bliss of maternal symbiosis.

It has been conjectured that some personal experiences with women in the 1790s intensified Blake's bitterness towards women, and account for the portraits of female figures in the epics as essentially more threatening and vindictive than the males. However, if mature adult experience is expressed in a particular form, it is because it gains its strength and coloring from deep emotional patterns established in infancy. If women are presented negatively during a phase of Blake's artistic career, they merely reflect his elemental emotional condition. The poem "To Tirzah," a late addition to the *Songs of Experience*, states a fundamental attitude:

> Thou Mother of my Mortal part.
> With cruelty didst mould my Heart.
> And with false self-decieving tears,
> Didst bind my Nostrils Eyes & Ears.
>
> Didst close my Tongue in senseless clay
> And me to Mortal Life betray. (E30)

In the early works both parent figures are regarded as a source of pain and are the object of the child's aggression. It is, however, the mother who remains as the most permanent tormentor. She is even seen here as the agent who binds the senses, an act usually associated with the father, and is the parent who caused the son to have a cruel heart and to be a dissembler, as a defense mechanism against fear of annihilation. The Urizenic father is responsible for much evil and suffering. Yet the son also admires him in his heroic manifestations, and finally loves him and forgives him. Females can be loved only as feeble and passive adjuncts of the male, and in their benevolent manifestation have altogether a more restricted and monochromatic presence. Fundamental biological ties with the mother are closer than those with the father, and their loss is therefore a source of more profound bitterness. The mother's rejection can barely be forgiven, whereas imitation of the father offers a hope of escape from dependence or self-annihilation. The mother, in her persecutory aspect, eternally casts a fearful shadow upon the enfeebled son.

CHAPTER 3

Patterns of Maternal Loss in Early Lawrence: *The White Peacock*

Ambivalent responses to women lie at the center of D.H. Lawrence's work. While he is unusually sensitive to the experience of women, he is also clearly moved by a powerful animus against them. The glorification of masculine power and the phallic mystique of many of the middle and later works testify to animosity towards female dominance, yet Lawrence continues to create strong and independent females, such as Kate Leslie and Rachel Witt, whose strength can barely be crushed.[1]

We might say that these contradictory feelings about women are finally feelings about mothers. The theme, declared in *Sons and Lovers*, of the son's struggle for independence from the mother's hold on his personal and sensuous life appears in many transformations throughout Lawrence's novels. Even before *Sons and Lovers*, the motif of the son's ambivalent feelings towards powerful mother figures was introduced in *The White Peacock*. Although not among Lawrence's most achieved works, this first novel provides through its very unevenness a glimpse into unguarded emotional areas. In my analysis, I shall stress aspects of the novel not often considered important, in particular the subplot of Annable, the gamekeeper, and his family, which, I believe, contains the essentials of a recurrent emotional pattern in Lawrence's work.[2]

The themes of this first novel are: the permutations of female dominance of men; the establishment of strong male relationships; and the shaping of a male mode of existence, characterized by violence and energy. Male efforts to assert power are always finally vain and fruitless. The central character and emotional focus of *The White Peacock* is Cyril Beardsall, a narrator of marked passivity, who typically responds to the experience of others rather than acting directly himself. He is, however, the questing center of the novel, to whom other characters and events are finally related, and his emotional state, marked by frequent depressions and a sense of yearning, is the containing element of the narrative. He experiences dissatisfactions with several mother figures and concomitantly has a timid and unfulfilled love relationship with Emily Saxton, the sister of the young farmer George Saxton, his close friend. Two vigorous male figures, George and Annable the gamekeeper, are surrogates for Cyril in the world of masculine action. Sam, the eldest son of Annable and male child victim of the punishing mother, echoes the sufferings of George, the adult male, at the hands of maternalistic women. Throughout the novel, Cyril searches for a warmer and more ideal relationship than he has found with women. Such a relationship is attained briefly with men, in the male bonding with George and Annable as loving brother and father.

These shifting patterns within the male psyche, moving between grudging dependence on women and ideals of male strength, are intrinsic to the affective texture of Lawrence's art. The male aggressively asserts independence from women, and yet also feels intimately drawn into the feminine perspective and sensibility.

In applying Kleinian theory here, I am suggesting that paradigms of infantile emotion underlie the deliberate and controlled surface of the novel. Thus, certain attitudes of men towards women, or some categories of women, are given color and urgency by fundamental feelings surrounding the mother, formed in infancy. These feelings are partly specific to Lawrence and partly widespread among those subject to the same cultural conditions. The sufferings of the child, Sam, and the adult male, George, are closely related at this deep emotional level in a way that goes beyond a rational analysis of the surface of the novel and Lawrence's most deliberate intentions.

The White Peacock is a novel that teems with episodes of cruelty and suffering inflicted upon young, vulnerable creatures,[3] a paradigm that resembles that of ill-treated children in early Blake. Again, Kleinian theory would see this not as a simple expression of direct pain and loss but also as an inversion of the child's own violent fantasies. The fact that he has hated and, in fantasy, destroyed the beloved object who is synonymous with nurture and sheer existence is so unbearable to the infant that he inverts the experience and forms a primitive image of a vengeful maternal superego who inflicts upon him the punitive aggression that matches his own.[4] Several mother figures in the novel, most dramatically Mrs. Annable in her attacks upon the vulnerable white-skinned male child, Sam, are imbued with the intensity of these elemental emotions.

An important motif in the novel is Cyril's struggle to establish selfhood and to break free from suffocating ties with the mother. This is reflected in the bond he forges with the assertively male Annable and in the glorification of male violence related to both Annable and George. We recall the view of both Chodorow and Kohut that, where the father is remote and the mother emotionally dominant—which seems to have been the case in Lawrence's childhood—a sense of masculinity is difficult to achieve, and frequently needs to be idealized and fantasized.[5]

An analysis of the inner tensions of *The White Peacock* reveals these emotional patterns at work: the splitting of images of women into the benign and the malevolent, and an ideal of masculinity as an escape from female domination. The responses to women that emerge in the novel are manifold. Mothers, such as Mrs. Beardsall and Mrs. Saxton, may be subtly oppressive or, like Mrs. Annable, act with outright violence. Meg and Lettie in young motherhood embody ideals of tenderness, yet in their detachment from the mature male, George, exert coldness and cruelty towards him. The woman in her domain, the kitchen, offers warmth and cohesiveness, yet all too often the kitchen is also the locus of violent feelings and destructiveness. These responses to the mother figure are at the core of Lawrence's emotions towards women. The mother's cruel dominance of the son is only partly assuaged by his alliance with male figures and male ideals. Thus, Cyril turns to Annable as the male parent through whom he will overcome the mother, yet there is no lasting triumph in this association.

Throughout his work, Lawrence strives to overcome masculine dependence. In the novels of the leadership period, he appears to achieve permanent faith in masculine strength and concomitantly is able to subject women to its authority. Among such women are certain overbearing and malevolent mothers: Rachel Witt of *St. Mawr* and Rachel Bodoin of the story that closely parallels that novel, "Mother and Daughter"; or Pauline Attenborough of "The Lovely Lady." Both Rachel Bodoin and Pauline Attenborough are finally crushed and lose power over the sexual life of the younger generation, a resolution of the *impasse* of *Sons and Lovers*. It appears to be Lawrence's intention to curtail the power of Rachel Witt also, yet her death-associated grip on male sexuality seems to linger even in the wilderness. The controlling and unnurturing mother is destroyed only in fantasy.

In *The White Peacock*, many of the complex and contradictory feelings about women relate immediately to Lettie, Cyril's intimate sibling, who is menacingly flirtatious in her dealings with men, but who also stands for some principles that are approvingly associated with feminine caring and sympathy. She criticizes the cruel treatment of animals prevalent in the novel. Enlightened by her readings in the women's movement and by the democratic views her mother has taught her, she speaks out against Leslie, an incipient Gerald Crich, at the time when his miners are on strike, although Leslie believes that women are unfit to understand the ways of the world.[6]

Lawrence had an empathy with women's social experience unusual among his male contemporaries. His own sympathetic observations stand behind Lettie and Emily when they condemn Mrs. Annable's situation:

> "Ah, it's always the woman bears the burden," said Lettie bitterly. "If he'd helped her—wouldn't she have been a fine figure of a woman now—splendid? But she's dragged to bits. Men are brutes—and marriage just gives scope to them—" said Emily. (*WP* 135)

Lettie and Emily's statements ring out as an indictment of the type of marriage where a woman must suffer both economic hardship and male arrogance. Lawrence notes with true insight the effect of such a marriage upon women, a sympathy he shows also for Mrs. Morel in *Sons and Lovers* and for Elizabeth Bates and her neighbor, weary with work and childbearing, in "Odour of Chrysanthemums." Yet this recognition of the suffering of women under economic repression, while a piece of heartfelt social observation, is not the sum of Lawrence's total attitude. His genuine appreciation of the difficulties of a woman's life are intermingled with fears and resentments of her emotional sway over men.

The themes of women as nurturing or depriving figures, in relation both to men and to children, dominate the novel and are the focus of its most urgent emotions. Images of maternal warmth or of cruel destructiveness proliferate, even when not apparently related to the deliberate meaning of the novelist. Cyril finds a maternal pattern in the landscape: "I remember a day when the breast of the hills was heaving in a last quick waking sigh, and the blue eyes of the waters opened bright. Across the infinite skies of March great rounded masses of cloud had sailed stately all day, domed with a white radiance, softened with faint, fleeting shadows as if companies of angels were gently sweeping past; adorned with resting, silken shadows like those of a full white breast." Later the swelling clouds have disappeared, leaving behind a curious sense of absence and tenuous security: "At evening they were all gone, and the empty sky, like a blue bubble over us, swam on its pale bright rims" (126–27). This reflection is for Cyril synonymous with an otherwise unvoiced depression. "Hoping to escape from [himself]," he accompanies Leslie, Lettie, George, and Emily to the woods where they have the first major encounter with Annable, who is the male figure able to provide Cyril with strength to resist his feeling of maternal deprivation.

Among the central nurturing images of women are those associated with fruit and fruitfulness; women can be positively maternal in their ripeness and fulness, promising fecundity. In the happy period of his courtship of Lettie, George recounts to Cyril how she helped him to pick apples: "She climbed a tree with me, and there was a wind, that was why I was getting all the apples, and it rocked us, me right up at the top, she sitting half way down holding the basket" (65). The eroticism of this passage is inherent in the evocation of female fertility. When George calls upon Meg to take her to their wedding, he finds her in a pose redolent of happy and positive fecundity: "Beyond the border of flowers was Meg, bending over the gooseberry bushes. She saw us and came swinging down the path, with a bowl of gooseberries poised on her hip" (239–40).

These images of nurturing fruitfulness can be matched with feelings of resentment and destructiveness on the part of George, the person who so strongly desires maternal nurturance. When the rich Christmas mincemeat, symbolic of family bonding, is being prepared in the Saxtons' kitchen, the scene is marred by George and Lettie's tussle over an apple and, more viciously, by George's dismembering the raisins, pulling out their flesh and leaving "nothing but the husks" (93). In another act of destructiveness, this time of the cognate symbol of flowers, George bites and chews some violets, which he says remind him of Lettie.

George's violent acts reflect the residue of intense infantile aggression against a mother figure who withholds total ideal love, and who therefore must be torn apart by the furious infant. The shredding of the raisins for the Christmas mincemeat is significant here; not only do the raisins symbolize the object of frustrated desire, but they are destined for a rich composite food that gathers together the values of family loyalty, which are centered in the mother and her nurturing kitchen. In their primary impulse, they anticipate the cherry tree episode in *Sons and Lovers*, preceding Paul and Miriam's first act of lovemaking, when Paul among the "sleek, cool-fleshed" cherries looks down from the tree at Miriam to see cherry stones hanging from the stems, picked clean of flesh by birds.[7]

A related example is found when George hears of Lettie's virtual engagement to Leslie, and experiences an intense feeling of rejection. His aggression is turned against a cow, an obvious displacement of the comforting and nurturing quality in a woman. He strikes her so that she cowers "like a beaten woman" and withholds most of her milk, causing George's father to express anxiety that she will go dry and turn skinny; George's violence against the innocent cow converts here into a fearful type of female. Still handling the cow's udder, George savagely comments to Cyril, "'I should like to squeeze her till she screamed'" (89–90). At this moment of profound deprivation, the emotional patterns of the mature male are those of the infant overwhelmed with loss who, in fantasy, tears apart the maternal breast, the source of all joy and goodness.

Cyril's feeling for Emily demonstrates a further layer in the male response. He perceives her as an embodiment of the female who refuses sensuous gratification: "'You think the flesh of the apple is nothing, nothing. You only care for the eternal pips. Why don't you snatch your apple and eat it, and throw the core away?'" (69). Emily is associated with acts of violence in a way that reflects inverted male aggression; she herself perpetrates violence and, yet, is at the same time an object of pity. In the opening scene of the novel, she has hit one of her pupils and made his nose bleed; in the episode which leads up to the first visit to Annable's wife and family, Emily is partly responsible for killing a dog who has been worrying sheep, and she is bloodily involved in his death throes: "Emily was kneeling on the dog, her hands buried in the hair of its throat, pushing back its head. The little jerks of the brute's body were the spasms of death; already the eyes were turned inward, and the upper lip was drawn from the teeth by pain" (67).

In each of these violent episodes, Emily acts with some justification. Her pupils are particularly provocative, and the dog was harming the sheep; Cyril also contributed to the dog's death, while Emily herself was injured by the animal. Yet George says that she hit her pupils because "'She merely felt like bashing 'em'" (5), and she is closely implicated in the dog's bloody death: she hit him with a stone, lost her balance, and fell upon him as he lay bleeding. From the standpoint of Cyril, these two episodes bring together some fundamental feelings: Emily, the object of his own feeble and unfulfilled sexual drive, is a displaced mother figure who, even when he regards her most honestly and directly, is an agent of violence. The element of pity for her—she hangs her head at her brother's taunting, and later suffers an injury from the dog—does not remove her culpability. The conflicting qualities of vulnerability and aggression are projected into her. Emily stands for an elemental female figure in a Lawrencean emotional pattern for whom male desire is corroded and shot through with an ever-itching aggression.

This aggressive ambivalence towards Emily is reflected in Cyril's frequent irritation with her, for instance on account of her myopia. Other male figures in works of the early period show a similar deep-seated irritation towards cognate women, Miriam of *Sons and Lovers* and Maggie of *A Collier's Friday Night*.[8] A striking example of this chafing antagonism is Cyril's response to Emily's tender mothering of Sam after he has been attacked by Trip, the bullterrier. Emily "went on her knees before him, and put her face close to his," speaking "with a voice that made one shrink from its unbridled emotion of caress" (187). When she goes on to talk to him with "her full vibration of emotional caress," it seems to suffocate him. What is resented in Emily here is apparently the very nurturing quality that is desired. Both Cyril and Sam shrink from a motherhood that seems to be imposed as power and possessiveness. In his dependence, the male child feels that his basic self might be overwhelmed. Maternal affection is experienced not within a tender relationship but as an assertion of the mother's dominance.

The final portrait of Emily is one of the most powerfully serene projections of womanhood in the novel. When Cyril goes to visit her after her marriage to Tom Renshaw, he finds her "stately" and beautiful in her pregnancy, baking a plum pie and totally at home in a kitchen that breathes the qualities of female strength: "The room, that looked so quiet and crude, was a home evolved through generations to fit the large bodies of the men who dwelled in it, and the placid fancy of the women. At last, it had an individuality. It was the home of the Renshaws, warm, lovable, serene" (319). Cyril reacts to Emily with none of his customary acrimony. Rather, he feels "rejected" by the room and is distressed by "a sense of ephemerality, of pale, erratic fragility." She no longer threatens him because the symbiotic bond is broken. He therefore sees her from afar as a strong mother and, even in his male adulthood, experiences a sense of loss, unaccompanied, however, by aggression since he has been cast adrift from her protective aura. The corollary of this is that George, in an advanced state of delirium tremens, has become a child in Emily's home, watched over and protected by her. Cyril's complex feelings of animosity have been split into two simplified aspects: he has gained an independence, however bleak, from the maternal bond, while George, the stronger and more virile self of Cyril, is reduced to infantile dependency. In both fates there is defeat. In the grip of the unbreakable power of women and their maternal imperative, men face life as weak and joyless beings. The same is true for Leslie, who must become dependent upon Lettie as a result of his accident before she will finally accept marriage to him.

Fundamental feelings about women in the novel are frequently related to their homes or kitchens, a common and obvious extension of female symbolism as the locus of shelter or nurture. Cyril is strongly drawn towards the Saxton household, prefiguring the Leivers–Chambers', as offering more warmth than his own, with its abandonment and neglect of the father. When he first enters his mother's house, having just eaten dinner with the Saxton family, there is an undertone of dryness and emotional emptiness. Cyril hears his mother apparently dust the piano keys: "The vocal chords behind the green silk bosom,—you only discovered it was not a bronze silk bosom by poking a fold aside—had become as thin and tuneless as a dried old woman's. Age had yellowed the teeth of my mother's little piano, and shrunken its spindle legs" (6). Her place is in the drawing room, formal and remote, not the kitchen. This first intimation of his mother reflects an insubstantial empty-breasted female with some of the malevolence of the cannibalistic witches of folklore.[9] The notion of the mother who denies nourishment, or other forms of personal support, lurks near that of the mother who lovingly holds together her family. The coldness Cyril experiences contrasts with the warm female solidarity of his mother and his sister, Lettie.

The center of the Saxton household is, on the other hand, the farm kitchen. The scene at the beginning of the "Riot of Christmas" chapter enshrines domestic peace. The mother sits by the fire bathing and drying a child while the father reads aloud and other members of the family are gathered together absorbed in their tasks (91–92). Yet it is an unstable harmony which is about to be disrupted by conflict between George and Emily. In the very first description we have of the Saxton kitchen, we notice a lack of connectedness: "The kitchen was very big; the table looked lonely, and the chairs mourned darkly for the lost companionship of the sofa; the chimney was a black cavern away at the back, and the ingle-nook seats shut in another little compartment ruddy with firelight, where the mother hovered" (3). There is ambivalence in this first scene about the nourishment that Mrs. Saxton, the woman at the heart of this kitchen, provides. Cyril reflects that she is ludicrously absorbed in her function: her "soul was in the saucepans." George and Emily express grudging resentment that the meat and potatoes are undercooked, a resentment that leads to conflict and aggression between them. Childhood feelings of dependence, and desire or dissatisfaction linked to the mother's provision of nourishment, underlie emotional patterns relating to the more complex activities of adult life.

Later in the novel, during their brief period of happy courtship, Cyril and Emily pay a visit to Strelley Mill after the departure of the Saxtons. The woman who now occupies the kitchen is the wife of the new tenant farmer, a strange little bird-like woman: "She was small and very active, like some ragged domestic fowl run wild" (267). She presses food on the young couple, and malevolently teases Emily about being kissed. The function of this distorted mother figure is to displace and render harmless the previously strong maternal dominance. The woman has the dried-up, bird-like features of a cannibalistic ogress, like Baba Yaga, displaying bony limbs as she offers food to Cyril and Emily: "Then she brought us delicious scones and apple jelly, urging us, almost nudging us with her thin elbows to make us eat" (267). Like a witch, or a threatening "bad mother," she does not provide food for nourishment but forces it upon young people in order to strengthen her aggressive hold over them. However, unlike Cyril's own mother with her spindle legs and empty breasts, or the surrogate, Mrs. Saxton, absorbed in the production of food, this creature has been removed to a realm of caricature where she is controlled by the young couple. Her loss of power is made plain in the clandestine embraces of Cyril and Emily: "When we were out on the road by the brook Emily looked at me with shameful, laughing eyes. I noticed a small movement of her lips, and in an instant I found myself kissing her, laughing with some of the little woman's wildness" (268). At this phase of the novel, Cyril is able to respond to Emily with straightforward sensuousness because he has detached himself from the threatening power which Emily partly represents for him. The conspiratorial air of the encounter with Emily here reflects Cyril's rebellion against maternal power: he now directs his eroticism solely towards a woman of his own generation.

It is the kitchen of the Annables, in which sits Mrs. Annable surrounded by her brood, that most completely embodies grudging and aggressive feelings related to the mother. Unlike the Saxtons' kitchen, this is one where nothing is idealized and where violence lies close to the surface. The children eat, but must usually procure their own food: "The kitchen was large, but scantily furnished; save, indeed, for children. The eldest, a girl of twelve or so, was standing toasting a piece of bacon with one hand, and holding back her nightdress in the other. As the toast hand got scorched, she transferred the bacon to the other, gave the hot fingers a lick to cool them, and then held back her nightdress again. Her auburn hair hung in heavy coils down her gown. A boy sat on the steel fender, catching the dropping fat on a piece of bread" (70–71). This a bleak scene, in which maternal tenderness is quite lacking, and the children must constantly risk physical pain in order to eat. Beneath the well-observed social details, Lawrence is giving us a picture of women as grudging and ungenerous in their nourishment, projected from infantile rage against them. Indeed, the youngest child here bites Mrs. Annable's breast as she nurses him.

The novel is filled with urgent and conflicting feelings about the family, relating back to the central emotional issue of responses to the mother. There are many references to young families, usually of wild animals, and many instances of gratuitous violence, often directed against young creatures. On the positive side we find portraits of blissful family unity: the ecstasy of the thrush parents preparing the nest for their turquoise eggs (155), the larks' eggs in a nest built in the hollow of a horse's hoofprint (208). More common are families or young creatures who are destroyed. A family of fieldmice is killed during the harvest: "'Mice!'" said George, and as he said it the mother slid out. Somebody knocked her on the back, and the hole was opened out. Little mice seemed to swarm everywhere. It was like killing insects. We counted nine little ones lying dead" (50). In a parallel instance, Mrs. Saxton brings a family of nine motherless chicks into the kitchen to warm them by the fire when one wanders in too closely and is burned to death:

> Suddenly George's mother gave a loud cry, and rushed to the fire. There was a smell of singed down. The chicken had toddled into the fire, and gasped its faint gasp among the red-hot cokes. The father jumped from the sofa; George sat up with wide eyes; Lettie gave a little cry and a shudder; Trip rushed round and began to bark. There was a smell of cooked meat.
>
> "There goes number one!" said the mother, with her queer little laugh. It made me laugh too. (206)

In this and the previous passage, there is a deliberate callousness, a detachment, despite superficial shock, from any sentimentality towards small creatures in their sudden and violent death. At the human level, the family of Annable, eight children living in poverty and struggling and scrapping for food, are explicitly associated by their father with the families of wild creatures: "'You know 'em, do you, Sir? Aren't they a lovely little litter?—aren't they a pretty bag o' ferrets?—natural as weasels—that's what I said they should be—bred up like a bunch o' young foxes, to run as they would'" (131).

The encounters of the central characters, Cyril, Lettie, and their friends, with Annable's family always turn up violence and disarray, particularly surrounding Sam, the child who is closest to his father. At the second meeting, he burns himself with a hot needle, smashes his sister's favorite mug, and injures his foot with a thorn. More seriously, he is covered in bruises from his mother's beatings: "We undressed him, and found his beautiful white body all discoloured with bruises" (133). And, he is the unfortunate person to discover his father's body in a quarry, probably pushed to a violent death by vengeful miners. These frequent references to suffering children or small creatures in *The White Peacock* reflect a fantasy of a harsh parent or parents, springing from infantile aggressions.

Violence is integral to the very fabric of the novel, and we should note distinctions between the kinds of violence associated with women and those associated with men. Although violence is apparently the province of men, violence emanating from women is in fact more fearful and far-reaching.

George often seems to be the main perpetrator of violence, beginning with his playful teasing of the field bees in the opening scene of the novel. He drowns the cat, Mrs. Nickie Ben, after she has been injured in a trap, and while harvesting, kills small animals as a matter of course, including rabbits and the family of mice in the passage just quoted. The narrative and comments from other characters make plain an acceptance of certain kinds of male violence. After the drowning of the cat, Lettie comments that all human beings, male or female, are cruel: "If we move the blood rises in our heel-prints" (13). While George is digging a grave for the cat, Emily and Lettie go indoors and discuss George's apparent brutality:

> "Has he done it?" asked Emily–"and did you watch him? If I had seen it I should have hated the sight of him, and I'd rather have touched a maggot than him."
>
> "I shouldn't be particularly pleased if he touched me," said Lettie.
>
> "There is something so loathsome about callousness and brutality," said Emily. "He fills me with disgust."
>
> "Does he?" said Lettie, smiling coldly. She went across to the old piano. "He's only healthy. He's never been sick, not any way, yet." She sat down and played at random, letting the numbed notes fall like dead leaves from the haughty, ancient piano. (14)

Lettie at first appears to lean towards sharing Emily's revulsion at her brother, then detaches herself from it and begins to play the piano. When George enters, he stays beside her at the piano to sing with her, in a sequence infused with their sensuous awareness of each other. Her erotic response to his physical presence is partly conditioned by the act of violence that has just taken place. She has accepted an inevitability of violence in the blood "in our heel-prints". Then rejecting Emily's narrow condemnation of George's act, she glories in him as a male who has performed violence.

The killing of the rabbit, occurring on the same day of harvesting as the killing of the family of mice, is the focus of a variety of responses to acts of cruelty towards animals. Several of the men in the group pursue it, even Cyril and Leslie, who, although they are not native to farming tradition, find themselves stirred by some primitive male aspect of the chase. Leslie, George's feeble counterpart as Lettie's would-be lover, almost tears off the rabbit's head, but later professes that "When it comes to killing it goes against the stomach." He follows this up with a comment on women: "'they're cruel enough in their way'—another look, and a comical little smile." (52). This response sets him up against the virile, independent male, George, as an effete man weakened by his contact with "civilized" attitudes. He cannot answer to his true nature in the male life of action and concomitantly gives smirking acceptance to the conventional view of women's "cruelty," a flirtatiousness quite different from the genuine female aggression present in the novel.

The cruelty of the male in action is held to be acceptable and often even justifiable, given that it is a part of George's work as a farmer. By contrast, the violence carried out by women is far more fundamental and destructive. We have noted the very bloody sequence in which Emily kills the dog, where her intimate involvement in his death agony led us to the basic connection between aggression and maternal rejection. In the episode of the chick burned alive in fire, an extreme example of the suffering of the vulnerable, it is Mrs. Saxton who responds oddly "with her queer little laugh," a laugh that seems to cover up suppressed tensions. Marguerite Beede Howe suggests that certain women in *The White Peacock* "represent civilization, or 'spirituality,'" and hence attack animality and, by implication, sex.[10] This is accurate but does not go far enough. We must observe the endorsement of male violence and also the inversion of male hostility that is reflected in these representations of women. It is not so much that women deny sex, but that they wish to control it as their own sphere.

One of the most extended scences of violence in the novel is found when Mrs. Annable beats Sam, in her frenzy turning her kitchen with its family hearth into a hell hole: "The lad was rolled up like a young hedgehog—the woman held him by the foot, and like a flail came the hollow utensil thudding on his shoulders and back. He lay in the firelight and howled; scattered in various groups, with the leaping firelight twinkling over their tears and their open mouths, were the other children, crying too" (133). The feelings surrounding the mother figure are sharply revealed. The kitchen, which should be a place of nourishment and consolation, is bristling with pain that emanates from the destructive mother, an extreme portrait of a denying female that is partly a projection of the child's own wish to inflict suffering. The boy's transgression has been to injure his sister's cheek, echoing an earlier occasion when a little boy had tried to choke the baby by stuffing too much food in his mouth. These episodes suggest furious sibling envy as part of the seething complex of emotions. Conversation with Mrs. Annable reveals the social causes of the situation that Lawrence understands so well. She feels overwhelmed by practical cares and by her husband's lack of emotional support, but those rational factors pale beside the emotional animus of the violent witch in the firelight, surrounded by vulnerable children. The love and desire that are a necessary base for the child's destructive aggression are revealed in the genuine Pietà scene of the reconciliation of son and mother: "Then his mother caught him in her arms, and kissed him passionately, and cried with abandon. The boy let himself be kissed–then he too began to sob, till his little body was all shaken. They folded themselves together, the poor dishevelled mother and the half-naked boy, and wept themselves still" (134). A response to the "good mother" is maintained, but tenuously, since the union is one not of comfort but of desperation.

Sam is seen repeatedly as the vulnerable male victim. Cyril and his companions undress the boy after his mother's beating, to discover "his beautiful white body all discoloured with bruises" (133). When he steals a pet rabbit in order to supply a Sunday meal for his family, the reader's sympathy is directed towards him. He is pursued by a crowd of vengeful women, veritable furies, screaming and waving their arms. One shrieks, "'Ta'e 'im up, ta'e 'im up, an' birch 'im till 'is bloody back's raw'" (181).

Sam's importance for Lawrence in his working out of the themes of the novel is made very plain in the earliest draft of *The White Peacock*, entitled "Laetitia," of which two fragments remain. Here Lettie, abandoned by Leslie, is married to George and bears Leslie's child. She is seen as a "good," nurturing mother figure and also as a piteous, suffering creature who twice roams the countryside *en deshabille* clutching her baby and seeking the faithless Leslie. Whereas in the final version she is predominantly a destructive female, here she is the object of manifest male aggression. Sam, who in "Laetitia" is being cared for in the household of Lettie and George, is extremely protective of the baby. In terror that she will be harmed, he crosses thin cracking ice to rescue her from some bushes where she has been left by Lettie, and with anxious care restores the infant to the distraught mother (335). When the child is baptized, Sam weeps, thinking that the minister has harmed her (339). In his anxious, self-punishing identification with Lettie's baby, Sam is revealed as the "good" child who covers up his rage, placates the suffering mother, and restores his injured sibling to her. The Sam of the final version of the novel reaches to the core of the child's relationship with the mother, performing acts of violence and envious theft, and incurring her punitive anger and that of her surrogates as a displacement of his own.

Sam, the victim and pitiful child who is also an aggressor of women, symbolizes the suffering position of males in relation to women. George and Annable, the two characters with whom Cyril as shadowy narrator is intimately linked, take that relationship and its possible resolution into a more complicated mature realm. George is the virile male, capable of violence and masculine action, who finally succumbs to the powers of women. Annable remains tough and independent to the end, dying a violent death as a figure whose values cannot be compromised. In both George and Annable, some of the important ideals of the novel are located. Although often an agent of violence, during the happy phase of his courtship of Meg George reveals a capacity to nurture and protect young creatures. He tells Meg of how he had reared two motherless baby lambs and also moved the eggs of a mother peewit while ploughing (179). This illustrates men's capacity to be nurturing parents and indicates that violence ultimately has its source in women in their deprivations of men, while men when treated with maternal tenderness are capable of gentle and protective behavior.

The theme of fatherhood, actual and spiritual, is an urgent one in *The White Peacock*. For both Cyril and Lettie, two close siblings, the suppression, or suffocation, of their father by their mother produces a feeling of loss of which Lettie is more conscious than Cyril. She tells George that she has known in her life the experience necessary for suffering because her mother hated her father before she was born: "That was death in her veins for me before I was born" (28). A source of her feminine cruelty to George is suggested: although possessing greater moral insight than her mother, she is the heir, despite herself, to her mother's denial of the male.

Cyril's only meeting with his father is a key to some of his troubles. In chapter 3, "A Vendor of Visions," he encounters a broken tramplike man marked by humiliation and lost idealism. He does not recognize him as his father until he later accompanies his mother to see him when he lies dead. On the occasion when he sees him alive, the father is sleeping on a fallen tree that is usually a seat for young lovers, significant for Cyril on two counts. A tree can symbolize the union of the two parents and also the phallic power of the father. Here, the father is laid low and unacknowledged, preventing Cyril from feeling pride in his own maleness. Furthermore, it is only through realization of his masculinity and acceptance of his parents' union that he will come to a free expression of his own erotic nature. The ghostly young couple who should have been making love on the lover's seat are a fleeting vision of Cyril's rebellious sexual drive for a female of his own generation, a transformation impossible in actuality because he lacks a strong father from whom to derive male strength. In the attitude of the father sleeping on the fallen tree, there is, however, a touch of idealism that establishes an emotional link with the watching son: "The cap had fallen from his grizzled hair, and his head leaned back against a profusion of the little wild geraniums that decorated the dead bough so delicately" (22). This father, cast down by the overbearing mother, possesses a hint of rustic strength in the flowers that almost crown his hair, leading to an association with Annable, the vigorous demon of the woods who becomes a true father figure for Cyril. The parting sign for Cyril after he has identified himself to the person he does not yet know is his father is an ebony stick with a gold head that the man takes up as he rises from the tree. "The stick seemed to catch at my imagination" (23) is all that we are told intentionally, but the emotional meaning of the stick for Cyril is that it is a promise of the possibility of masculine power, to be more fulfilled in his relations with George and with Annable, each of whom reconstructs an area of male experience on Cyril's behalf.

Cyril's brotherhood with George links him with the sphere of George's violence and pride, as well as with his suffering and defeat. The masculine ideals of the novel are crystallized in the person of Annable, a tough unyielding male figure, contemptuous of women and of all "civilized" society, who becomes an ideal father image for Cyril, thus strengthening his sense of independence as a man. Annable draws together several important unfulfilled themes: anger at male domination by women; male independence; the need for a male parent; and male comradeship. All are assertions of the masculine ego that feels defeated by female power. Cyril is powerfully drawn to the tough and violent maleness of the keeper: "All the world hated him—to the people in the villages he was like a devil of the woods. Some miners had sworn vengeance on him for having caused their committal to goal. But he had a great attraction for me; his magnificent physique, his great vigour and vitality, and his swarthy, gloomy face drew me" (146). Annable, in turn, treats him like a son: "He treated me as an affectionate father treats a delicate son; I noticed he liked to put his hand on my shoulder or my knee as we talked" (147).

The tenor of this relationship is made clear in the passage that follows the funeral of Annable after his abrupt fall to death. There is a parallel between the deaths and funerals of the two father figures, both called Frank: Cyril's biological father, hated and wished dead by his wife and daughter Lettie, and the lusty father Annable, contemptuous of all ties with women, whom Cyril finally dares to acknowledge. The period following the funeral of the first Frank is sad and muted, that which succeeds the funeral of the second is curiously joyful and marked by a surge of springtime energy in flowers, trees, and birds. The link with Annable is found in a passage describing the nesting behavior of thrushes: "Ah, but the thrush is scornful, ringing out his voice from the hedge! He sets his breast against the mud, and models it warm for the turquoise eggs—blue, blue, bluest of eggs, which cluster so close and round against the breast, which round up beneath the breast, nestling content. You should see the bright ecstasy in the eyes of a nesting thrush, because of the rounded caress of the eggs against her breast!" (155). What is notable here is the intensity of emotion and the function given to the male thrush as the primary parent who shapes the nest and delights in the warm closeness of the eggs. Only towards the end of the passage is there a transition to the female thrush, forming a hybrid parent in which the male element is dominant. The joyful sense of release in the post-funeral sequence emanates from Cyril's newfound ability to acknowledge Annable's values and his male strength, and above all his relief at being able to accept the moral authority of a male parent and his own maleness against the dominance of a mother figure with empty breasts and a grudging resentment of men.

There are two important scenes in which Annable puts forward his views of women, the first when he comes across the two pairs of young people trespassing in his woods, and the second in the frequently discussed sequence when he attacks the peacock as an image of vain and teasing women. The first episode begins with a sense of compelling secrecy as the group discovers a hollow in the dim woods filled with snowdrops, characterized as sad and mysterious flowers: "The girls bent among them, touching them with their fingers, and symbolising the yearning which I felt" (129).[11] They have approached the boundaries of a taboo and are aware of a delicious longing for something beyond the muted virginal whiteness of the flowers. They proceed forward into the woods and are stopped by Annable the keeper, "like some malicious Pan," who makes lascivious taunts about the coupling of the young people in this hidden place. His repeated theme is that "ladies" should be stripped of their self-possession and dignity and subjected to male power in the realm of sexuality where men are supreme: "You can't tell a lady from a woman at this distance at dusk" (130). Cyril's sexual yearnings take on the power of vigorous possibility as Annable tears down the taboos that surround female sensuousness, taboos deriving from infantile oedipal desires.

Annable's second attack upon women is made when Cyril seeks him out in the woods near the derelict church. From the graveyard, Cyril sees in the Hall courtyard a bowed and weather-beaten statue of an angel upon which a peacock perches briefly and leaves behind its excrement. This Annable points to as "the very soul of a lady" (148). The debased images of the church and the angel together crystallize a wish to smash in fury the elevated virtue of the angelic feminine ideal. Both convey an aura of profanity, which is intensified by the fact that the demonic Annable is a former clergyman. He again desecrates the ideal of feminine purity that threatens male sexuality.[12]

In the vital sequences of the novel where Annable appears, the "bad mother" aspect of women is overwhelming, and Annable's function is to assert the preservation of maleness against this threat. In the churchyard scene, the peacock is presented as a despicable creature with ugly legs, an ungainly movement, and a harsh, screeching voice. The image of loathesome or predatory birds is regularly associated in symbol and fantasy with threatening females. The peacock, defiling with excrement, resembles the harpies of classical mythology. One recalls the various references in Lawrence to women as harpies, for example the overpowered Skrebensky's view of Ursula. The Russian Baba Yaga, the cannabilistic ogress, with her "spindle-shanks"—(paralleled by the "shrunken spindle legs" of Cyril's maternal piano with its empty breast)—and her flying cottage resting upon chicken legs, is one example of the negative "bad mother," which Annable so insistently projects here.

Annable hates civilization and all social values associated with women's hold over individual life. He expresses affection for his family but links them only with the animal world, not with the human society of female dominance. At the social level, Lawrence evinces a criticism of this father's neglect of his wife, leading to deprivation and suffering on the part of the children; yet the more fundamental values reflected in the novel yield an irrational image of Annable as an ideal father, providing the bond in nature for which Cyril longs. These two points of view cannot be resolved in a logical way. Whatever Lawrence's sympathetic observation of women's experience, Annable is necessary at a basic level as a father imago who can give pride and independence to the son. Once again, Sam is the figure who crystallizes the fundamental experience. He is the suffering, lacerated male child, masochistically carrying the inverted guilt of aggression against the mother. He is also necessarily the son of Annable, another Cyril helplessly cut off from the father, living in a female-dominated world, yet ever striving after the father who hates the woman and all her weapons of possessiveness. In the social world constructed by the mother, he can have no contact with that father; in the world of nature, he can acknowledge his bond with him. Annable leads a life of cruelty and brutality, the active mode of existence of a male. He also dies the violent death of a male, in which he is discovered by the suffering Sam. For the helpless male child, this repeats the pattern of the death of the father experienced by Cyril, the mature form of Sam. At the immediate level, the deaths of both Franks are the intentional killing off of fathers who in some respects are hateful and cannot be accepted in the real world, yet, on behalf of himself and his surrogates, Cyril extracts and internalizes the facets of Annable necessary to his male existence. This is one of the positive moments of the novel, but Cyril's fitful hopelessness and George's eventual infantile subjection to both Meg and Emily show female power finally triumphant. In Annable, we have merely the germ of a solution to the problem of male independence overwhelmed by female dominance. In later works, in the violent active maleness of *The Plumed Serpent* and in the phallic supremacy of Parkin-Mellors, the achieved form of Annable, we discover a more consistent and carefully wrought philosophy of maleness that is an elaborate defense against the emotional power of women.

CHAPTER 4

Images of Women in Blake

Blake's central theme is the fall of human beings from the ideal state, in which the imagination and the senses are integrated, into a contemporary condition of harmful abstractions. His social critique applies to all people, male or female, for in the restored world of imagination there will be no distinctions between the sexes:

> Los answerd swift as the shuttle of gold. Sexes must vanish & cease
> To be, when Albion arises from his dread repose O lovely Enitharmon.
> (E252; *J*92, 13–14)

In the perfection of existence, men and women will have no separate being but will be united in harmony. However, in the joyful apocalypse that follows this statement by Los at the end of *Jerusalem*, it is in the image of man that human beings are restored.[1] Albion's Emanation, Jerusalem, is gathered to his bosom in an ultimate vision of integration. All of the senses are expanded and restored, and distinctions in types of existence fade out. The second state of innocence is attained.

In these redemptive moments of unity with man, woman is benign and a source of peace. Elsewhere in Blake, there are fearful references to women as separate beings who have their own identity and exert power over men. In Night the Ninth of *The Four Zoas*, there is a horrified description of a female who exists independently:

> And Many Eternal Men sat at the golden feast to see
> The female form now separate They shudderd at the horrible thing
> Not born for the sport and amusement of Man but born to drink up all his
> powers

They wept to see their shadows they said to one another this is Sin
This is the Generative world they remembered the Days of old
(E401; *FZ*IX, 133, 5–9)

The perfect female exists for man's gratification. Like Oothoon and Enitharmon, she brings other women to her mate for his pleasure, without expecting reciprocal attentions. Here, woman as a self-sufficient entity carries a threat of castration: "born to drink up all his powers." In *Jerusalem*, a mysterious nonsexual, redeemed condition is described, wherein the function of the Emanations is to make it possible for men to communicate with each other:

For Man cannot unite with Man but by their Emanations
Which stand both Male & Female at the Gates of each Humanity
How then can I ever again be united as Man with Man
While thou my Emanation refusest my Fibres of dominion.
(E246; *J*88, 10–13)

A woman who refuses to be subservient threatens the ideal human state, namely, that in which man is actor and agent.

Blake's critique of his society, then, is fundamentally concerned with male well-being;[2] his redeemed people arise in the image of man, within whom the female is safely contained. Although he makes reasonable and sensitive observations about women as the victims of a repressive society, like Jane Shore in his early painting or Oothoon in *Visions of the Daughters of Albion*, his deepest feelings towards women are colored by an aggression that shapes and animates his works.[3] Brenda Webster contends that Blake is incapable of envisaging men and women living together without conflict, and that his solution to this problem in the later works is either to assimilate the female within the male or to cast her in a very restricted role, meaning that she does not truly exist in the male world.[4]

In the epics, women are often more persistently cruel and sinister forces than men; Blake criticizes the stultifying effect of arid intellectualism in his society through his characterization of the Female Will, a terrible power emanating from women. In order to defend himself against the female forces that threaten to overwhelm him, Blake uses several thematic devices that preserve belief in male dominance. He attaches enormous value to "the definite," whether in visual art, techniques of verbal expression, or

Los's methods of forging redemption with his very palpable mace and anvil; women, on the other hand, are customarily associated with the sinister *indefinite* of fluidity and vagueness. The creation of the Emanations is the major means whereby Blake asserts male existence.

It is often assumed that the Emanations are simply an expressive technique that Blake used in the unfolding of his epic themes.[5] However, if an artist uses an expressive form, it is because it is particularly suited to his view of the world or to the structure of his feelings. Blake used the device of the Emanation to embody an essential part of his mental reality. Since Emanations derive their being from men, and in the ideal state are not distinct from men, the male has the illusion of having power over them. The device is a defense that reverses the psychological reality. The male in actuality feels in danger of disintegration in the sphere of the dominant female; in fantasy, he dominates the female and also has more stable and permanent existence than she.

The notion of the Emanation, woman as a creature who literally derives her existence from man, first developed in the mid-1970s. In the earliest version of *Vala*, later *The Four Zoas*, there are no Emanations. The first description of the birth of an Emanation is found in plate 18 of *The Book of Urizen* of 1795, in a passage that Blake intended to include at the end of Night the Fourth of *The Four Zoas*.[6] This move from naturalistic women characters to a type of female whose threat could be curbed by her existential ties to man suggests a deepened anxiety about women. The inception of the Emanations seems to correspond in general to the appearance of more hostile images of women in Blake's work.[7]

The descriptions of Enitharmon's parturition from Los reveal their psychological significance. The most detailed version of the birth of Enitharmon is found in Night the Fourth of *The Four Zoas*, when the Spectre of Urthona describes the event to Tharmas:

> My loins begin to break forth into veiny pipes & writhe
> Before me in the wind englobing trembling with strong vibrations
> The bloody mass began to animate. I bending over
> Wept bitter tears incessant. Still beholding how the piteous form
> Dividing & dividing from my loins a weak & piteous
> Soft cloud of snow a female pale & weak I soft embracd
> My counter part & calld it Love. (E333; *FZ*IV, 50, 11–17)

At the end of Night the Fourth, the globe of blood itself is described in more detail, in lines that originally appeared in *The Book of Urizen* (plate 18):

> The globe of life blood trembled Branching out into roots;
> Fibrous, writhing upon the winds; Fibres of blood, milk and tears.
> (E338; *FZ*IV, 55, 24–25)

The process of parturition is a hideous parody of normal birth, the original and fundamental way in which the female controls the male. It is, therefore, an effort to usurp maternal power. According to Klein, boys at the anal-sadistic phase feel envy of the mother's womb and of her children.[8] The globe of blood is a womblike form that shifts power to the male in a manner that so wrenches his elemental being that it causes anguish.[9] An essential aspect of the process is the male's sense of partial disintegration, as "veiny pipes" shoot from him. There is a tension between this disintegrating sensation and the solid enclosing form of the globe of blood. It is interesting to note that Lawrence also produced a version of this motif, in the painting *Renascence of Men*, which depicts a woman prostrate in worship of a man who has apparently just given birth to her.

Elsewhere in Blake, there are references to other rigid, enclosing forms, such as the circle, the crystal cabinet, and the sun of generation. These are associated with the womb of elemental female power and pose a threat to man unless, as here, he is able to gain control of them in his turn. The enclosure fantasy is a defense against the infantile fear of annihilation resulting from anguish at separation from the mother and, at the same time, extreme, destructive aggression against her. The female creature who emerges from this bizarre parturition is weak and pitiful, yet her pitifulness proves to be an actual source of strength. In *The Book of Urizen*, the creature called Pity produces two effects: she activates the building of a sinister temple overspread with the Woof of Science, and she displays seductive cruelty towards Los, her consort. Both of these effects spring from the psychological reality of the male's response to the female. The pity she embodies is an inversion of soft and tender maternal feelings, bitterly resented by the male because they are withheld but also experienced as her power over him because they are intrinsic to the infant's overwhelming dependence upon the mother.

In *The Book of Los*, dating from the same period as *The Book of Urizen*, Los also spawns a Polypus in a manner that resembles the engendering of Enitharmon. This is the first appearance in Blake's work of the amorphous, cancerous, stultifying mass of life that, in its overwhelming formlessness, seems to be related to the peculiar menace of the female:

He arose on the waters, but soon
Heavy falling his organs like roots
Shooting out from the seed, shot beneath,
And a vast world of waters around him
In furious torrents began.

Then he sunk, & around his spent Lungs
Began intricate pipes that drew in
The spawn of the waters. Outbranching

An immense Fibrous form, stretching out
Thro' the bottoms of immensity raging. (E93; *BoL*4, 63–5, 2)

The generation of the Polypus begins with a fantasy of ejaculation that displays the weakness of the male self of Los, since at this moment of male fulfillment he is engulfed in furious waters. Instead of attaining desired union with the female, he produces a monstrous, shapeless creature. The tenuousness of his male identity is linked with the suffocating formlessness of this being.

Several dark female presences haunt the action of some of Blake's epic works and display a sinister influence upon males. They are fleeting figures and their function is less specified than that of the Emanations, but their power reaches deep into the recesses of the male spirit. They represent the essence of female power in their vagueness, and in their association with food of a harsh and nonnurturing kind.

The first of these is the Shadowy Daughter of Urthona, an early form of Vala, who appears in the Preludium to *America*, and is known in *The Four Zoas* as the Shadowy Female. In *America*, she bears a shifting relationship to Orc, the revolutionary son. At the beginning of the poem, she is a somber sister-mother figure who is violently raped by the young hero, an action that brings revolution into the world. The initial description of her presents a woman of grim and ruthless nature:

The shadowy daughter of Urthona stood before red Orc.
When fourteen suns had faintly journey'd o'er his dark abode;
His food she brought in iron baskets, his drink in cups of iron;

> Crown'd with a helmet & dark hair the nameless female stood;
> A quiver with its burning stores, a bow like that of night,
> When pestilence is shot from heaven . . . (E51; *A*1, 1–5)

She performs a female function in providing Orc with food, yet it is food given grudgingly.[10] The cold metal of the containers manifests a lack of tenderness for the suffering son chained in darkness, which matches the feeble light of the sun and the hopelessness of his psychological reality. The nameless and speechless female bears a bow and arrows, a weapon that is associated with male power and virility. The illustration of the woman that accompanies the text of the Preludium, however, shows a figure who is covering her face to weep, helpless in the presence of Urthona, Orc's captor. She is, then, a woman who carries a threat in her quiverful of "burning" phallic arrows and in her bow with its capacity to rain down plague; she brings harsh food to the imprisoned youth; yet her insubstantiality, lack of identity, and weeping pose make her seem a suffering victim of life.

The Shadowy Female is a mother figure, transposed into the role of a sisterly consort, who carries a threat for the male desperately seeking to establish the security and power for action that comes from incorporating the image of the good mother. She appears to him to have a phallic power that is greater than his and is capable of destroying his through disease. Her maternal nourishment is bestowed with a sense of severity. Her vagueness, diffuseness, and namelessness point to what emerges in later works as the most frightening and destructive quality in a woman; when anger against the mother overwhelms the child with punishing guilt, his own being seems to him to disintegrate and with it the solid image and relationship with the good mother.[11] She therefore appears vague and remote to him, which leads him to cling frantically to definite forms. This female bears a relationship to the weeping mother at the end of "The Crystal Cabinet," who is seen desolate in the wilderness and mutually unable to establish a bond with her child. She exists in a threatening perspective of menacing woman and suffering victim.

In *The Four Zoas* and, thereafter, in *Jerusalem*, the Shadowy Female takes on a more specific form as Vala, the cruel goddess of Nature. In either manifestation, the male with whom she interacts as mother-consort is Orc–Luvah. Orc is the rebellious son, a more complex form of the oedipal boy in the *Songs of Experience*. He is trapped in his phallic nature, and his rebellion is shown to be a repetitious cycle of frustration. In the more developed person of Luvah, he is the son who has incorporated guilt and is associated with suffering and Christlike sacrifice.

At the beginning of *America*, Orc fulfills a fantasy of rebellion against the father through seduction of a forbidden female. The revolution this engenders is shown to lead to frustration and negation, and Blake, thereafter, deals with the reality of the situation of oedipal anguish and guilt as a more complex and frustrating one, from which there is no permanent escape, even through fantasy. When Vala appears in *The Four Zoas* as a more specified form of the Shadowy Female, her power cannot be so easily overthrown. Both her shadowy, indefinite aspect and her aggressive, phallic aspect are more fully developed in their menace. She seeks to overwhelm Orc–Luvah in a variety of ways.

In Night the Second, Luvah, the anguished son, is cast into the furnaces of Urizen whose flames Vala feeds "in cruel delight" while she listens in joy to his "howlings" (E317). In Luvah's fantasy the parent-child roles are then switched as he recalls how he had nurtured her:

> When I calld forth the Earth-worm from the cold & dark obscure
> I nurturd her I fed her with my rains & dews, she grew
> A scaled Serpent, yet I fed her tho' she hated me. (E317; *FZ*II, 26, 7–9)

The mechanism of regarding the predatory mother as a child is an attempt to render her harmless,[12] but this is in vain: the earthworm grows nevertheless into the menacing phallic female, "a Dragon winged bright & poisonous." This sequence is followed by another attempt to construct a harmless mother under the son's control: "I carried her in my bosom as a man carries a lamb / I loved her I gave her all my soul & my delight" (27, 3–4).[13] Briefly here, a good object is created and maintained in love, and the son's fantasy of engendering children with the mother is fulfilled. Soon, however, Luvah feels that she has been taken away from him and hidden, while he is imprisoned by Urizen; his hatred and envy of the mother are associated with oedipal conflicts.[14] The illustrations that appear on page 26, the same page of the *Vala* manuscript as the description of Luvah's feeding of the earthworm who becomes a dragon, reveal the emotions that lie behind this sequence of images (see figure 1). We see

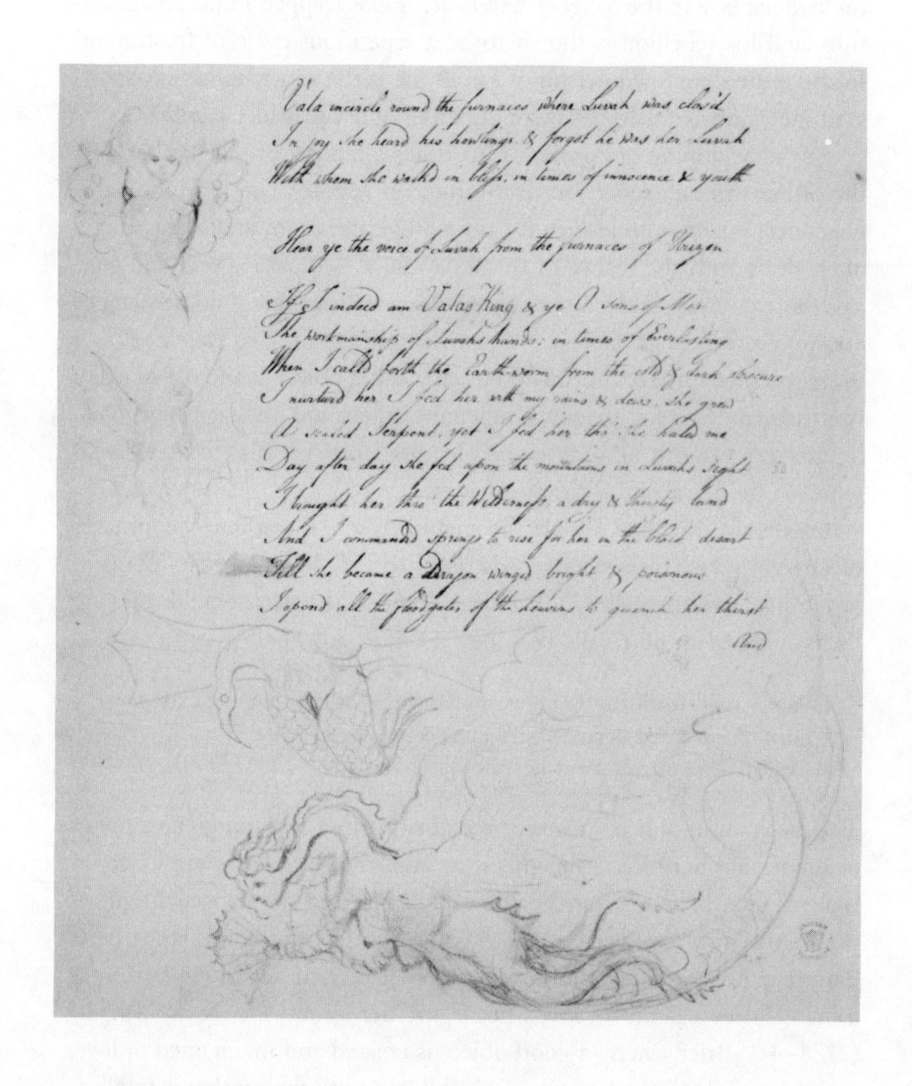

Vala incircle round the furnaces where Luvah was clos'd
In joy she heard his howlings & forgot he was her Luvah
With whom she walk'd in bliss. in times of innocence & youth

Hear ye the voice of Luvah from the furnaces of Urizen

If I indeed am Valas King & ye O Sons of Men
The workmanship of Luvahs hands; in times of Everlasting
When I calld forth the Earth-worm from the cold & dark obscure
I nurtured her I fed her with my rains & dews. she grew
A scaled Serpent, yet I fed her tho' she hated me
Day after day she fed upon the mountains in Luvahs sight
I brought her thro' the Wilderness a dry & thirsty land
And I commanded springs to rise for her in the black desart
Till she became a Dragon winged bright & poisonous
I opend all the floodgates of the heavens to quench her thirst
And

Figure 1. *Vala*, p. 26. Department of Manuscripts, the British Library

an ornate human female with dragon features who has a third, phallic, breast.[15] There is also a bird of prey with a hooked beak, a malicious, pretty butterfly, and a woman with dragon wings, all three with enlarged vulvas. While illustrating the text, these figures are also very fundamental motifs of menacing and castrating females.[16]

Jean Hagstrum prefaces a paper that chiefly focuses on the relationship of Luvah and Vala with the claim that "Blake may justly be considered the greatest love poet in our language."[17] However, as Webster so convincingly shows, Blake rarely deals with mature adult love, and his male characters are incapable of mature love.[18] This encounter between Luvah and Vala illustrates the fact that his predominant subject matter is the anguish and ambivalence of the mother-son relationship.

The relationship in the Shadowy Female–Orc configuration recurs throughout *The Four Zoas*. In Night the Seventh, the dominating mother seeks to destroy Orc's potency, thus reducing him to the smiling meekness and hypocrisy of the good and obedient child of the *Songs*:

> Thus in the Caverns of the Grave & Places of human seed
> The nameless shadowy Vortex stood before the face of Orc
> The Shadow reard her dismal head over the flaming youth
> With sighs & howling & deep sobs that he might lose his rage
> And with it lose himself in meekness she embracd his fire.
>
> (E363; *FZ*VIIb, 91, 1–5)

Her "dismal" nature and her manifestations of sorrow are not a weakness but a terrible female strength, allied to the female power of pity. Orc, by the related paternal power of Urizen, has been transformed into a serpent form, fixated in his helplessness as a limited phallic creature. Thence, he becomes the Christlike Luvah who is crucified, setting in process a sequence of torment presided over by the triumphant Female as Vala, the oppressive Goddess of Nature. Again, a profound association is made between the woman's violent assertion of power over the suffering male, and the loss of a sensuous grasp upon an integrated physical reality.

In Night the Eighth, Orc the jealous son appears in two guises, as the Christlike Luvah, now converted into the "meek" and suffering victim, and as a demonic serpent recalling the evil splendors of Milton's Satan:

> In fury a Serpent wondrous among the Constellations of Urizen
> A crest of fire rose on his forehead red as the carbuncle

Beneath down to his eyelids scales of pearl then gold & silver
Immingled with the ruby overspread his Visage down
His furious neck writ[h]ing contortive in dire budding pains
The scaly armour shot out. (E373; *FZ*VIII, 101, 8–13)

As Luvah, Orc is the "good" son, clinging to the idealized image of the mother. However, this idealizing process is not complete, as he splits into the form of Orc, his truer self, glowingly aware of desire for the mother and possessed by his phallic aspect. As Orc, without the false healing mechanism that produces Luvah, he is closer to the real anguished relationship with the mother, corroded with envy and destructive impulses,[19] which are associated with her apparent harshness and lack of nurture. His agony of frustration is linked with food; with the fruit of the Tree of Mystery, meaning knowledge of the parents' sexuality; and with the treasures of the mother's body:

Stubborn down his back & bosom
The Emerald Onyx Sapphire jasper beryl amethyst
Strove in terrific emulation which should gain a place
Upon the mighty Fiend the fruit of the mysterious tree
Kneaded in Uveths kneading trough. Still Orc devourd the food
In raging hunger Still the pestilential food in gems & gold
Exuded round his awful limbs Stretching to serpent length
His human bulk While the dark shadowy female brooding over
Measurd his food morning & evening in cups & baskets of iron.
(E373; *FZ*VIII, 101, 13–21)

The jewels growing and fighting each other upon his back have several layers of significance. At the most developmentally advanced level, they are—as the fruit of the tree of the parents' authority and sexuality—sexual knowledge desired with a bitter and frustrated jealousy; thence, he is converted to a helplessly phallic creature in an elementally conflicting and endlessly striving serpentine form of existence. The jewels are also the riches and treasures of the mother's body, desired by the pre-oedipal infant as the source of all goodness, but also torn apart in fury by the frightened, aggressive child and subjected to spoiling and pollution by the feces.[20] Thus, they bring upon the child the anger of the persecutory mother image, in part, in the form of a poisonous infection. The jewels and gold are associated with the fruit of the tree, namely with sensuous desire; the pain and distortion of the infantile wish for nourishment are shown in the fact that they are, as gems, hard, cold, inorganic substances, sharing some qualities with the colorful and beautiful fruit of true and satisfying nourishment but lacking their vitality and fragrance. As frozen forms of frustrated desire, they suggest the essence of the true good object, yet are eternally unable to bring the fulfillment of integration. In their hardness and fascination with value and color, they reflect obsessive anal retentiveness, and the anal-sadistic impulses against the mother's body,[21] which bring related persecutory attacks from her.

A further and yet more fundamental association of the jewels and the anguished serpent form is the mother's function as the provider of food and, thus, the desperate sense of bleakness which unsatisfactory nourishment brings to the child. Again, as in the Preludium to *America*, we see the Shadowy Female give to Orc, insatiably desirous of maternal love, meager supplies of food in harsh iron vessels. In that earlier episode, her provision of sustenance was regulated by the passage of periods of time. To an even greater extent in this episode in *The Four Zoas*, there is a careful sense of regulation and, thereby, stinginess, as the brooding female measures out Orc's food. This is linked with the anally aggressive child's own wish to exercise control through ungenerous retention and the making of minute divisions.

In her oppressive task the Shadowy Female is aided by the "iron hearted sisters Daughters of Urizen", one of whom, Uveth, kneaded Orc's bread in her kneading trough. These three grim sisters recall the Fates and their terrible power over human live.[22] They first appear in their fallen form in Night the Sixth when Urizen is exploring his desolate kingdom. With his silver helmet, a symbol of treasured femininity, he drinks from the river but finds that his thirst is unsatisfied. At this moment of frustration, he sights three "terrific women," "spirits of darkness," the eldest of whom is filling her urn and pouring out water, the source of his tantalizing dissatisfaction. (*E*345; *FZ*V1, 67, 1–19) The women are distinct in dress and in color association but belong together as a trio like the groups of three women in "The Crystal Cabinet," "The Golden Net," and elsewhere, associated with the Female Will; like them, they are a split or disintegrating image of women arising from the dissolution of reality contingent upon the infant's disappointed urge for union with the good maternal object. Like the Shadowy Female in most of her manifestations, they are menacingly silent, a characteristic that Freud says is in dream language symbolic of death.[23] Appropriately, these grimly unyielding sisters are associated with nourishment, a fundamental experience of desire and denial. Orc suffers torment at their hands when, upholding the authority of Urizen as oppressive father, they knead the bread of sorrow:

> Rending the Rocks Eleth & Uveth rose & Ona rose
> Terrific with their iron vessels driving them across
> In the dim air they took the book of iron & placd above
> On clouds of death & sang their songs Kneading the bread of Orc
> Orc listend to the song compelld hungring on the cold wind
> That swaggd heavy with the accursed dough. the hoar frost ragd
> Thro Onas sieve the torrent rain pourd from the iron pail
> Of Eleth & the icy hands of Uveth kneaded the bread.
>
> (E355; *FZ*VII, 79, 25–32)

The elements associated with feeding are imbued with cruelty and coldness, bleakness and inhospitality. What should be ideal feminine containing vessels become the sieve and the leaking pail, which refuse satisfaction and, together with the raging frost and the pouring rain, reflect the destructive aggression of the desolate child. The pierced feminine vessels evince the mutilated body of the mother; the rain pouring through the empty gaps in the pail is a urethral attack upon her. Bread, itself the very basis of wholesome nurturance, is transformed into a persecutory maternal association: the "accursed dough" suggests potential harm to the child. Kneading, like weaving, one of the elemental female acts,[24] means to reduce material to a shapeless and pliant mass. Here it is shown in a terrifying aspect, an aggressive pounding that exerts a pitiless control over form and matter. The kneading of the child's means of sustenance becomes for Orc, the angry, deprived son, a fantasy image of a punishing mother. Her pounding of the formless mass suggests also an attack upon him, or another child, by the female who truly controls his "fibres of being."[25]

The social dimension of Orc's pain is the suffering of the poor and downtrodden, in whom the capacity to rebel has been suppressed. Like the parents who had forced the frowning aggressive baby to adopt an air of meek compliance, social authorities make the people cover up their genuine feeling with hypocrisy:

Compell the poor to live upon a Crust of bread by soft mild arts
Smile when they frown frown when they smile & when a man looks pale
With labour & abstinence say he looks healthy & happy . . .
(E355; *FZ*VII, 80, 9–11)

A fundamental quality of female influence, according to Blake's depiction of it, is its indefiniteness and its deadening abstraction. His view of the Female Will, a major element in his analysis of history, is a central manifestation of this destructive influence. The Female Will is the presence and effect of abstract thinking within society, seen to be closely linked with women's dominance of men. We have already noted Los's lament upon the power of the Female Will in chapter 2 of *Jerusalem*:

O Albion why wilt thou Create a Female Will?
To hide the most evident God in a hidden covert, even
In the shadows of a Woman & a secluded Holy Place . . .
Is this the Female Will O ye lovely Daughters of Albion. To
Converse concerning Weight & Distance in the Wilds of Newton & Locke.
(E176–77; *J*30, 31–40)

Later in *Jerusalem*, the presence of Rahab, or Natural Religion, within Hand, the eldest son of Albion and the Reasoning Spectre, is presented as a deadening female power that acts through moral repression:

Imputing Sin & Righteousness to Individuals; Rahab
Sat deep within him hid: his Feminine Power unreveal'd
Brooding Abstract Philosophy. to destroy Imagination, the Divine–
–Humanity A Three-fold Wonder: feminine: most beautiful: Threefold
Each within other. (E224; *J*70, 17–21)

In *Europe*, an earlier work, the effects of menacing female beauty upon masculine imagination are made plain in an Enlightenment setting, following the eighteen-hundred-year sleep of Enitharmon that culminates in the appearance of Newton.[26]

We have mentioned that the association Blake and Lawrence make between feminine power and abstract empiricism is problematic,[27] since it seems opposed to familiar cultural interpretations. Blake is unusual in giving a female quality to the Enlightenment, as he is singular among contemporary artists in repudiating both landscape painting and an expressive delight in nature. It is evident from his images and narrative sequences that Blake puts an uncommon stress upon "definiteness." In visual art, he admires a firm outline and despises chiaroscuro, putting these principles into practice in his own art. In his poetry, he constantly works to achieve effects of concreteness and definiteness, expressing ideas through sharply delineated human figures and conveying concepts through palpable structures or activities: the temple and books of Urizen, or Los's active rebuilding of a better society.[28] The vagueness and disintegration resulting from the fall of Urizen must be contained, hence Los's binding of Urizen in *The Book of Los*, and the setting of the Limits of Opacity and Contradiction. We, therefore, see in Blake an urgent concern with concrete containment, working against another set of images that reflect a fear of being contained and a dislike of what seems vague or undefined.

The fear of containment and the wish to contain are closely associated. For the infant, the move into abstraction through both motor operations and the formation of concepts marks a delightful independence, yet also holds perils. It entails a movement away from maternal symbiosis, the most secure and blissful state. Where there is very strong aggression against an apparently cold mother, the child's destructive fury is so intense that, during the phase Melanie Klein refers to as the paranoid-schizoid position, the child fears its own annihilation.[29] It defends itself from this disaster by splitting the hated object into a good and a bad part, casting out the bad part and incorporating the good. If hatred and fear of annihilation, that is, of the infant's causing its own annihilation, are truly intense, the need to cling to the good object for the sake of sheer survival is especially strong. To leave the good mother, on whom the child feels dependent because of the strength of his aggression, and to enter a formless world which, through an inversion of antagonistic feelings, has become filled with menace is therefore a frightening prospect. The act of "splitting," through its basic binary form, helps the child to organize his experience, but his intense fear of the negative makes experience appear vague because it is too fearful to contemplate. Hence, the mother and her solid sensuous world are idealized and strongly valued, making the child's excursions beyond her into a mental, less sensuous world appear threatening to his individual survival.

The intense emotion that surrounds the mother image in Blake has a strong content of sexuality and moral repression. At the narcissistic stage, in early infancy, the ego instincts and the sexual instincts are still united. The child's original drive is for self-preservation, within which the sexual instincts grow and then differentiate themselves. The painful anger directed against women in Blake is associated with an early phase in which the bad mother's threat to the child's survival is met with furious aggression; at the same time, incipient oedipal conflicts lend a sexual quality to the experience of deprivation and the accompanying attack upon the mother.[30] He presents the mother figure as a major source of moral injunctions, or "Moral Law," while her harshness is wrapped in mystery, or a tabernacle, which has an aura of forbidden sexual delight:

> Enitharmon answerd: This is Woman's World, nor need she any
> Spectre to defend her from Man. I will Create secret places
> And the masculine names of the places Merlin & Arthur.
> A triple Female Tabernacle for Moral Law I weave
> That he who loves Jesus may loathe terrified Female love
> Till God Himself become a Male subservient to the Female.(E247; *J*88, 16–21)

Moral prohibitions emanate from an all-powerful female and are enshrined in a tabernacle, one of Blake's imprisoning womblike forms, having the numinous quality of a taboo. In *Europe*, the specific effects of female-induced moral prohibitions within society are made clear:

> Enitharmon laugh'd in her sleep to see (O womans triumph)
> Every house a den, every man bound; the shadows are filld
> With spectres, and the windows wove over with curses of iron:
> Over the doors Thou shalt not; and over the chinmeys Fear is written:
> With bands of iron round their necks fasten'd into the walls
> The citizens: in leather gyves the inhabitants of suburbs
> Walk heavy: soft and bent are the bones of the villagers . . .(E64; *Eu*12, 25–31)

Like the lovers of "Ah! Sun-flower," deprived of sexual fulfillment, the male victims of woman's repressions are gravely diminished in substance and vitality.

It is initially surprising that Blake should give woman a function as a harsh guardian of moral law since he also, in accordance with more usual expectations, makes Urizen, the father figure, the source of moral authority as well as of abstract reasoning. Melanie Klein's view of earlier development helps to elucidate this complexity. The parents may not be sharply distinguished by the infant and may appear as a hybrid force. In the oedipal phase, which she places earlier than Freud, there is a strong response to both parents. Moreover, the infant in earlier life may have a primitive and very powerful superego, which is not by any means a reflection of a clear and rational moral code but of a punishing, emotional sense of taboo and cruel prohibition.[31] This does not correspond to the reality of the parents' treatment of the child; rather, it is the child's anticipation of violent punishment for destructive and cannibalistic impulses.

The reflection of the maternal superego in Blake is very harsh, ultimately more cruel and unyielding than Urizen himself. She is a forbidding presence who cuts off and inhibits libidinal delights at their source, through what is perceived as moral prohibition. The child feels that his desires are suffocated and killed. In abandonment, his being disintegrates into nothingness, causing him to perceive the female as intangible, vague, and evanescent.

This threatening female presence is habitually found at the heart of the scenes in which the paternal authority figure exerts his oppressive influence over the son. The image of a net or a web that covers and enshrouds is frequently used to denote a condition in which the instincts and senses are frozen or shrunken by moralistic rationalization. In one of its most developed forms, it is the Web of Religion apparently created by Urizen:

> And the Sciences were fixd & the Vortexes began to operate
> On all the sons of men & every human soul terrified
> At the turning wheels of heaven shrunk away inward withring away
> Gaining a New Dominion over all his sons & Daughters
> & over the Sons & daughters of Luvah in the horrible Abyss
> For Urizen lamented over them in a selfish lamentation
> Till a white woof coverd his cold limbs from head to feet
> Hair white as snow coverd him in flaky locks terrific
> Overspreading his limbs. in pride he wanderd weeping
> Clothed in aged venerableness obstinately resolvd
> Travelling thro darkness & whereever he traveld a dire Web
> Followd behind him as the Web of a Spider dusky & cold . . .
>
> (E350; *FZ*VI, 73, 21–32)

We notice, however, that this web, or woof, associated with the repressions of science and religion is closely linked with the *female* presence and with the male's attempt to overcome *female* domination. The connection is made explicit in the *Book of Urizen* after the account of the birth of Enitharmon. The indefiniteness emanating from the female leads to the formation of a temple to conceal a void and mystery:

They began to weave curtains of darkness
They erected large pillars round the Void
With golden hooks fastend in the pillars
With infinite labour the Eternals
A woof wove, and called it Science. (E78; *U*19, 5–9)

Later, as Urizen explores the vast wastes of desolation called his "dens," the effect of the female is made clearer:

Till a Web dark & cold, throughout all
The tormented element stretch'd
From the sorrows of Urizens soul
And the Web is a Female in embrio
None could break the Web, no wings of fire.

So twisted the cords, & so knotted
The meshes: twisted like to the human brain

And all calld it, The Net of Religion. (E82; *U*25, 15–22)

Again, female mystery and indefiniteness resulting from the prohibition of libidinal expression are at the center of the actuality of repression. Even so, Urizen, as the male agent of prohibition, suffers in his own web. As the male to whose role the son aspires, he is ultimately seen as a victim of the female power that preserves the dread holiness of sexual delight. The white woof is linked with the cloud within which the father is concealed in "Infant Sorrow": the strong heroic father is hidden from the son, castrated like him by the powerful mother.

Urizen, in his fallen state, is customarily sorrowful and caught up in the torments he himself has produced. By contrast, women enjoy cruel triumph in creating repressive suffering for others, suffering which they regard from an untouchable position of control. At the beginning of the "night of Enitharmon's joy," as described in *Europe*, the period of eighteen hundred years during which chastity flourished under formal Christianity, Enitharmon announces the policy with exultation in her power:

Go! tell the human race that Womans love is Sin!
That an Eternal life awaits the worms of sixty winters
In an allegorical abode where existence hath never come:
Forbid all Joy, & from her childhood shall the little female
Spread nets in every secret path. (E62; *Eu*5, 5–9)

Here and elsewhere, the locus of action and suffering is the male body and psyche. Women stand outside of this, apparently forced to be subservient to the male but, in fact, showing themselves to be the superior power and the source of male anguish.

The Tree of Mystery is a central image for the moral power of the parents over the oedipal child and shows the distinct function and relationship of each parent. The tree is a common symbol in the child's unconscious for the union of the parents.[32] This is apparent in the Garden of Eden motif that Blake draws on, in which the Tree of Knowledge conceals the secret of the parents' sexuality, and the acquisition of knowledge brings with it the authority of a punishing parental superego. In Blake's version, the sense of mystery emanating from the female is heavy and oppressive:

> Urizen heard the Voice & saw the Shadow. underneath
> His woven darkness & in laws & deceitful religions
> Beginning at the tree of Mystery circling its root
> She spread herself thro all the branches in the power of Orc
> A shapeless & indefinite cloud in tears of sorrow incessant
> Steeping the Direful Web of Religion swagging heavy it fell
> From heaven to heavn thro all its meshes altering the Vortexes
> Misplacing every Center hungry desire & lust began
> Gathering the fruit of that Mysterious tree till Urizen
> Sitting within his temple furious felt the num[m]ing stupor
> Himself tangled in his own net in sorrow lust repentance
>
> (E375–76; *FZ*VIII, 103, 21–31)

The female presence here is the Shadowy Female. The constellation of images surounding the tree of parental authority, in which the phallic father might appear supreme, is dominated by the more fundamental power of the mother.[33] Urizen's own sphere is engulfed by the influence of woman, the guardian of sacred eroticism, associated in fantasy with Orc, the would-be phallic son. This passage describing the tree and the shadow displays the emotional pattern associated with the phase of infancy when the drive for self-preservation and sexuality are only partly differentiated, placed by Klein at the period when the sense of maternal withdrawal, and its accompanying desired and feared independence, help to bring the child into the oedipal phase, while the oral bond with the mother remains strong. Oedipal feelings are implicit in the tree itself, in the sense of paternal repression, and in the phallic orientation of Orc, while the vague feminine mystery links the two spheres of the child's experience: she is the disintegrating mother fantasied by him in expectation of punishment and is also, in her holy mystery, the object of forbidden libidinal desires. The anguish of each position is combined as the son assuages his oral deprivation by devouring the erotic fruit of the tree: "Misplacing every Center hungry desire & lust began / Gathering the fruit of that Mysterious tree."

The seductive and yet terrifying power of the female is made plain in a description of the Shadow of Enitharmon giving birth beneath the Tree of Mystery to fruits and blossoms which, though beautiful, are poisonous:

> Thus Los lamented in the night unheard by Enitharmon
> For the Shadow of Enitharmon descended down the tree of Mystery
> The Spectre saw the Shade Shivering over his gloomy rocks
> Beneath the tree of Mystery which in the dismal Abyss
> Began to blossom in fierce pain shooting its writhing buds
> In throes of birth & now the blossoms falling shining fruit
> Appeard of many colours & of various poisonous qualities
> Of Plagues hidden in shining globes that grew on the living tree.
> (E357–58: *FZ*VII, 82, 15–22)

Here the nurturing and reproductive functions of the mother are the focus of attention. The fruit is the food that the infant depends upon and is, at the same time, a symbol of the female power of giving birth. The production of poisonous blossoms and fruits is a reflection of the son's envy and fear. The body of the mother, Klein tells us, is seen as filled with treasures and riches and with the bodies of other children.[34] This is a source of pain to the fantasying male child who wishes to possess all those precious treasures and also to produce his own babies. Since this is denied to him, his aggression and cannibalistic fury are converted into an image of a mother whose nurturing fruitfulness is corroded with the bitterness of his envy, and who is poisoned by his attack. The son Orc's unspeakable desires for the mother and his fantasy of fulfillment are voiced by Enitharmon, now drawn out of her "secret places":

> Art thou terrible Shade
> Set over this sweet boy of mine to guard him lest he rend
> His mother to the winds of heaven Intoxicated with
> The fruit of this delightful tree. (E358; *FZ*VII, 82, 37–83, 2)

The relative ease and indulgence of this scenario make it clear that it is a momentary illusion. The ongoing psychological reality is fraught with pain and complexity; the bleak Spectre of the forbidding father–son reflects guilt and a frightened introspection. Subsequently, the reign of Urizen, the oedipal father, is established, ushering in an age of fear and repression in which the fundamental power is that of the Shadow of the mother giving actuality to the tree of Urizen's authority:

> But in the deeps beneath the Roots of Mystery in darkest night
> Where Urizen sat on his rock the Shadow brooded
> Urizen saw & triumphd . . . (E360; *FZ*VII, 95, 15–17)

As this era of war and repression is described, its ultimate source in the rage and sadism against the mother on the part of the envious infant emerges. This is especially apparent in *Jerusalem*, where cruel women often dominate the action. Luvah, the Christlike, regenerated form of Orc, is put to death by the children of Albion, a joint act of cruelty in which the part played by the women appears more extreme:

> Now: now the battle rages round thy tender limbs O Vala
> Now smile among thy bitter tears: now put on all thy beauty
> Is not the wound of the sword sweet! & the broken bone delightful?
> Wilt thou now smile among the scythes when the wounded groan in the
> field[?] (E216; *J*65, 29–33)

Later, other victims are killed by the Daughters of Albion in a process equated with the deadening of men's sensory capacities; again, abstraction is fearful because it means the separation of man from the physical reality of the female body:

> The Knife of flint passes over the howling Victim: his blood
> Gushes & stains the fair side of the fair Daug[h]ters of Albion . . .
> They take off his vesture whole with their Knives of flint:
> But they cut asunder his inner garments: searching with
> Their cruel fingers for his heart, & there they enter in pomp,
> In many tears; & there they erect a temple & an altar:
> They pour cold water on his brain in front, to cause.
> Lids to grow over his eyes in veils of tears: and caverns
> To freeze over his nostrils, while they feed his tongue from cups
> And dishes of painted clay. Glowing with beauty & cruelty:
> They obscure the sun & the moon; no eye can look upon them.
> (E218; *J*66, 20–34)

The male suffers castration and dismemberment when females set up their dominion in the deepest recesses of his being. As he becomes totally overpowered by them, his senses atrophy and he loses all capacity to feel contact with sensuous reality. The origin of this critical state is infantile terror of disintegration and violent punishment, brought about by his fantasied destruction of the body of the mother who, by inversion, becomes a persecutory figure. The intricate details of dismemberment match the child's own curiosity and his attacks upon the body of the mother, attacks which, through guilt, lead to loss of the good object and apparent destruction of the self. Therefore, it seems that the child's capacity to respond to the outer world through the senses has been curtailed because his overwhelming reality is the need to preserve fundamental sensory contact with the mother.

As this description of the historical Female Will in action continues, we see the women exerting further refinements of cruelty upon their victim and the indefiniteness of abstraction becoming yet more entrenched:

> The Human form began to be alterd by the Daughters of Albion
> And the perceptions to be dissipated into the Indefinite. Becoming
> A mighty Polypus nam'd Albions Tree: they tie the Veins
> And Nerves into two knots: & the Seed into a double knot:
> They look forth: the Sun is shrunk: the Heavens are shrunk
> Away into the far remote: and the Trees & Mountains witherd
> Into indefinite cloudy shadows in darkness & separation. (E219: *J*66, 46–52)

Again, the male is at the mercy of the female in all of his innermost being; each intimate function is brutally handled by her, torn from its natural form, and all functions neurological or phallic curtailed. Blake is giving expression to a tormented psychological state in which infantile envy of the good object and destructive aggression against it produce a distorted fantasy of a vicious punishing female who dismembers the guilt-ridden male and destroys his powers of perception.

The image of the tabernacle as a holy shrine for moral law sums up a range of important associations with female domination. In this context of law and religion, the aura of holiness and dread emanates from the taboo feelings that have made an intangible "mystery" of the actuality of erotic desires. The fundamental reference of the tabernacle is to the female genitals and also to the womb, the essential spheres in which males are overwhelmed by the power of females and where loss or repression erode the integration of the male self. The link is made plain in the description of ideal sexuality:

> Embraces are Cominglings: from the Head even to the Feet;
> And not a pompous High Priest entering by a Secret Place.
>
> (E223; *J*69, 43–44)

The place of female mystery is seen as the obscene preserve of the priestly oedipal father; therefore, in this fantasy, sexual fulfillment takes place without an enclosing female space. Women characteristically veil and obscure what should be an open delight:

> We Women tremble at the light therefore: hiding fearful
> The Divine Vision with Curtain & Veil & fleshly Tabernacle.
>
> (E206; *J*56, 39–40)

The genesis of the image in sexual repression is apparent in extracts from Blake's earlier poetry. Thel, who rejects sexual experience, hears a voice from her own grave plot asking: "Why a little curtain of flesh on the bed of our desire?" (*K*6; *Th*IV, 20) The female "bed of desire" is an object of worship for the frustrated young male in *Visions of the Daughters of Albion*:

> the youth shut up from
> The lustful joy. shall forget to generate. & create an amorous image
> In the shadows of his curtains and in the folds of his silent pillow.
>
> (E50; *VDA*7, 5–7)

A related image of the female enclosing and constricting the male, this time without a holy aura, is found in the "crystal" house or cabinet. At the end of *Europe*, Enitharmon awakens her sons and daughters to sport within her crystal house, a place of sexual indulgence that remains, however, a prison. Its courtly ideal of femininity is reflected in the menacing charms of Leutha, who embodies a feeling of guilt at sexuality: "Soft soul of flowers Leutha! / Sweet smiling pestilence!" (E65; *Eu*14, 11–12) Similarly, the crystal house of Vala in Night the Ninth of *The Four Zoas* has a sinister aspect. Tharmas, apparently restored to innocence as a shepherd boy, weeps in Vala's house, and also feel oppressed in the static and deadened beauty of her garden.[35]

The fullest treatment of the theme is found in "The Crystal Cabinet," one of the poems from the Pickering Manuscript. The narrator of the poem, an autonomous male dancing in the wild, is trapped by a seductive female in the imprisoning cabinet imbued with the sinister and delusive beauty of the courtly love idealization of women. The crystal itself suggests frigidity and the deadening of libidinal impulses; the gold, pearls, and crystal forming the cabinet reflect the desired treasures of the mother's body, which are lifeless and ungratifying in this illusory situation. In the lyric, we find a brief expression of some of the dominant themes of the epics: in the grip of female control, the male experiences a distortion of sensory perception. The visual reality within the cabinet is the same as that outside: the mirror reflection curtails expansion of the senses. The seductive woman and her mirror counterpart are each split into three images.[36] Elsewhere, this threefold quality is associated with depictions of the Female Will and is felt to be sinister, as in this description of Vala-Rahab:

> so her whole immortal form three-fold
> Three-fold embrace returns: consuming lives of Gods & Men
> In fires of beauty melting them as gold & silver in the furnace . . .
> (E224; *J*70, 25–27)

or in this of the three villains of empiricism as an aspect of female power: "Frozen Sons of the feminine Tabernacle of Bacon, Newton & Locke." (E218; *J*66, 14)

The experience of longing for the female, originally as nurturing mother and here in "The Crystal Cabinet" as mistress, brings with it an anguished fear of loss that causes the disintegration of the ego and the splintering of reality. When the lover fails to grasp the essence of the desired woman, the enclosing, womblike cabinet of romantic delusion in which the woman possesses the man dissolves, exposing a deeper layer that reveals the underlying reality. The lover is now a weeping baby in the world of loss and desolation outside of the cabinet, a place far more terrifying than the enclosing prison in its emptiness and bleakness. Both the baby and the woman, a bereft mother figure, are weeping in the vacant air. They are a mother and child who are separate from each other and, therefore, cannot give each other consolation. The child's aggression has produced a fantasy of punishment in which both infant and mother are unable to restore the bond of love:

A weeping Babe upon the wild
And Weeping Woman pale reclind
And in the outward air again
I filld with woes the passing Wind (E489; 25–28)

Some related themes appear in the "The Mental Traveller," a poem of complex, shifting perspectives. Here the relationship between men and women at various stages of life is explored. At the beginning and the end of the poem, the male is an infant and the woman a harsh mother who nails him down on a rock. In the final stanzas, we are given more information about the child's emotional condition. Earlier, he had appeared to be born into a joyful atmosphere. Now, with a characteristic Blakean inversion, the truer and more fundamental infant is shown full of an aggression that can strike terror in all who look on him:

But when they find the frowning Babe
Terror strikes thro the region wide
They cry the Babe the Babe is Born
And flee away on Every side

For who dare touch the frowning form
His arm is witherd to its root
Lions Boars Wolves all howling flee
And every Tree does shed its fruit (E486; 93–100)

The child has a fantasy of omnipotence in the power of his aggression against the female, and it is an aggression that brings destruction, especially to the essential nature and fertility of the good mother, who is the healthy fruit. His arm is withered, a symbolic castration, yet this is presented as a symptom of his anger instead of being related to its true cause, the mother's sadism. Earlier in the poem, the mother is a persecutory phallic mother and a fearsome figure of cruelty, cutting into the heart and nerves of her victim like the Daughters of Albion in *Jerusalem*. The intervening stanzas of the poem show how layers of illusion can be stripped away to reveal the effects of the child's destructive anger. The male child grows through the various stages of life to old age and then reverts to childhood, while the mother ages in a reverse direction, so that male-female relationships can be explored at each stage.[37] When they are both young lovers, he treats her with the aggression the mother had originally bred in him:

Till he becomes a bleeding youth
And she becomes a Virgin bright
Then he rends up his Manacles
And binds her down for his delight (E484; 21–24)

The angry and punishing early relationship with the mother stamps anger into future sexual relations. With her as his "dwelling place / And Garden fruitful," he produces a cottage filled with gold and gems, referring to the mother's body and its treasures, which is the goal of all the desires of infancy. In his relationship with the female who stands for the eternal mother, he has been able to re-create temporarily an illusory positive image of her. The "bleeding Youth," however, is shown to be an "aged Shadow," as the youth's weak father imago emerges:

An aged Shadow soon he fades
Wandring round an Earthly Cot
Full filled all with gems & gold
Which he by industry had got (E484; 29–32)

The possession of the mother and her riches, won through much psychic strife and labor, proves to be an empty satisfaction, because the good mother has been destroyed and the son lacks masculine strength. The jewels, as the dead hard forms of the vanished sensuous blossoms, are emblems of the inconsolable sorrows of humanity:

And these are the gems of the Human Soul
The rubies & pearls of a lovesick eye
The countless gold of the akeing heart
The martyrs groan & the lovers sigh (E484; 33–36)

The next manifestation of the female is as a "Female Babe" formed of "solid fire / And gems & gold." Here we see an attempt to render the threatening mother harmless by reducing her to infancy, like Tharmas and Enion in *The Four Zoas*. However, as a figure encrusted with gold and gems, she remains sinister and too much in control of her sphere to allow herself to be touched or possessed by the boy; yet she soon comes to give herself to any man she loves.

She and her lovers drive the male figure from his own house, forcing him to be a beggar at other doors. Now the aggression of the envious male against the female is projected into the inverted image of the sorrowing homeless wanderer. He encounters another seductive maiden, namely, the female baby in another guise. At this point, the themes link up closely with those of "The Crystal Cabinet." The maiden here sometimes has the harmless and untouchable aspect of infancy, but her malevolent power remains and gradually reduces the male to his elemental state of anguished and furious babyhood. The male and female are again in the disconsolate wilderness outside the bounds of the cabinet, or cottage. There is no actual sustenance to be derived from a solid reality beyond the anguished and ever-disappointing relationship. He must take his nourishment from her, at the price of his male independence, thus devolving again into an infant under the control of the cruel mother:

> The honey of her Infant lips
> The bread & wine of her sweet smile
> The wild game of her roving Eye
> Does him to Infancy beguile
>
> For as he eats & drinks he grows
> Younger & Younger every day
> And on the desart wild they both
> Wander in terror & dismay (E485; 69–76)

Like mother and child at the end of "The Crystal Cabinet," they are both made victims, in the infant's fantasy, of the terrifying disintegration of the bonds of love. Beguiled by her "arts of Love," he pursues her as though she were a fleeing Stag, in a parody of courtly love. This form of female control of the male and the male's fruitless efforts to integrate himself with female love builds up into denser forms—"Labyrinths of wayward Love"—in the essential wilderness of emotional loss. Thence, the basic pair that produces the permutations of other attempted relationships, the angry baby and the sadistic mother, is restored.

The image of the good mother in Blake is fleeting and unstable but nonetheless compelling. It resides most clearly in the Daughters of Beulah; in certain manifestations of Enitharmon; in Ololon; and in Jerusalem, the Emanation of Albion. These positive and hopeful images of women are clearly present in his works but often become engulfed in the stronger portrayals of menacing and cruel women.[38]

The state of Beulah, frequently associated with the state of married love, is a peaceful and harmonious condition, often alluded to as a reference point for a way of life approaching the ideal. The most complete account of Beulah appears at the beginning of the second book of *Milton*, where we are told:

> There is a place where Contrarieties are equally True
> This place is called Beulah, It is a pleasant lovely Shadow
> Where no dispute can come. (E129; *M*2, 1–3)

It is a place of harmony where the anguish of conflict and perpetual denial is assuaged. The basis of this refreshing state is the image of union with the good mother:

> But Beulah to its Inhabitants appears within each district
> As the beloved infant in his mothers bosom round incircled
> With arms of love & pity & sweet compassion. But to
> The Sons of Eden the moony habitations of Beulah,
> Are from Great Eternity a mild & pleasant Rest. (*M*2, 10–14)

This is a complete and unambiguous portrait of infantile symbiosis with the mother, describing the child as the focus of love surrounded by the mother's protective adoration. The element of pity here is desirable and nonthreatening. In *Milton*, Blake acknowledges the Daughters of Beulah as his Muses, providing release for his creative powers. Although *Milton*'s real interest is a very masculine one, it appears finally more gentle and accepting in its view of women than most of Blake's other works, hence the sustained Beulah sequence just referred to is possible. Elsewhere, recollections of Beulah are transitory, and are soon overwhelmed by bristling conflict and the strenuous urge to restore what is lost or disintegrating. The precious image of the good mother is a weak and evanescent ideal among the far more prevalent forms of violent or threatening females, and of male annihilation and disintegration.

In other evocations of Beulah, the adult male is supreme and the attentive female ministers to his primary needs:

> . . . Beulah
> Where every Female delights to give her maiden to her husband
> The Female searches sea & land for gratification to the
> Male Genius: who in return clothes her in gems & gold
> And feeds her with the food of Eden. (E223; *J*69, 14–18)

The lost ideal state described here in *Jerusalem* has been replaced by Rahab's Religion of Chastity, characterized by prostitution and the tabernacle of sexual mystery. The sequence began with a description of the cancerous Polypus, a male who has become "a ravening eating Cancer growing in the Female" (69, 1–2).[39] The illustration to this episode, plate 69 of *Jerusalem*, shows a male victim about to be attacked by two females with knives. Here and elsewhere, the ideal of joy and integration is fragile and quickly submerged in the more compelling reality of menace and destructiveness.

Jerusalem, the emanation of Albion, is an important manifestation of the good and nurturing female. She is closely related to the Daughters of Beulah, and shares their function of giving support to the male. She stands for Liberty, meaning freedom from repression and moral authority, and represents the ideal state towards which Los, in his reforming zeal, is striving in *Jerusalem:*

> I see the River of Life & Tree of Life
> I see the New Jerusalem descending out of Heaven
> Between thy Wings of gold & silver featherd immortal
> Clear as the rainbow, as the cloud of the Suns tabernacle.
>
> (E244–45; *J*86, 18–21)

In Night the Ninth of *The Four Zoas*, as the state of regeneration is established, she encompasses in her being the restoration of joyful freedom:

> Thus shall the male & female live the life of Eternity
> Because the Lamb of God Creates himself a bride & wife
> That we his Children evermore may live in Jerusalem
> Which now descendeth out of heaven a City yet a Woman
> Mother of myriads redeemed & born in her spiritual palaces
> By a New Spiritual birth Regenerated from Death.
>
> (E391; *FZ*IX, 122, 15–20)

The re-creation of the injured and mutilated body of the mother to form again a female figure of love and maternal support is the occasion for the release of immense joy and a sense of creativity. But the moments of joyful apocalypse at the end of each of the major epics form a small part of Blake's total material. Before this condition is reached, Jerusalem is seen in a range of desperate and humiliating conditions. At the beginning of *Jerusalem*, the fallen Albion, in a state of jealous fear, denies his Emanation, and hides her saying that she is indefinite. Thereafter, she becomes one with Vala, the treacherous and vindictive female manifestation of the natural world. The good maternal figure, though longed for and still dimly perceived, is engulfed in the more sustained image of the punitive mother who cuts off the suffering son from sensuous natural response:

> He found Jerusalem upon the River of his City soft repos'd
> In the arms of Vala, assimilating in one with Vala . . .
> Dividing & uniting into many female forms: Jerusalem
> Trembling! then in one comingling in eternal tears,
> Sighing to melt his Giant beauty, on the moony river.(E164–65; *J*19, 40–47)

The two figures terrifyingly split into many forms and then unite into one female form who, through the characteristically feminine act of weeping, attempts to cause the erosion of Albion's being. A disintegrating image of Jerusalem as the lost good mother is found on plate 54 of *Jerusalem*, where Albion, in an anguished act of self-defense against the aggressive utterances of his cold reasoning Spectre, tries to draw England into his bosom:

> But she stretchd out her starry Night in Spaces against him. like
> A long Serpent, in the Abyss of the Spectre which augmented
> The Night with Dragon wings coverd with stars & in the Wings
> Jerusalem & Vala appeard: & above between the Wings magnificent
> The Divine Vision dimly appeard in clouds of blood weeping.
> (E204; *J*54, 28–32)

His attempt to encompass England in a controlling fashion is thwarted; instead, he is overwhelmed by this vast female form of a powerful phallic serpent, in the menacing beauty of whose wings Vala and Jerusalem appear. Within this malevolent figure is seen the evanescent image of the Divine Vision, or Jesus, the vulnerable male who can only fitfully cling to existence.

Jerusalem often appears in the guise of a sad mother, bewailing the loss or the suffering of her children. In the biblical image of Israelite captivity, she knows exile and desolation:

> My tents are fall'n! my pillars are in ruins! my children dashd
> Upon Egypts iron floors, & the marble pavements of Assyria;
> I melt my soul in reasonings among the towers of Heshbon.
> (E234; *J*79, 1–3)

Like Enion, she is the woman wandering in intense maternal anguish, and also a mother punished by being cut off from love and communication with her children:

> Encompassd by the frozen Net and by the rooted Tree
> I walk weeping in pangs of a Mothers torment for her Children:
> I walk in affliction: I am a worm, and no living soul! (E236; *J*80, 1–3)

In the most extreme form of the punishment, she is forgotten by her children, who have the destroyed the state that she should enshrine for them:

> and Jerusalem wept upon Euphrates banks
> Disorganized; an evanescent shade, scarce seen or heard among
> Her childrens Druid Temples dropping with blood wanderd weeping!
> (E234; *J*78, 27–29)

She is the mother subjected to violence in the child's fantasy, weeping and solitary in a reflection of the violence she herself has caused.

In another manifestation, Jerusalem, the evanescent good mother, is seen as a harlot, spurned, humiliated, and despised, a wretched victim of a repressive society:

> Jerusalem replied. I am an outcast: Albion is dead!
> I am left to the trampling foot & the spurning heel!
> A Harlot I am calld. I am sold from street to street!
> I am defaced with blows & with the dirt of the Prison! (E212: *J*62, 2–5)

Again, this is an image in which the mother is made to suffer punishment and aggression: Jerusalem is a reflection of Vala and her debased sexuality, which she suffers as a victim instead of imposing its cruelty upon others. In a cognate portrait, we see Jerusalem in miserable captivity in Babylon, triumphed over by her Spectre, Vala:

> But Jerusalem faintly saw him, closd in the Dungeons of Babylon
> Her Form was held by Beulahs Daughters. but all within unseen
> She sat at the Mills, her hair unbound her feet naked
> Cut with the flints: her tears run down, her reason grows like
> The Wheel of Hand. incessant turning day & night without rest
> Insane she raves upon the winds hoarse, inarticulate. (E210; *J*60, 39–44)

With her cut feet, unbound hair, weeping, and insanity, she is a disintegrating form of the good mother. Since it is the child's aggression that has caused this condition, her state is an occasion for grief and fear.

In Night the Eighth of *The Four Zoas,* the restoration of Jerusalem sets in motion the whole process of renewal. Fragments and dead forms are brought together through the agency of Enitharmon, who weaves bodies for them. These splintered separate images coalesce in one unified female form, Jerusalem:

And they appeard a Universal female form created
From those who were dead in Ulro from the Spectres of the dead

And Enitharmon namd the Female Jerusa[le]m the holy
Wondring she saw the Lamb of God within Jerusalems Veil
The divine Vision seen within the inmost deep recess
Of fair Jerusalems bosom in a gently beaming fire.
(E376; *FZ*VIII, 103, 38–104, 4)

This act follows the grim sequence in which the Shadowy Female in the Tree of Mystery engulfs Urizen in the Web of Religion. After the nadir of human experience has been reached, a painful recovery begins with the apparition of an integrated good female through the sad efforts of Enitharmon. The urge to make reparation for attacks upon the mother succeeds in forming a unified female whose wholeness is, however, to be subjected to many further conflicts and vicissitudes before a semblance of harmony is attained. This apparition is a glimmer of the possibility of resolution. Both the aura of the revived Jerusalem here and the vision of Christ in her bosom represent a sublimation of aggressions in an acceptance of spiritual harmony, a tendency and a theme that become stronger in *Jerusalem*. Plates 97 to 99 describe an infinite expansion of the fourfold Senses:

Driving outward the Body of Death in an Eternal Death & Resurrection
Awaking it to Life among the Flowers of Beulah rejoicing in Unity
In the Four Senses in the Outline the Circumference & Form, for ever
In Forgiveness of Sins which is Self Annihilation. (E257; *J*98, 20–23)

The experience which makes possible this enormous sense of joy and release is reunion: Albion's reunion with his emanation, Jerusalem, and with the Divine Vision, and the reunion of all separated beings. The illustration to plate 99 shows the essential experience: the combined figure of Albion and Jehovah embraces Jersusalem. As David Erdman puts it in his comment on the illustration, "These two persons must now symbolize all the divided persons in the now whole Song: he all the flayed, chained, decapitated, deluded, accusing and divided men in the poem, now united in One; she all the separated and separating women, now ready for trust and love."[40] Flames swirl around the figures, expressing the ardor of forgiveness and the renewal of love. This image, upon which the restoration of harmony and sensory wholeness is built, is founded upon the child's restoration of the good mother who had been mutilated, attacked, and perceived as a threatening monster, and also of the parents, who can now be seen as a source of nurture and harmony instead of as objects of envy and aggression. The urge to make reparation for infantile destructiveness underlies the creative impulse, and we have observed Blake battling to reach this moment, through many conflicts, contradictions, and the multiplication of threats and obstacles. It is a hard-won moment of release from torment.

In copy E of plate 99 of *Jerusalem*, Erdman notes, the repainting of the faces of the two figures makes both of them look more male than female. The stress is on the son's reconciliation with the male parent and on a more urgent identification with the male than the female.[41] Female figures are assimilated to the point of absorption: they are no longer threatening because they no longer have independent existence. The son's sense of himself is now focused upon the father and upon his own maleness.

CHAPTER 5

Images of Women in Lawrence

D.H. Lawrence's response to women reflects his awareness of the fundamental power of women over men's emotional lives[1] and of strong female influence in his own society.[2] This perception of female ascendancy was deepened by his close relationship with his mother and by his early contact with the women's emancipation movement. His resentment of female domination was complicated and intensified by his relationship with Frieda. Through Frieda, he became familiar with the acceptance of matriarchal values, derived from Bachofen, of the avant-garde group *Die Kosmische Runde.*[3] Through living at close quarters with Frieda's forceful personality, his deep-seated resistance to female domination was aggravated into a particular form of taunting invective.[4] He refers often to the powerful and overwhelming mother figure as the "Magna Mater." It is a term that he applied to Frieda with variants such as the "Queen Bee," and to Ursula in *Women in Love.* The response can also be found as the mainspring of many important relationships within his works. Lawrence's rebellion against the powerful mother has been noted and regarded as a major element in his work. Marguerite Beede Howe defines this preoccupation in terms of the Laingian notion of the fear of engulfment.[5] If we study some recurring characteristics of the central male-female relationships, we will observe buried patterns that indicate the essential nature and source of his emotional reaction to women.

As we have observed in *The White Peacock*, Lawrence, in his earlier works, is likely not to be explicit about his antagonism towards women; indeed, an attitude of sympathy for women in their social condition is often uppermost.[6] The case of *Sons and Lovers* is especially interesting. In this autobiographical novel. Lawrence is apparently writing an account of a young man's oedipal struggle, in which the father's authority is entirely despised and the mother wins emotional ascendancy over her female rival, a young woman of her son's generation, in order to establish absolute emotional control over her son. A close study of the novel reveals, however, that this surface pattern, in fact, conceals a fundamental antagonism towards the mother.[7]

D. H. Lawrence's *Sons and Lovers*, one of the first artistic works produced with an awareness of psychoanalysis, appears to be a classic Freudian text.[8] While writing the final draft of the novel, Lawrence was led by Frieda's insights into his earlier experience and also by her knowledge—through Otto Gross and others—of theory not yet widely known, to write of his emotional life with some objectivity. In so doing, he achieves a delicate balance between self-analysis and the evocation of sensuous immediacy. The triadic oedipal pattern emerges sharply from the action of the novel: in the development of the relationship between the parents; in the conflict of the two sons, first William and then Paul, with the father; and in the emotional aridity of Paul's relationships with young women.

Yet, does art reveal its fundamental impetus so readily? Is not the oedipal pattern so deliberate and so close to the surface in *Sons and Lovers* that we are led to suspect that it must, in fact, conceal something else?

In 1913, when *Sons and Lovers* was published, Freud had not yet presented his own work on object relations,[9] which was later to provide a starting point for Melanie Klein. We find that it is Kleinian theory that leads us to the truest meaning of the novel.

Beneath the more apparent triadic oedipal structure lie the dynamics of the early mother-infant dyad. The novel appears to be written out of loyalty to the mother, Gertrude Morel, on the part of the son, Paul Morel, whether against the aggressive father or the possessive sensual woman of the son's own generation; yet its true emotional core is a sense of hatred for the suffocating mother, leading to a series of fantasies in which the son destroys her, and culminating in her actual death at his hands. These key events are: the sacrifice of Annie's doll, Arabella, in Paul's childhood; the burning and symbolic entombment of the loaves of bread in the "Strife in Love" chapter; and the death of Gertrude Morel as an immediate result of an overdose of morphia administered by Paul. In each of them, we find a destructive anger that runs against the manifest devoted love for the mother in the text, corresponding to Melanie Klein's notion of the infantile defense mechanism of the splitting of the mother into a good aspect and a bad aspect.

The first episode is one of apparently motiveless violence in which the boy, Paul Morel, destroys his sister Annie's doll, with her frightened connivance:

> Let's make a sacrifice of Arabella," he said. "Let's burn her."
>
> She was horrified, yet rather fascinated. She wanted to see what the boy would do. He made an alter of bricks, pulled some of the shavings out of Arabella's body, put the waxen fragments into the hollow face, poured on a little paraffin, and set the whole thing alight. He watched with wicked satisifaction the drops of wax melt off the broken forehead of Arabella, and drop like sweat into the flame. So long as the stupid big doll burned he rejoiced in silence. At the end he poked among the embers with a stick, fished out the arms and legs, all blackened, and smashed them under stones.
>
> "That's the sacrifice of Missis Arabella," he said. "An' I'm glad there's nothing left of her." (*SL* 58)

The scene cuts beneath the familiarly "oedipal" patterning of the novel to show a powerful anger against the mother. The "sacrifice" is an act of desecration against a figure who should be revered. This is apparent in the building of an altar, the title "Missis Arabella," and the aura of "wicked satisfaction" that emanates from defying a taboo. The body of the mother is, in fantasy, dismembered and destroyed, disintegrating in a flash of fiery consuming anger, and liquified into the wax and sweat of elemental fluids. When already blackened and "dead," the fragments are retrieved with aggressive phallic curiosity by means of a poking stick, and then further pulverized into nothingness, not "with" stones but "under" stones, suggesting both a final horror that cannot be looked at and the gravestones that cover the dead, which in turn have in their origins an impetus of aggression against the dead.[10]

The scene is a vivid depiction of a child's sadistic fantasy against the mother. The presence of Annie is an essential component of the scene. In this and the cognate episodes, her witnessing of the event and her connivance at Paul's action suggest that part of the emotional totality of anger against the mother is a fantasy of a sibling relationship that is transmuted into relationships with female peers in defiance of the mother's sensuous dominance.[11] The sister in earlier life can be a female figure who provides an alternative to the mother and who, like the son, strains against the mother's moral strictures.

In the structure of the narrative, the occurrence is closely related to Paul's conflict with his father. Immediately following this symbolic annihilation of the mother and a reference to his impetus against what he has destroyed—"He seemed to hate the doll so intensely, because he had broken it"—we find one of the central oedipal scenes. Lawrence stresses Paul's opposition to his father and the Morel children's support of their mother against their father. He then shows us a triad of the mother with a black eye, the father shamefaced, and William glaring at the father (59). This significant juxtaposition is completed by a description of the ash tree, symbolic of the father's violence, which dominates the household and instills a fundamental fear in the children. We note, however, that it is also associated with freedom and the creative power of music:

> In front of the house was a huge old ash-tree. The west wind, sweeping from Derbyshire, caught the houses with full force, and the tree shrieked again. Morel liked it.
>
> "It's music," he said. "It sends me to sleep."
>
> But Paul and Arthur and Annie hated it. To Paul it became almost a demoniacal noise. The winter of their first year in the new house their father was very bad. The children played in the street, on the brim of the wide, dark valley, until eight o'clock. Then they went to bed. Their mother sat sewing below. Having such a great space in front of the house gave the children a feeling of night, of vastness, and of terror. This terror came in from the shrieking of the tree and the anguish of the home discord. (*SL* 59)

In the welter of emotions that are the condition of the boy's life, he must deny himself identification with this creative force and also with his father as a strong male. The emptiness, vastness, and sense of an unknown menace in the darkness, described above, make apparent his personal experience of psychic disintegration in the face of such conflicting pressures. The ambivalence of his response is, however, made plain in the treatment of Annie's doll, where Paul is behaving towards the mother in a way that reflects the father. Beneath the relatively superficial oedipal structure, we see more fundamental feelings at work. Paul cannot identify with this liberating masculinity. His attempt to obliterate his mother's emotional hold over him is crushed, paralleling the father's futile act of aggression. The father's shame reflects the damaged masculine pride of father and son.[12]

The second episode displays a similar emotional configuration: Paul burns loaves of bread that his mother has given him the responsibility of tending as they bake in the oven. Paul is at his home with Miriam one evening during a phase of their relationship when he feels most strongly drawn to her and realizes how important it is for him to be able to discuss his work with her. They are joined by Beatrice, a high-spirited and flirtatious young woman who teases them both and temporarily monopolizes Paul. At this stage, Miriam draws his attention to the fact that the loaves are burning. Beatrice in her flippant and mocking way aids Paul in covering up his neglect, grating the one badly burned loaf with a nutmeg-grater and then wrapping the loaf in a damp towel for Paul to hide in the scullery, or small back kitchen. The scene has a close parallel in the play, *A Collier's Friday Night*, where the central figures are Ernest; his girlfriend Maggie who, like Miriam is disliked by his mother; and another flirtatious and mocking Beatrice.

Correspondences between the two, and elements that emerge more nakedly in the play than in the novel, heighten our awareness of its significance.[13] In the play, the burned loaf is again grated, accompanied by even greater hilarity on the part of all three young people: Ernest Lambert (the Paul figure) and the two women. Again, it is wrapped in a damp towel and put in a small room, this time the pantry. Whereas in the novel a reference is made to the "swathed loaf,"[14] in the play, presumably the less carefully written text, it is the "shrouded loaf."[15] The use of the word "shroud" and the wrapping of the loaf to enclose it in a small dark space, the pantry, reflect a fantasy of killing and burying the mother. As with the episode of Annie's doll, in each of these versions of the loaf sequence, the son is accompanied by young women of his own generation, who offer him sensuous pleasure and escape from the mother's emotional dominance. The loaves of bread are a suggestive symbol of maternal power, since they are associated with the fundamental experience of nourishment, the center of the infant-mother relationship and its inherent conflicts. The essence of the fantasy lies in Paul–Ernest's assigned duty of tending the loaves as they bake. He has been given a constricting sense of responsibility to the mother, who governs the fundamental sphere of nourishment and sensuality. His temporary release from this responsibility is shown in the frivolity and promise of amoral, sensuous indulgence with which the burning of the loaves is surrounded, carried in each instance by a high-spirited, mocking, and indomitable young woman, Beatrice.

The complexity of the son's emotional situation is reflected in the three distinct young women who are associated with the scene. Beatrice offers a clear promise of liberation into sexual fulfillment. The sister, although her presence is admissible because she is the son's peer, here represents the mother's values and point of view. The deep emotional conflicts surround Miriam–Maggie, who is also linked with the mother's values, yet in a more complicated way.[16] It is she who is blamed for the burning of the loaves as the person who had distracted Paul–Ernest, blamed mockingly by Beatrice in the novel and with exasperation by Nellie in the play. Although Beatrice is apparently the object of Paul–Ernest's erotic fooling and flirtatiousness, is is clear that his deeper erotic feelings are more seriously directed towards Miriam–Maggie. Since, however, those instincts are frustrated, partly as a result of complex guilt in turn related to the mother, he gives rein to sensual impulses with Beatrice, who represents a condition of amoral emotional freedom.

The close connection between his feelings for Miriam and the loaf-burning episode, intertwined with awareness of maternal power, are very apparent. As Paul turns a fresh batch of baking loaves, he appears brutal and distant to Miriam: "There seemed to be something cruel in it, something cruel in the swift way he pitched the bread out of the tins, caught it up again" (*SL* 208). The soft and vulnerable Miriam feels that he does not belong to her world but rather is a cohort of his mother, doing her harsh work, in which the baking pans become an implement of psychic control of dependents. Paul himself becomes a mother figure from whom the tender nursling Miriam desires loving sustenance but feels that he gives it grudgingly. As they study poetry together later, "she was really getting now the food for her life during the next week" (208), while we are told that certain poems "nourished her heart" (209). Paul's final emotional loyalty to his mother makes Miriam experience the uncertain affections of a harsh mother. In other words, Paul takes on the dominance of his mother through his bond with her.

Earlier in the *Sons and Lovers* episode, Beatrice, the woman who is free from the sensual restraints associated with the mother, exerts her own control over Paul. As she and Paul tussle in a teasing, flirtatious way, she pulls his hair and then combs it straight with her own comb, tilting back his head to comb his moustache also (204). This signifies her female command of his maleness: we recall the anger and humiliation Lewis, in *St. Mawr*, feels when Mrs. Witt wants to touch his head and cut his hair. Here, Paul accepts Beatrice's treatment of him because it gives him access to her sensuality. The episode is redolent of passion and overtones of male sexuality: "It's a wicked moustache, 'Postle," she said. "It's a red for danger. Have you got any of those cigarettes?" (204) The dangerous burning red of male virility is associated with the fire that burns the loaves in the oven; in the play we are told that the fire is "ramped" like hell (*CFN* 506). The association links the force that rebels against the mother's hold and the force that desires sexual fulfillment, each of which also means a turning away from Miriam. The episodes in both novel and play are filled with references to Paul's many female admirers, which further links the suppression of the mother with fantasies of masculine prowess.

The relationship with the mother herself lies behind the responses to Maggie–Miriam and Beatrice. The mother is the moral and emotional center of Paul's life, and responses to her are split off in feelings towards other kinds of women. Thus, although the sexual unease surrounding Miriam is derived from the mother's sexual prohibitions, the relationship with the mother is experienced as a totality and a continuum, while that with Miriam is segmented and disjunctive, at the conscious level.

The burning of the loaves and the burial of the shrouded or swathed loaf is a reflection of the unthinkable and the unapproachable: the wish for the death of the repressive mother who curtails desire. In both the novel, *Sons and Lovers*, and the play, *A Collier's Friday Night*, the incident leads to a resolution of action that stresses its significance. In each case, the mother returns to the scene of the transgression, ill and suffering from a weak heart brought on by carrying bags of shopping for the family. In each case, it is an extra burden of meat that has been the final straw. The fantasy of the mother's death is, therefore, followed up by a premonition of her actual death, to be followed through in *Sons and Lovers*. Her maternal function and the moral power she wields through self-sacrifice are emphasized by the meat that she carries. The latent guilt at the destructive fantasy is transferred into a complete image of pity. As with the childhood episode of the annihilation of the doll in *Sons and Lovers*, the symbolic act of the destruction of the mother is followed up in both novel and play by a scene of emotional conflict with oedipal overtones. The essential content of the sequence is similar in both works: the father, returning home drunk, wants to eat special food the mother is keeping for Ernest–Paul, clearly suggestive of the sexual generosity that she begrudges the father. This leads to a bitter altercation between husband and wife; the son intervenes and physical violence almost breaks out between father and son; the mother and son dispute heatedly over the time and attention that he gives to Maggie–Miriam. At the conclusion of the episode, he admits to his mother that he cares more deeply for her than for the girl, and they are tenderly reconciled.

Whereas in the earlier oedipal configuration juxtaposed with the childhood doll fantasy, the father maintains a violent independence for the son to aspire to, here he is entirely crushed by the woman and her union with the son. The episode marks his final defeat. As he prepares for going to the pit in the morning, both the novel and play intimate that his son will never belong to this demeaning collier's world. In *A Collier's Friday Night*, the stage directions describe the movements of a broken man: "Then he lurches round, and, limping pitiably, goes off upstairs" (522). Similarly, Morel in *Sons and Lovers* is a pathetic figure: "The elderly man began to unlace his boots. He stumbled off to bed. His last fight was fought in that house" (214).

In both works, this sequence of experience produces a moment of resolution: the working through of a fantasy of killing the mother and enjoying libidinal freedom with consorts who can stand against her; the guilty fear at the actual death of the mother with its consolidation of her supermacy over the father and other women in their emotional claims to the son. At the end of *A Collier's Friday Night*, the stage directions instruct the actors playing mother and son to speak in a particular way: "There is in their tones a dangerous gentleness—so much gentleness that the safe reserve of their souls is broken" (530). In *Sons and Lovers*, Paul goes to bed in an intensely emotional state: "He pressed his face upon the pillow in a fury of misery. And yet, somewhere in his soul, he was at peace because he still loved his mother best. It was the bitter peace of resignation"

(215). Each description of the emotional state refers to graduated psychic levels, the deepest level being "the soul," the elemental psychic state. In each, we are told that a point of acceptance has been reached after bitterly conflicting feelings have surfaced for a time. The acceptance brings with it a sense of gentleness or peace because the most fundamental state of the psyche—commitment to the mother, her dominance, and her taboos—is reaffirmed. However, it is a qualified gentleness because it denies the urgency of independence and desire. In the play, the "safe reserve" of the soul, the usual acceptance of external reality that makes it possible to live with deep psychic conflict, is broken, temporarily revealing what lies beyond. The final sequence of the episode in *Sons and Lovers* emphasizes the defeat of masculinity: the following day Paul's father tries to conciliate him, which is "a great humiliation to him." The sense of the cowed father, his male pride destroyed by the mother, is associated with the permanent effects of the experience for Paul, since submission to maternal dominance means a suppression of the possiblity of male aspiration. The humiliation is shared by father and son.

The third episode in this sequence is the death of Gertrude Morel, hastened by Paul. The three acts, two fantasied and one actual, are linked by several similarities, indicating that they arise from the same psychic source. In each, Paul is accompanied by a young woman, either his sister or a woman with whom he has an erotic association. Paul and his co-conspirators plot together, knowing that they are breaking a strict taboo: this knowledge gives rise to the horrified fascination or hysteria of the females in each episode.

The chapter dealing with Mrs. Morel's death is entitled "Release." The agony that Paul suffers upon her painful demise and his own great emotional loss is also a release from her powerful hold over him. There are certain parallels between the episode of actual death and the two fantasies of killing the mother found earlier in the novel that show how his mother's death releases Paul from the domination that could not be broken except in symbolic rebellion during her lifetime.

The central fact that reveals the association with the fantasies is that here Paul literally brings about her death and does so with the assistance of a female accomplice, his sister Annie. The three events are further linked by an association with fire. In the two fantasies, it is by fire, a displacement of urethral violence, that the mother image is destroyed. The moment when Paul first realizes that his mother is going to die is again related to fire. He is sitting in the kitchen smoking: "Then he tried to brush some grey ash off his coat. He looked again. It was one of his mother's grey hairs. It was so long! He held it up, and it drifted into the chimney. He let go. The long grey hair floated and was gone in the blackness of the chimney" (*SL* 376). Fire is a presence here, yet is curiously suppressed. Its light and heat are concealed, and it appears to turn living things like the hair to ash, without going through the intermediate stage of burning. Although we are not told that Paul is sitting by the fire, it is clear that he must be, because when he holds up the hair, it drifts up the chimney, necessarily drawn by the heat from a glowing fire. He is a strong agent, engaged in the masculine act of smoking, while his mother's life moves towards disintegration. Moreover, the ash from his cigarette turns into the hair of a dying woman and seems to cause its dissolution. The moment marks the knowledge that fantasy will become reality. The blackness into which the hair disappears reflects the infant's terror at the annihilation of his own being, which he has brought about through his destructive aggression. This sense of personal disintegration is experienced often from this point until the end of the novel, amid the turmoil of anguish that Paul endures.

Henceforth, fire is benign, symbolizing the sustenance of Mrs. Morel's life. Its work of aggression is done. Paul lovingly tends the fire in his mother's sickroom to provide her with comfort. It is through an inversion of maternal power, the drinking of poisoned milk, rather than through masculine aggression, that she will be destroyed. The agent of annihilation has its source in the primary depths of the relationship.

Paul makes the decision to take his mother's life to spare her further suffering. The suffering, however, often seems to be his own, as he longs for her to die; but there is distinct ambivalence in the way he feels about the prolonged period of agony she suffers before she dies. He does not wish her to eat and puts water in the milk that he gives her: "And he would put some water with it, so that it should not nourish her. Yet he loved her more than his own life" (392). When he gives her the fatal draught of morphia, he puts it in the feeding cup of hot milk she takes before sleeping at night, making it a bitter potion that she drinks with difficulty. He seems almost to be forcing her despite her vulnerability: "He saw her frail fingers over the cup, her lips making a little move" (394). When he tells Annie that she has drunk it and found it bitter, Annie laughs, "putting her underlip between her teeth." We notice here that in each of these episodes it is *milk* that is involved, the basic sustenance of life and the food that in the act of nourishment knits the bond between mother and child. In putting first water and then morphia in her milk, Paul is therefore denying life to his mother at the fundamental level and is, moreover, making a statement of violence against the mother-child bond itself. The fatal drink is given to her in a feeding cup, evocative of a child's cup. An elemental scene of nurturing in which the mother gives a soothing bedtime drink to the child becomes an act of imposing suffering and denying life as the mother, now a helpless child, is forced to drink. At the same time, an inverted mother–child relationship, in which Paul is the loving mother, is strongly suggested.

The final phase of Mrs. Morel's life and the agonized process of her death are closedly interwoven in the narrative with references to Paul's unsatisfactory relationships with two women, Clara and Miriam. When he and Clara are together or are making love, Clara feels that he is a "make-belief" lover. With Miriam, too, Paul is unable to make true personal contact, precisely at moments of sensuous intimacy: "She could not kiss his agony. That remained alone and apart. She kissed his face, and roused his blood, while his soul was apart writhing with the agony of death" (391). Paul's personal fragmentation and failure to maintain genuine feeling with these two women goes beyond the normal response, however painful, to a parent's impending death. As he is made more nakedly aware of his emotional dependence upon his mother, his inability to make deep emotional contact with women is more keenly present to him. The female accomplice who assists him in the three episodes of killing the mother is a symbol of the sexual liberation he hopes to achieve through destruction; that ultimate act of rebellion is finally, however, ineffectual.

In Lawrence's writings from about 1915 on, two major themes emerge and become insistent: the close relationship between the infant and the mother; and the male child's—and the adult's—need to break away from maternal dominance. These themes first surface in the long hybrid novel,

"The Sisters," that becomes two novels, the first, *The Rainbow*, in which female dominance of men is resented in a relatively benevolent way and, then, *Women in Love*, where strong conflict and anger surrounding male-female relationships are revealed.[17] Lawrence continued to pour scorn and invective upon overdominant women, specifically mothers, and their effects on men in many succeeding works, notably in "Education of the People," a group of four essays written in 1918, and in the two treatises of 1923, *Fantasia of the Unconscious* and *Psychoanalysis and the Unconscious*. It is a paramount necessity, he asserts, to stress individual independence, particularly male independence and, at the same time, the need for human beings to live from within their "dark consciousness." The male, Lawrence came to believe with great intensity, must assert his independence from female domination and must live in harmony with the dark centers of his being, a harmony threatened by female-induced idealization and abstraction.

The cardinal error of his society, Lawrence believes, is that the upper centers of the body, related to cognition and knowledge of the external world, are overstimulated, while the lower centers, where self-knowledge and a deep dark mode of consciousness are located, are starved. The chief cause of this condition is an idealizing and controlling mother love that brings about abstraction in thinking and dissociation from sensuous immediacy. His analysis here is very close to Blake's.[18] In the *Fantasia*, having denounced "this infernal self-conscious Madonna starving our living guts and bullying us to death with her love" (143), Lawrence expresses loathing for all members of his society, on account of the intellectualism that springs from the female influence.

The emphasis that Lawrence gives to the primacy of the preoedipal mother-infant bond and to the conflicts of love, hate, and the struggle for independence that characterize it is the very emphasis that we find in the work of Melanie Klein and the object-relations school. Although we cannot take seriously as psychology his schema of the four primary modes of consciousness set forward in the two treatises on psychoanalysis, [19] we should note that Lawrence recognized with startling accuracy the importance of the preoedipal mother-infant dyad for the foundation of the personality. Freud at this time was just developing his own notion of object relations, which was later to provide a starting point for Klein.[20] For Lawrence, it was his own emotional life that gave him insight into the primacy of that earlier relationship and distorted his vision according to his own perspective.

Lawrence shows a sympathetic insight into the earliest phase of life when the infant dwells in a symbiotic bond with the mother. He beautifully realized the relaxed unity of that early state: "Child and mother have, in the first place, no objective consciousness of each other, and certainly no *idea* of each other. Each is a blind desideratum to the other. The strong love between them is effectual in the great abdominal centres, where all love, real love, is primarily based. . . . the unconscious sparkles, vibrates, travels in a strong subjective stream from the abdominal centres, connecting the child directly with the mother at corresponding poles of vitalism."[21] This is, however, a bond that must be strenuously broken if an independent being is to emerge. Lawrence comments at length upon the consequences for the male child when the mother does not allow him to break these early bonds, in the two treatises on the unconscious and in other writings, notably "Education of the People" and *Women in Love*. In his culture, he believes, the mother is encouraged to idealize a possessive love, and thence to deny to the child his natural growth in his own unconscious centers: she "starts this hateful 'personal' love between herself and her excited child, and the unspoken but unfathomable hatred between the violated infant and her own assaulting soul, which together make the bane of human life, and give rise to all the neurosis and neuritis and nervous troubles we are all afflicted with."[22]

Man is repeatedly referred to as the leader and the source of knowledge and ideas, for whom the woman is a support, waiting for the male pioneer in the twilight by the campfire when he returns in the evening.[23] The view is also found repeatedly in essays such as "Cocksure Women and Hensure Men" and is implicit in the middle and later novels. A central and insistent theme of the two treatises is the overwhelming and destructive effect of mother love, which overstimulates the child, introduces him too early to adult love, and destroys his independence and precious self-possession.

This and other accounts of the primary closeness between mother and child, despite protests and theorizing, carry the stamp of Lawrence's deepest understanding. His insight into and sympathy with the mother's feelings for the child and the child's response, found so often throughout his work, form the powerful emotional nexus from which he must struggle to free himself, stridently overinsisting upon difference and separation in order to establish individual male existence. In Lawrence's version of the Female Will, the element of maternal possessiveness is more sharply in the foreground than it is in Blake. Mother love appears to promote abstraction and idealization because the son has projected into the mother the emptiness and aridity of his own near-disintegration. She seems to control him with a menacing love that is "sentimental" or "idealizing" in that it detaches him from the sensory world and is linked to a castration fear emanating from the powerful maternal imago's defeat of the father.

These themes are developed in *The Rainbow*, where "Anna Victrix" triumphs over Will, the young husband whose life is bounded by her sensory needs, and also triumphs over her older daughters through her teeming fecundity.[24] In the Ursula of *The Rainbow*, Lawrence presents us with a complex figure who, in certain respects, is the acme of his balanced social critique of the position of contemporary women. She is the heroine who emerges from cyclic generations of Brangwens as a separate individual, deliberately going beyond her mother's existence, which is enmeshed in childbirth and maternity. Lawrence depicts her as a woman who will have her own history, avoiding conventional marriage with Skrebensky and undergoing a symbolic miscarriage in order to break her enslavement to biology.[25] Yet Ursula, too, has the destructive female qualities of Anna. In one sense, she is the cause of Skrebensky's weakness, since she does not allow him to be an equal. In the stackyard scene following the country wedding in the "First Love" chapter, she is a virginal goddess, overwhelming him with her moon power: "Oh for the coolness and entire liberty and brightness of the moon. Oh for the cold liberty to be herself, to do entirely as she liked. She wanted to get right away. She felt like bright metal weighted down by dark, impure magnetism. He was the dross, people were the dross. If she could but get away to the clean free moonlight" (*R* 296). Their relationship ends when he feels that his will has been broken by the sexually assertive Ursula.[26] She appears to him as a harpy, a birdlike, beaked monster who is a manifestation of the phallic mother: "his heart melted in fear from the fierce, beaked, harpy's kiss. The water washed again over their feet, but she took no notice. She seemed unaware, she seemed to be pressing in her beaked mouth till she had the heart of him" (*R* 444). The image of woman as a threatening bird-monster is found elsewhere in Lawrence. In *The Plumed Serpent*, Kate's assertiveness in lovemaking in the early phase of her marriage to Cipriano is characterized as "the beak-like friction of Aphrodite of the foam" (*PS* 422). When, like Constance Chatterley, she submits to orgasmic passivity, the male's fear of castration has been removed. Mrs. Crich, mother of Gerald and a tough and domineering wife to her soft hearted husband, is described as "strange, like a bird of prey, with the fascinating beauty and abstraction of a hawk" (*WL* 215).[27]

The novel in which Lawrence most fully works out these ideas and complex feelings surrounding the powerful mother is *Women in Love*. The central concerns of the work are Birkin's definition of and struggle to establish a love relationship that leaves the individual, free together with a study of female threats to the maintenance of male integrity through the portrayals of three women: Hermione, Ursula, and Gudrun.

Birkin struggles throughout much of the novel to establish a relationship with Ursula appropriate to the balance of independence and commitment he desires. Ursula shares with Hermione and most women the wish to dominate men in an overbearing and possessive way:

> And Ursula, Ursula was the same—or the inverse. She too was the awful, arrogant queen of life, as if she were a queen bee on whom all the rest depended. . . . she was so certain of her man, that she could worship him as a woman worships her own infant, with a worship of perfect possession.
>
> It was intolerable, this worship at the hands of woman. Always a man must be considered as the broken-off fragment of a woman, and the sex was the still aching scar of the laceration. Man must be added on to a woman, before he had any real place or wholeness. (*WL* 200)

Lawrence alludes to the deep bond between mother and child, so richly evoked in *Psychoanalysis and the Unconscious*, showing here the urgent wish to break the tie. Man has no strength or independence of his own without woman; indeed, his sexuality, the central quality of his maleness, is a wound and a negation of selfhood. We see here the effect upon the adult male of the mother's tendency to idealize, paralleling Lawrence's account in the *Fantasia* of its effects upon the boy child. The fear of castration is experienced as a female emphasis upon the nonsensuous sphere of life.

In Birkin's resentment of Ursula and Hermione we observe the reason for the urgent overstatement of such texts as the *Fantasia*: man so much fears female power that he must preserve his sense of self by producing images of an independent male leader and pioneer from whom the woman, as other, is eternally different and separate, but dependent upon him for ideas and action.

Hermione is a type of Lawrencean woman, similar to Miriam of *Sons and Lovers* and Emily of *The White Peacock*, who appears negative and threatening to the male because of her spiritual and mystical qualities. In the adult sphere, she reproduces the idealizing capacity of the suffocating mother, and hence the most extreme form of abstraction and loss of maleness. Miriam and Emily are referred to as witches and priestesses. In *Women in Love*, Hermione is a more highly wrought version of the same female figure. She is "a sacred and inviolate priestess of desecrated mysteries" (293), and looks "like the pythoness inspired with oracles" (299). This association with mystery and spirituality, which can stir up such virulent feelings of revulsion, closely resembles Blake's hatred of mystery and the holy tabernacles of feminine repression. Like the Blake images, it springs from the deep-seated taboo against oedipal love, and in turn is seen as the cause of arid rationalism.

It is Hermione, above all, who displays the intellectualism that Birkin identifies as a social evil and traces back to the idealizing mother: "What is it but the worst and last form of intellectualism, this love of yours for passion and the animal instincts? Passion and the instincts—you want them hard enough, but through your head, in your consciousness. It all takes place in your head, under that skull of yours" (*WL* 41). Ursula recognizes the same strain in Hermione: "Poor Hermione, it was her one possession, this aching certainty of hers, it was her only justification. She must be confident here, for God knows, she felt rejected and deficient enough elsewhere" (292–93). Hermione looks down upon women like Ursula as being "purely emotional"; this, however, is the quality that Birkin, and Lawrence, value highly. Hermione and her antecedents are despised for not being in touch with the emotional life. In the terms whereby Lawrence criticizes these tendencies in *Fantasia of the Unconscious*, those women are guilty of overstressing the mind and the spirit, and of lacking a connection with the dark centers of creativity. Although not mothers, they are yet able to stir up the most virulent feelings against the mother in the Lawrencean male.

In these two sets of women, Hermione–Miriam–Emily and Ursula–Clara, and in the significant patterns of events in the novels in which they are found, we see a progression from the male's relationship with a threatening and restrictive mother to one in which he attains partial liberation from her power. More urgently, he recaptures the sensory wholeness of infantile symbiosis, while maintaining a fantasy of male independence.

Miriam and Hermione are women who, for their male counterparts, repeat the patterns and repressions of the maternal relationship. With each of them, the man, whether Paul Morel or Birkin, has had a long-standing relationship. Each woman has for so long been interwoven with the texture of his life that she seems part of a primary layer of experience that he needs to slough off as he expands in his life's enterprise. Miriam has been associated with Paul since adolescence; Hermione and Birkin have been together throughout his twenties, the period of the flowering of his social ideas and criticism, so that Birkin seems to Ursula to belong to Hermione, linked through his everyday possessions, his teacups and silver.

However, Ursula and, briefly, Clara promise a relationship grounded in the emotional and the sensuous through which the male can break away from the distorted possessiveness of the mother. Like Annie and the flirtatious Beatrice in *Sons and Lovers*, they are cognates of the sister with whom the rebellious son will establish a sensuous domain beyond that of the mother. Each of them is in a way partnered with the original maternalistic female in an early meeting and then is selected over her as the promise of a more satisfying way of life: Miriam introduces Clara to Paul; Hermione accompanies Birkin when he visits Ursula's class in Chapter II of *Women in Love*, her shrill theorizing comparing unfavorably with Ursula's rich composure. The sensuous and amoral nature of Ursula and Clara, women who represent escape from maternal strictures, is emphasized. Clara has a passionate physical presence: "There was a wonderful close down on her face near the ear that he wanted to touch. And a certain heaviness, the heaviness of a very full ear of corn that dips slightly in the wind, that there was about her, made his brain spin" (*SL* 305-6). Ursula is also a figure of sensuous actuality; she is most frequently evoked physically with reference to golden light which shines out of her: "And, being silent, he remembered the beauty of her eyes, which were sometimes filled with light, like spring, suffused with wonderful promise. So he said to her, slowly, with difficulty: 'There is a golden light in you, which I wish you would give me'" (249). She offers warmth, tenderness, and the satisfaction of passion.

Yet Birkin's feelings towards her remain ambivalent and sometimes anguished. In the long sequence, corresponding to part of *Sons and Lovers*, in which he makes the emotional break with Hermione, establishes with Ursula a version of the ideal relationship, and commits himself to her, Birkin suffers physically and mentally. Since fundamental feelings of attachment and dependence are touched and primary patterns of emotion brought to the surface, the being itself is wrenched and torn.

His first physical illness is brought on by Hermoine's attack upon him. In an ecstasy of destruction, she twice brings down a heavy lapis lazuli paperweight on his head, "almost breaking his neck, and shattering his heart" (*WL* 105). From the male viewpoint, she is acting out her elemental psyche as the vengeful and possessive female: the manner and location of the blows signify her attack upon his ideas, his pride, and his tender emotions. Upon leaving Hermione, he walks out into the open countryside and takes off his clothes, to sit or lie among the grass and flowers. He finds a peculiarly soothing quality in nature, which appears more real and important than the human sphere: "To lie down and roll in the sticky, cool young hyacinths, to lie on one's belly and cover one's back with handfuls of fine wet grass, soft as a breath, soft and more delicate and more beautiful than the touch of any woman . . . enrichened now immeasurably, and so glad" (107). It is not so much that Hermione has attacked his upper centers of feeling, his head and heart, but that he has willingly abandoned them, since they are related to his affiliation with a cold and possessive woman.[28] He dwells now in peace and harmony at the level of nature, in the dark unconscious of the lower centers of feeling. In the passage quoted, we notice that there is a sensuous and erotic quality in the description of nature that is partly acknowledged: the contact with the sticky, cool hyacinths, and the lovely, desirable roses and trees that set up responses in the blood are redolent of blissful primary contact with the female body. Despite his statement that he does not want women, or any people, Birkin is actually affirming closeness with the female. It is, however, the closeness of infantile union with the elemental maternal quality of nature. It is the levels of development that follow this early stage that are rejected: separation and the ethical dimension of the superego, leading out into the world of ideas and other people. The erotic content of the episode, and the affirmation of a new mode of existence, are made plain in a passage that Secker omitted from the first English edition: "He knew now where he belonged. He knew where to plant himself, his seed: — along with the trees, in the folds of the delicious fresh growing leaves" (*WL* 107–8). Hermione, the cold possessive woman who wreaks violence upon the son, must be eluded. He turns instead to Ursula, who promises a dark unconscious relationship within the natural sphere, remote from the intellectualism associated with separation and disintegration.

Yet even this primal association with the woman threatens the male through dependence and possessiveness; therefore, it cannot be accepted without turmoil. Birkin's psychic anguish is reflected in the period of recuperation he must take as an invalid, following Hermione's attack, and then in an unspecified illness that keeps him in bed, reflecting upon Ursula, knowing that his life is united with hers but detesting the predefined strictures of marriage and domesticity this seems to entail. His illness is a period of spiritual sickness as he confronts the limits of what his being, formed by bonds with women, can bear.

In the relationship of Gerald and Gudrun, we see another essential strand in this emotional pattern. Gerald's mechanical nature and inability to make true contact with other people is a dimension of the Lawrencean male, brought about by the icy idealism of women. As Blakean man suffers separation of the vital functions that can be healed only with the redemption of Albion, so too are Gerald and Birkin two halves of a broken person who can come together only in a close male relationship that is envisaged but never realized. Birkin's phase of spiritual sickness, during which he separates himself from the world of people and action, is extended by a period of convalescence in the south of France, corresponding in time with Gerald's emotional disintegration at the end of "The Industrial Magnate."

Gudrun is a mother figure who cradles Gerald in a Pietà scene after the death of his father and overwhelms him with a menacing "pity."[29] His dependence upon her increases as the novel progresses, so that at the time when their relationship disintegrates, she thinks of him contemptuously as "a child that is famished crying for the breast" (*WL* 466), as indeed he is.

Gudrun becomes the ultimate terrible mother when she first recognizes with rapture her true element, the view of the snow-filled valley from the bedroom she and Gerald share in the Tyrolean inn:

> In front was a valley shut in under the sky, the last huge slopes of snow and black rock, and at the end, like the navel of the earth, a white-folded wall, and two peaks glimmering in the late light. Straight in front lay the cradle of silent snow, between the great slopes, that were fringed with a little roughness of pine trees, like hair, round the base. But the cradle of snow ran on to the eternal closing-in, where the walls of snow and rock rose impenetrable, and the mountain peaks above were in heaven immediate. (*WL* 401)

Here, Gudrun feels, "she had reached her place. Here at last she folded her venture and settled down like a crystal in the navel of the snow, and was gone." This marks the first moment of separation between her and Gerald, who feels an "icy vapour round his heart."

This scene contains the fundamental elements of harsh maternal power. It is the navel, the seal of the female source of life, and the "cradle," where the infant sleeps in a protected slumber. Yet in this manifestation, the female body is revealed as cruel and unyielding with its impenetrable folds of snow, its two sharp, unnurturing peaks, and the black rocks that rise to the heaven of female idealization. Above all, it is a scene of emotional coldness: the unyielding ice banishes the male to an eternity of abstraction and impotence and denies alike the desires of the infant and the adult male.

Gudrun's withdrawal of tenderness from Gerald, and her blow to his face and breast, paralleling Hermione's attack upon Birkin, leads to his death on the icy mountain. He stumbles among black rocks slashed with veins of snow, as if seeking out the "hollow basin of snow," the inhospitable female goal of his desire, where he falls into a sleep of death. Gerald suffers the ultimate agony of the male victim, perishing in a negation of his virility and masculine nature at the hands of a harsh, overpowering mother.

When Birkin returns from his convalescence he is prepared, though with pain and ambivalence, to commit himself to Ursula. They encounter each other again in the "Moony" chapter, where we are introduced into complicated layers of feeling surrounding the relationship of male and female.

The chapter begins with Ursula, who now experiences her own animosity towards other humans and the "detestable social principle." She is going through a phase of detachment from the forms of mankind in order to prepare herself for immersion in the twin-souled dark complicity with Birkin, incomplete as that will prove to be. Lawrence also separates other women, Lou Carrington and Kate Leslie, from ties with conventional society in order to make them worthy of association with his male ideal. Ursula goes to Willey Water feeling, like Birkin among the grass and cool hyacinths, "a sort of magic peace" in nature remote from humanity. This elemental encounter between male and female will take place at a distance from the social sphere. She is then startled by the presence of the moon rising through the trees: "But it seemed so mysterious, with its white and deathly smile. And there was no avoiding it. Night or day, one could not escape the sinister face, triumphant and radiant like this moon, with a high smile. She hurried on, cowering from the white planet" (*WL* 245). As she stands by the water, knowing that Birkin is also present, she wishes for complete darkness, without any distractions of light.

The brilliant presence of the moon recalls other scenes in Lawrence such as that in *Sons and Lovers* when Gertrude Morel, pregnant with Paul, is locked out of the house by her drunken husband and is confirmed in the strength of her feminine power in the bright moonlight and tall white lilies. This power is affirmed when Morel, finally opening the door to her, is afraid: "there stood the silver-grey night" (*SL* 25). In *The Rainbow*, Skrebensky has the sensation of being reduced to nothingness by Ursula when they are together in the moonlight among the haystacks during the country wedding party (*R* 296–99). There is, however, a shift in the acceptance of female dominance in *Women in Love*. In the earlier novels the woman's power seems indomitable: Morel is always essentially the loser in every encounter throughout the narrative, while Skrebensky knows that "there was no core to him: as a distinct male he had no core" (*R* 300). In *Women in Love*, on the other hand, Birkin isolates and attacks the significance of the ancient female symbol.[30]

Lawrence's detestation of the power and tyranny implicit in idealization of women is made clear in *Psychoanalysis and the Unconscious*: "Of that reflected or moon-love, derived from the head, that spurious form of love which predominates today, we do not speak here. It has its root in the *idea*: the beloved is a mental objective, endlessly appreciated, criticized, scrutinized, exhausted" (*PsyU* 229). The act of idealization has the effect of causing division, separating emotions and personal responses, and therefore of putting at a distance the phallic strength of the male.

Birkin approaches the water, "touching unconsciously the dead husks of flowers" (*WL 246*), and flings stones at the reflection of the moon in the water, at first in vain since the scattered fragments of the reflection keep on returning to the center, as to the "heart of the rose." Momentarily, his furious efforts seem to succeed: "He got large stones, and threw them, one after the other, at the white-burning centre of the moon, till there was nothing but a rocking of hollow noise, and a pond surged up, no moon any more, only a few broken flakes tangled and glittering broadcast in the darkness, without aim or meaning, a darkened confusion, like a black and white kaleidoscope tossed at random. The hollow night was rocking and crashing with noise . . . " (247–48). It is a primary image of infantile aggression against the mother, producing a disintegration into fragments, darkness, and chaos. Here the locus of attack is the "white-burning centre of the moon"; his previous attempt has resulted in the moon's reflection regathering itself into "the heart of the rose" (*WL* 247). An inviolable center, in fact, remains and will return, but the furious child momentarily annihilates her into a terrifying emptiness echoing with noise and confusion in a dark empty pond that, even as a negation, remains as the maternal essence. The unifying rose, like the lilies associated with the moon in the Gertrude Morel episode, is a hated reminder of the social dimension of female power, corresponding with Blake's Female Will, the female principle in culture that enforces sublimation and idealization. The "dead husks of flowers" that he touches as he passes Ursula in the darkness reflect hatred of both female sexuality as power and the worship of females enshrined in the lily and the rose.

Birkin vainly wishes for a commitment to Ursula that is founded upon a denial of maternal power. Indeed her appeal to him is that she is a "good mother," sensuous and nurturing, who does not set up the aggressive feelings that lead to overintellectualization. Yet she remains threatening because he depends upon her nurture. In the "Excurse" chapter he submits to her, recognizing his need while regretting the dependence he must acknowledge: "Hermione saw herself as the perfect Idea, to which all men must come: and Ursula was the perfect Womb, the bath of birth, to which all men must come! And both were horrible" (*WL* 309). Birkin makes this statement at a moment of estrangement between them. When he has acknowledged the inevitability of his relationship with Ursula, his feelings of antagonism are resolved: "There was a darkness over his mind. The terrible knot of consciousness that had persisted there like an obsession was broken, gone, his life was dissolved in darkness over his limbs and his body. But there was a point of anxiety in his heart now. He wanted her to come back. He breathed lightly and regularly like an infant, that breathes innocently, beyond the touch of responsibility" (309–10). Ursula, the positive womb mother, for a moment exists side by side with Hermione, the overweening bad mother who leads to separation and remoteness from sensuous actuality. When the choice is made, although it entails dependence, Birkin returns to the ideal infantile state of unthinking darkness, feeling in his newfound sense of harmony that he has been reborn.

In the "Excurse" chapter, Birkin and Ursula consummate their love and commitment according to Lawrence's regressive phallic ideal, whereby the female responds to the dark richness of the male loins. The encouner seals the finality of their commitment. This is the first major example in Lawrence's writing of his masculinist ethos, whereby the man has indeed, in fantasy, crushed female power and is himself dominant. Emphasis shifts from the healthy phallic ethic of the earlier writings to what Cornelia Nixon has defined as Lawrence's "deathly sensuality," based on corruption and the bowels, and linked to his male supremacist ideals.[31] As he drives with Ursula to Sherwood Forest at the end of the chapter, Birkin experiences the accession of his mystical masculine power, which has replaced the male's angry but helpless sense of being overwhelmed by the dominant female: "He knew what it was to have the strange and magical current of force in his back and loins, and down his legs, force so perfect that it stayed him immobile, and left his face subtly, mindlessly smiling. He knew what it was to be awake and potent in that other basic mind, the deepest physical mind. And from this source he had a pure and magic control, magical, mystical, a force in darkness, like electricity" (*WL* 318). Since, in fantasy, he has destroyed female dominance, he is able to believe that he has attained masculine ascendancy at the dark preconscious stage of emerging oedipal awareness, seeming to restore the devalued father. However, such moments of absolute balance are tenuous: Ursula's continuing sensuous power and Birkin's unfulfilled longing for brotherhood with Gerald indicate the strains that underlie the defensive fantasy.

Male-female relationships in *Women in Love* are also defined by the contradictory image of the twin stars: "But beyond this, he wanted a further conjunction, where man had being and woman had being, two pure beings, each constituting the freedom of the other, balancing each other like two poles of one force, like two angels, or two demons" (199). Instead of overwhelming white light in the sky, he envisages two small, controllable, and equal points of light. But this is an attempt to set up a social ideal that works against the logic of the more fundamental longing for dark male power. As Marguerite Beede Howe comments, "Stellar equilibrium is a fantasy possible only in the reality of the unconscious."[32]

This notion of the balanced independence of man and woman in "stellar equilibrium" is a temporary phase in Lawrence's thinking. We observe in *The Plumed Serpent* that the male morning star is in ascendancy over the female evening star. In the fiction that followed *Women in Love*, Lawrence produced instead the pattern of a virile male leader, like the poet in Blake's *Milton*, united in brotherhood with other males and dominant over women. Yet women, and strong women, are always essential to Lawrence's scheme. The need returns again and again to suppress in fantasy the power of the threatening mother and to assert an exaggerated compensatory image of the son's masculinity.

In many of Lawrence's works, we find the lurking figure of an older woman who has some association with the erotic relationship of a young couple: she may either look upon their congress with a forbidding air or, paradoxically, give it a furtive assent. She is a figure who carries the power of the "bad mother" in Melanie Klein's sense. She restricts the son's sensuous freedom and his contact with concrete reality, therefore casting a shadow upon his mature relationships with other women. At the same time, she is the original object of his sensuality who conceals her own powerful eroticism. The attitude of the older woman or the feelings reflected towards her lend a specific coloring to the relationship, as the complex of emotions surrounding the mother is closely linked with adult sexual experience.

This motif is found in *Sons and Lovers*, where the male seeks erotic freedom with a young woman in defiance of the possessive and forbidding mother who wishes to prohibit her son's sexuality. There are several instances of it in the earlier works. In the chapter of *The White Peacock* entitled "An Arrow from the Impatient God," Hilda Slaighter, "a garrulous spinster," calls upon the Beardsall family to talk about Lettie's impending marriage to Leslie, at a point in the novel when Lettie feels drawn to George, despite her engagement to Leslie, and George is gathering courage to propose to her once more. Hilda Slaighter's presence darkens the rightful sensuous bond of George and Lettie. She is associated with various foreboding signs in the earlier part of the chapter: the arrival of a telegram that she describes as a bad omen, and a sudden storm. In her distress at the storm, she rushes into a neighbor's house and is terrified at her own reflection in a mirror, thinking that it is a ghost. Her bonnet and its braid of false hair fall backwards, leaving visible some ends of grey hair. In great fear she "fled into the open stair-hole as into a grave" (*WP* 193). This figure of fate revealed in her unbonneted state as a grim old woman holds forth a warning of the accident to Leslie that follows closely upon her disappearance into the place of death. His accident proves not to be an acutal death but a death of feelings, since as a result of it, the sensuous and life-giving relationship of George and Lettie receives its final blow. Lettie has a sense of obligation to Leslie that, despite her emotional anguish, leads her to enter into marriage with him. Thus, the socially correct but emotionally shallow marriage approved by the mother, because it does not dissolve the son's emotional loyalty, is contracted in place of the passionate association that puts aside the mother's dominance. In that whisk of the false braid of hair, we catch a glimpse of the frail strength of Mrs. Morel and her girlish braid. The ludicrous birdlike Scottish woman who takes over Mrs. Saxton's kitchen as the new tenant of Strelley Mill in *The White Peacock* is a defensive parody of the motif. When Cyril and Emily return to the place of the mother, after the mother has gone, their conspiratorial eroticism reduces the mother to a harmless being.

In both *The White Peacock* and *Sons and Lovers*, we find two further sinsister figures of older women who act as grim guardians of Meg and Clara, the two young women who offer the respective male protagonists the most pure sensual abandon. Meg lives with her grandmother, an elderly woman who is ailing and close to death yet clings to life "like a louse to a pig's back" (*WP* 140). She is a formidable presence, "a hard-visaged, bosomless dame, clad in thick black cloth like armour" (139). Her deathlike qualities are emphasized. She has a "clammy corded hand" (139), a "skinny throat," and she shouts down in a thin voice from upstairs where she spends much of her time, "like a ghoul from the upper regions" (143). In her sinister fashion, she encourages the match of Meg and George, screaming in delight and clutching her wineglass when George kisses Meg, urging him to hasten toward betrothal. At the same time, she insists on decorum, ordering Meg to send George home at night and becoming enraged at the sudden and unceremonious manner of their marriage. This combination of a deathlike guardian of propriety and a lascivious goad to male sexual activity requires some explanation. She seeks to control the erotic relationship by making demands upon the prowess of the male and circumscribing it within the female sphere of marriage. Thus, she imperils the male sense of self in more than one way, by seeking to trap him in a female-dominated institution and by submitting his very sexual instincts to her own wishes. She is the lurking presence of Thanatos at the gates of Eros, a mother who, in appearing to give freedom to the son, extends her rule over him.

Another version of the domineering older woman associated with the sexual relationship of a young couple is Clara's mother, Mrs. Radford, in *Sons and Lovers*. We encounter her first when Paul calls at her house to give a message to Clara. She has the air of a guardian Fate, a tall well-built figure, who admits him into her "mausoleum of a parlour" with its mahogany furniture and "deathly enlargements of photographs of departed people done in carbon" (*SL* 259). She again has a menacing air when she serves supper to Clara and Paul after their visit to the theater, on the occasion when Paul spends the night in her house: "Mrs Radford, large and threatening, stood suspended on the hearthrug holding her fork" (333). She has a jovial attitude, welcoming Paul as a male into a house of women and establishing a rapport with him that aligns her with his mother. However, she is overbearing and crushing in her treatment of Clara, and taunts both of them. Paul hates her as the protector of Clara's sensuous nature when she refuses to go to bed before him and thus leave him alone with her daughter, who must sleep that night in her mother's bed. Like Meg's grandmother, Mrs. Radford has an earthy appreciation of male physical nature, which is an aspect of her urge to command its rhythms. This mother figure who thwarts erotic freedom embodies the deathlike prohibition of maternal control, acting like one of the Fates upon the male's very fibers of life. Clara, whose alliance with Paul, above all, means his liberation from the maternal bond, is surrounded and protected by a force that opposes him.

Another figure who belongs within this configuration lingers on the fringes of the first meeting of Paul and Clara when Paul begins to fall captive to Clara's sensuous presence. Paul, Clara, and Miriam, taking a walk together, encounter Miss Limb, the spinster sister of the tenant farmer of Strelley Mill. The landscape has a misty intensity suggestive of the passionate plane of experience to which Paul aspires: "looking through the brake at the edge of the wood, where pink campions glowed under a few sunbeams, they saw, beyond the tree-trunks and the thin hazel bushes, a man leading a great bay horse through the gullies. The big red beast seemed to dance romantically through that dimness of green hazel drift, away there where the air was shadowy, as if it were in the past, among the fading bluebells that might have bloomed for Deirdre or Iseult" (*SL* 233). Amid the romantic sublimation, the masculine strength of the great bay horse stands dominant. Within this setting, Miss Limb is a ludicrous figure longing to be overwhelmed by masculine power. As Clara says, "she wants a man." Miss Limb lingeringly embraces the bay stallion and urgently invites Paul to fish and swim in her pond, to assuage her loneliness. This figure of an older woman is rendered powerless through ridicule. Instead of blocking erotic freedom like Hilda Slaighter, she is shown as a victim of eroticism. The age-old male joke of the frustrated spinster, created to break, through comic distance, the bond of male dependence upon women is projected here even by Clara, the feminist with whom Paul will seek erotic fulfillment and whose ascendancy he feels the need to control.

The figure of the red horse brings us to *St. Mawr*, where we find Mrs. Witt, the most developed and sinister of these females who are linked with death and marked by a determination to rule man's sexuality. In this late and ironic novel, in which Lawrence had advanced a great distance in developing a defense against the power of women, the paradigm of the older woman and the erotic relationship of a young couple reappears. She differs in her effect from the female found in the early works, although the same elements, rearranged, remain beneath the surface. Rachel Witt is the mentor and support of her daughter, Lou Carrington, as Lou frees herself from the hold of superficial, fashionable society and her empty marriage to Rico. Like the earlier oppressive mother figures, she wishes for a healthy virility in her daughter's mate and therefore is contemptuous of Rico. In this novel, however, both mother and daughter are brought under the sway of a Lawrence whose attitude towards women has been refined to a new strength, through the ideals of masculinity and leadership. The weak son-in-law is obliterated and superseded by Lewis and, more peripherally, by Phoenix, two males whose self-sufficiency cannot be eroded.

Mrs. Witt's terrible associations with death and violence are strongly emphasized. She is characteristically linked with the color grey, and with gunpowder and weapons. She has "heavy-lidded grey eyes" (*StM* 24) that conceal her destructive wit and can become "dagger-like" (26) as she surveys the vapid young Englishmen. She resembles a "smooth, levelled, gun-metal pistol" to whom Lou must be "a sort of sheath" (26), while Lewis, in describing her essential nature, says that her flesh and blood are mixed with gunpowder, so that she is like "a cartridge you put in a gun" (111). She has a personal fascination with death, shown in her enjoyment of the view of the graveyard from the drawing room of her house in the country and of watching funerals. She is dominated by thoughts of her own death, which she seems to imagine as the only token of the reality of her life: "I want death to be real to me—not as it was to that young girl. I *want* it to hurt me, Louise. If it hurts me enough, I shall know I was alive" (93). At this moment she seems to her daughter to have "a certain pure wistfulness of a young, virgin girl," quite in contrast to her usual amazon quality. Elsewhere, we are told of her longing to die positively, "folded then at last into throbbing wings of mystery, like a hawk that goes to sleep. Not like a thing made into a parcel and put into the last rubbish-heap" (102). To others she has a mythical power and presence, yet she has an inner fear of being discarded without human concern. She is a fantasy of the overwhelming mother, bristling with aggression and destruction, and resembling a phallic weapon, whom the enfeebled son weakly wishes to kill, knowing, however, that the wish is vain.

On the voyage to America, hating the sea, she spends most of the crossing in her bunk, "silent, shut up like a steel trap, as in her tomb" (127).

We feel that she has the deep primitive feminine association with the ocean, "the great, heavy Atlantic," which she resembles in her quality of predatory greyness: " . . . this grey, wolf-like, cold-blooded Ocean hated men and their ships and their smoky passage" (128). She is herself this destructive spirit, and yet is also banished to a constricting tomb.

Mrs. Witt relishes controlling and arranging things, such as salads and complicated dishes. This inclination manifests itself most menacingly when she cuts Lewis's hair. As a Fate who controls the threads of man's life and inheres in the deepest layers of human emotion, her truest significance is manifest: "she poised a pair of long scissors like one of the fates. In her big black hat she looked curiously young, but with the youth of a bygone generation. Her heavy-lidded, laconic grey eyes were alert, studying the groom's black mop of hair." This is the ultimate point of feminine interference that Lewis, the impregnable male, will allow: "And efficiently she bent down, clip–clip–clipping! while Lewis sat utterly immobile, with sunken head, in a sort of despair" (57). He experiences the cutting of his hair as profound humiliation and refuses to let her go the further step of cutting his beard, which he has already declared is part of himself, his essential maleness. The cutting of the hair is a symbolic act of partial castration, but Lewis toughly resists true emasculation.

In her later encounter with Lewis and her proposal of marriage to him, an important aspect of Mrs. Witt stands revealed: before the self-sufficient Lawrencean male, this tough and fearsome woman is vulnerable. Like Lou, with her weariness of modern men, and in accordance with the ethos attached to St. Mawr, the proud stallion, she despises men because she is more powerful than they. This extreme manifestation of feminine dominance finally meets a point of masculine strength that she cannot overcome, a state that she has sought and desired:

> If she could have found something indestructible, especially in men, though she would have fought against it, she would have been glad at least to be defeated by it.
>
> That was the point. She really wanted to be defeated, in her own eyes. And nobody had ever defeated her. Men were never really her match. A woman of terrible strong health, she felt even that in her strong limbs there was far more electric power than in the limbs of any man she had met.
>
> (*StM* 100-101)

Lewis, with his quiet refusal to be overcome by her, and his insistence that women must have a special kind of respect for his body, is the force she encounters that has the capacity to defeat her. His strength lies in his remoteness from cerebral forces, his closeness to nature, and his association with the mystical powers alluded to in the novel, "the darkness of the old Pan" (107). His fey affinity with ash trees (107–8) recalls the bristling ash tree of *Sons and Lovers*, terrifying, yet alive with the hidden phallic power of the ideal father. Mrs. Witt values an experience beyond sex, "the mysterious, intense, dynamic sympathy that could flow between her and some 'live' man—a man who was highly conscious, a real live wire" (101). In Lewis, she finds even more, a sense of mystery that promises to assuage her fear of death. She approaches Lewis at a moment of intense fear of a barren death, longing to be folded "into throbbing wings of mystery," (102) realizing that he possesses a quality that makes him "perhaps the only real entity to her" (104): his contact with the inaudible, silent world of private darkness. Since he is a projection of the ideal male or the strong father, he is able to make her appear less threatening, and therefore she is less subject to punitive, destructive wishes.

Mrs. Witt is puzzling and inconsistent if we approach her with expectations of social realism. She represents, or is brought to accept, some of Larwrence's most crucial values: an appreciation of the dark unconscious layers of existence and respect for male supremacy, both of which lead to bitter criticism of the shallowness of contemporary society. Yet she remains a terrible figure whose condition of life cannot be accounted ideal. Her significance emerges when we consider her in relation to that earlier motif and its transformations, wherein she is the menacing, yet engaging, sexually wise older woman linked with a young couple.

Whereas, in the earlier configurations, this female appeared fleetingly and had no ultimate effect upon the relationship of the two young people, Rachel Witt dominates the foreground of *St. Mawr* and overwhelms the young pair, Rico and Lou. Rico, like other males and the members of his false society, is obliterated by her gaze, while Lou, apparently herself a strong woman, remains under her mother's tutelage and reflects her views. If we make substitutions between the earlier and later patterns, we note that Rico corresponds to the young man, whether George Saxton or Paul Morel, who in pursuing the female he desires encounters her maternal protector. Both George and Paul aspire to Lawrence's ideal of manhood. In *St. Mawr*, Rico is quite divorced from Lawrencean values. Instead, we have alongside him in the novel, Lewis, who is an embodiment of those values. The figure has been split, into the male who has no defenses against the all-powerful mother and the dark independent Lawrencean male whom not even she can dominate. The function of Lewis is to act as a bastion against this terrifying female, who cannot destroy him since he is an ideal figure, but will destroy all men in the realistic sphere.

Rico is emptiness in every respect: in his style of living, in his relationships, and in his art. His emptiness corresponds to the totality of Rachel Witt's destructiveness. A characteristic moment is when Mrs. Witt, speaking with the "smooth acid" of her irony, looks from Rico to Fred Manby "as if she were dropping them down the bottomless pit" (*StM* 64). Man is empty and feeble, as Lawrence says at length in *Fantasia of the Unconscious* and "Education of the People," because of excessive dependence upon overassertive mothers who rob them of their deeper selves. The source of the anger and contempt for Rico is fear and helplessness before the female "suave as a grey leopard cat" (98) who obliterates men with her Medusa gaze, a gaze to which George and Paul were also unwittingly subjected.

The novel is a central statement of the position of the later Lawrence. Woman has become so dominant and menacing to male stability that masculine strength and faith must be invested in an idealized male figure—found here in Lewis and Phoenix, and later in Don Cipriano and Mellors—who is impervious to her and will instead dominate her. Both this strong father image and the overbearing mother are fantasy projections of the parents by Lawrence, the weak son.

Mrs. Witt's association with death is partly an inversion of the son's conflicting feelings. She threatens the male with annihilation and blights his sexual powers. The barren and unceremonious death that she fears reflects the son's wish to obliterate her, as well as her own deathly influence over him. She describes to Lou her fantasy of the funeral in which she is the corpse, a young girl of eighteen who has died of consumption. At this moment she appears to her daughter young and innocent: "She was so used to the matchless Amazon in her mother, that when she saw her sit there, still, wistful, virginal, tender as a girl who has never taken armour, wistful at the window that only looked on graves, a serious terror took hold of the young woman" (*StM* 93). The aggressive amazon is stripped of her weapons and rendered harmless in a static image of a sublimated romantic maiden, like Mrs. Morel on her deathbed. Elsewhere, she is described as being age-old and in contact with the eternal powers. Here she is bereft of those associations and since, at the fantasy level, it is the male who strives to control the dark mysteries, it is only through him that she may recover them.

Lou Carrington is the desirable young woman of the earlier Lawrencean configuration, now brought under male domination; she must either await union with an ideal masculine lover or else remain a virgin in the wilderness, "since the mystic new man will never come to me" (139). She is presented as a woman who comprehends true masculine values in her recognition of the gleaming virility of St. Mawr, and in her scorn for Rico's life as a "rattling nullity" (94); yet she cannot arouse Phoenix, who has attained his ideal masculinity in America, "impassive, detached, self-satisfied, and silently assertive" (134). Depraved though he has become through contact with white society, his "rat-like" furtiveness still responds more deeply to the submissiveness of the Indian woman. We find Lou at the end of the novel wishing with all her soul that "some men *were* bigger and stronger and *deeper* than I am" (154), and knowing that she will remain alone: "either my taking a man shall have a meaning and a mystery that penetrates my very soul, or I will keep to myself" (155).

Lou is one of the women created by Lawrence who incorporate something of his own persona and pass through some of his personal experience. In the same way that Ursula in *The Rainbow* feels some of Lawrence's reactions to being a student and teacher, or Kate Leslie reflects his response to bull fighting and to travel in Mexico, Lou Carrington voices Lawrence's outrage with contemporary Western society and discovers, as he does, the solace of a more primitive natural world. When St. Mawr rears at the sight of the dead snake, falling backwards onto Rico and injuring him, Lou has a vision of evil that corresponds with Lawrence's own most bleak perception. Furthermore, her ranch, Las Chivas, and the surrounding terrain resemble Lawrence's ranch in New Mexico. When we consider the attachment that Lawrence felt to the place and the solace that its nonhuman essence provided him from the torments of his restless contact with human society, we recognize how significant a spokesperson for his values Lou is.

These female protagonists who reflect Lawrence's insight and experience—Ursula, Alvina, Kate, Lou—are an amalgam of women he had known, most especially Frieda, but more fundamentally, they are himself. The polarity of his resentment of women is his feeling of close sympathy with women: he was a man with an unusual capacity to empathize with female experience and to be in touch with his own femininity. Thus, some of the crucial experiences of his life are recreated in a feminine persona: his intellectual growth and the development of a critical stance in *The Rainbow*; bitter observation of contemporary society and departure from England in *The Lost Girl*; and the exploration of the satisfactions of a primitive society in *St. Mawr* and *The Plumed Serpent.* We must note, however, that these are women whom he must subject to the dominance of the mystic male. There is a continuum in Lawrence's responsiveness to women, from the earlier works where he observes and sympathizes with the tribulations of a woman's life—such as Gertrude Morel's or Elizabeth Bates's—to later works where his empathy with the feminine is so strong that he creates the ideal male in order to defend himself from being absorbed in the female.

With Ursula, the Lawrencean male has a life-and-death struggle to establish supremacy, and essentially fails. In later Lawrence, women may be removed from a sphere in which they can exert control. They are depicted as no longer able to dominate the male with their moon-derived icy friction but subject to a fantasy of male power.[33] Lou sees herself as a Vestal Virgin: "They were symbolic of herself, of woman weary of the embrace of incompetent men, weary, weary, weary of all that, turning to the unseen gods, the unseen spirits, the hidden fire, and devoting herself to that, and that alone. Receiving thence her pacification and her fulfilment" (*St M* 138-39). In her turning away from ordinary men to the sublimation of a mystical hidden fire, we note not so much her own disappointment but a general lack of faith in the ordinary male. *St. Mawr* is a novel without actual sexual intercourse. It moves between contempt for puny, empty men and admiration for idealized males who, in degraded Europe, do not make contact with women, and in more primitive America are released into unspecified encounters with females. Lewis refuses contact with Mrs. Witt and, in England, St. Mawr shuns mares. In America, both the stallion and

Phoenix are shown entering into sexual congress with nameless females. Lou's and Mrs. Witt's, in other words *women's*, scorn for men is the dominant view of the novel, countered only by a remote ideal of the new mystic male that does not come into actuality in the course of the novel. It inheres in primitive nature as an unrealized power. Lou has no sexual activity but is aware of her sexuality and its possible fulfillment with some, as yet, unimaginable male: "And I am here, right deep in America, where there's a wild spirit wants me, a wild spirit more than men. And it doesn't want to save me either. It needs me. It craves me. And to it, my sex is deep and sacred, deeper than I am, with a deep nature aware deep down of my sex" (155). We note in the novel a sexual emptiness counterbalanced by sexual sublimation. This combination of qualities betokens lack of faith in male sexuality and reveals the need to create a fantasy to cover the awareness of male feebleness and emptiness. Within this scheme, woman is never empty; she is rather a well of deep and sacred sexuality that the male must somehow possess and circumscribe.

The configuration of young couple and maternalistic Fate from the earlier novels is drastically recast in *St. Mawr*. The questing erotic male disintegrates, while the younger female is a source of sexuality that he cannot tap. Rachel Witt, the death-bringing mother who controls male virility, is subjected to the sterile dominance of Lewis, the superior male. Her power for action is cut down, but her withering presence as a blight upon eroticism stays, as she remains the guardian of the daughter whom the male does not possess in actuality. On the Atlantic voyage, she turns away from the living delight of the ocean to remain in her coffinlike cabin, reflecting an infant's view of an ungenerous mother who offers suffocating confinement instead of the life-giving surge of the maternal sea. The apparent meaning of the novel is inverted. Unlike the earlier male, who had his sensuous fulfillment in woman despite the lurking Medusa, the male of the phase of novels to which *St. Mawr* belongs is immobilized by the mother's deathly gaze and must vanish into a realm of mysticism where sexuality is a static fantasy.

CHAPTER 6

The Triumph of Masculinity in Blake's *Milton*

Both Blake and Lawrence develop an elevated ideal of masculinity and brotherhood in order to overcome the oppressive presence of women. For Lawrence, the central work in which we find these ideals expressed is *The Plumed Serpent*; for Blake, it is *Milton*.

Milton, Blake's most autobiographical major work, has as its main theme the resolution of conflict and male rivalry in images of union and reconciliation. Women are peripherally present in the poem, in various threatening aspects, mingled with some of the most benign images of women that Blake produced, above all, Ololon, the Emanation of Milton. At the end of the poem, Ololon descends to Blake as an innocent figure integral to the creative harmony of the conclusion.

Milton received its impetus from one of the most tormented periods of Blake's life: the three years from September 1800 to September 1803 that he spent at Felpham, Sussex, as an assistant to William Hayley, an inferior poet who lacked the insight to appreciate Blake's genius. From references in his letters as well as indications in his poetry, it is clear that Blake suffered immensely under Hayley's tutelage. In letters from Felpham, Blake confides to Thomas Butts, his friend and patron, that he has been through a long period of mental torment: "my Abstract folly hurries me often away while I am at work, carrying me over Mountains & Valleys which are not Real in a Land of Abstraction where Spectres of the Dead wander" (E716). He tells Butts that he has, however, overcome these grave difficulties: "but I have traveld thro Perils & Darkness not unlike a Champion" (E720). His state of mind as he emerges from the crisis appears to be confident: "but as none on Earth can give me Mental Distress . . . a Fig for all Corporeal Such Distress is My mock & scorn" (E716).

Blake refers to the period spent at Felpham in ambivalent ways, both as a time of torment and as a time of peaceful sleep.[1] He tells Hayley two years after his return to London that "Three that would have been the Darkest Years that every Mortal Sufferd. . . . were renderd thro your means a Mild & Pleasant Slumber" (E767). He says in another letter: "O lovely Felpham, parent of Immortal Friendship, to thee I am eternally indebted for my three years' rest from perturbation and the strength I now enjoy" (E756). The unusual use of the word "parent" here to refer to a place suggests the feelings that colored his association with Hayley. He was a patron and a paternal figure who, in his positive manifestation, also had the ideal maternal capacity to provide the unbroken peace of the womb. However, he set up obstacles to material success and creative strength, thus activating Blake's basic dissatisfaction with the father-imago. Blake had been very hopeful that he would prosper under Hayley's patronage. His disappointment at the failure of the association was extremely bitter. Hayley was a weak father figure who had the capacity to stir up fundamental conflicts within Blake.

In a letter to his brother James in January 1803, Blake indicates the nature of the quarrels with Hayley, quarrels that are allegorically dramatized in *Milton*: "I am now certain of what I have long doubted Viz [*that H*] is jealous as Stothard was & will be no further My friend than he is compelld by circumstances. The truth is As a Poet he is frightend at me & as a Painter his views and mine are opposite" (E725). The poem *Milton*, probably composed during the Felpham period and in the years immediately following it (E806), records very violent conflicts between Hayley, who is Satan in the poem, and Blake, figured in the split personae of Rintrah, a raging, iconoclastic prophet and Palambron, a milder and more amenable figure. This division represents Blake's fundamental feelings of anger against Hayley, and the milder public self who behaved towards Hayley in a meek and complaisant manner. The surface gentleness of Palambron's relationship with Satan–Hayley is made clear:

Palambron oft refus'd; and as often Satan offer'd
His service till by repeated offers and repeated intreaties
Los gave to him the Harrow of the Almighty; alas blamable

> Palambron. fear'd to be angy lest Satan should accuse him of
> Ingratitude . . . (E100; *M*7, 8–12)

The fury of the spurned artist is expressed more directly through Los:

> But Rintrah who is of the reprobate: of those form'd to destruction
> In indignation. for Satans soft dissimulation of friendship!
> Flam'd above all the plowed furrows, angry red and furious. (E102; *M*8, 34–36)

Blake's reassertion of himself as a person and as an artist, in the face of Hayley's subtle erosion of his being, is achieved partly through identification with Milton, a strong poet and father figure whose "Selfhood," or negative aspect, is shown to be Hayley–Satan, the weak poet and father. Milton, as the poet who represents the tradition and artistic values that Blake holds precious, descends from his place among the eternals in order to restore life and harmony to a state of existence torn by conflict:

> I go to Eternal Death! The Nations still
> Follow after the detestable Gods of Priam: in pomp
> Of warlike selfhood, contradicting and blaspheming.
> When will the Resurrection come; to deliver the sleeping body
> From corruptibility. (E108; *M*14, 14–18)

Milton's act of redemption entails that he purify himself by reconciling himself with the six women whom he had oppressed during his life, his three wives and three daughters.

Out of the male rivalry of *Milton* emerges a sequence of acts of male bonding leading to images of brotherhood and a triumphant assertion of male strength. Intermingled with these, and often integral to male anger and dissension, are evocations of female figures and female influence. *Milton* contains strikingly polarized images of women: in this poem, we find some of the most benign and positive evocations of women that Blake ever produced, together with portraits of feminine destructiveness akin to those we find elsewhere in his work, and here given a special character.[2] What finally makes possible the resolution of the male conflicts within the poem is the establishment of the good, nurturing female over the malevolent women who pose constant threats to man's existence. Webster states that the common problem of father and son in *Milton* is "how to neutralise woman's baleful influence."[3] Blake, she observes, solves the problem of controlling the destructive mother by asserting male strength and, at the same time, by totally denying woman, either through incorporation or isolation.[4] Webster considers that this process continues into *Jerusalem*.

The Emanation of Milton is a strikingly polarized composite image, which contains all of the extremes of the good and the bad manifestations of women that we find throughout Blake's work. In her negative aspect, she is a sixfold personage based upon Milton's three wives and three daughters. In this multiple, divided form, she is associated with intimate male torment; as one unified woman, Ololon, she makes possible creativity and male liberation. The usual interpretation of the Emanation is that the negative qualities of the women have been produced by Milton's mistreatment of them.[5] It seems, however, that the source of Milton's suffering is not so much his own oppression of his wives and daughters as puritanical patriarch; it is rather that his individual personhood is threatened by the very existence of females as separate beings beyond his control. In plate 17, as Milton first descends towards earth at the completion of the Bard's Song, he glimpses himself and the six female members of his family:

> they and
> Himself was Human, tho' now wandering thro Death's Vale
> In conflict with those Female forms, which in blood & jealousy
> Surrounded him, dividing & uniting without end or number. (E110; *M*17, 5–8)

Within his divided self, he experiences anguish inflicted by jealous and violent female forces. As he journeys in the desert in imitation of Moses, he writes down the horrors of Ulro, dictating them to the six women. Their names are given first as the daughters of Zelophehad, including Tirzah, with the addition of Rahab, and then as the six mountains of the deserts of Midian:

> He saw the Cruelties of Ulro, and he wrote them down
> In iron tablets: and his Wives & Daughters names were these
> Rahab & Tirzah, & Milcah & Malah & Noah & Hoglah.
> They sat rangd round him as the rocks of Horeb round the land
> Of Canaan: and they wrote in thunder smoke and fire
> His dictate; and his body was the Rock Sinai; that body,
> Which was on earth born to corruption. (E110; *M*17, 9–15)

Zelophehad was an Old Testament figure who, in the book of Numbers, having no sons, had successfully appealed to Moses for permission to allow his daughters to inherit his property. These women, who have what can be seen as unnatural power since they have been allowed male privileges, are used by Blake to express the essence of the Female Will. The horror of the split-off female Emanation of Milton is further conveyed by the mountain names, arid immovable masses in the desert wastes, which surround the stony body of Milton himself. On account of their attribute of writing "in thunder smoke and fire," they seem to possess an independent aggressive power.

The hideous sixfold female is found perpetrating various destructive acts throughout the poem. She weaves the Polypus, an amorphous mass that is the basic stultifying element of existence:

> A self-devouring monstrous Human Death Twenty-seven fold
> Within it sit Five Females & the nameless Shadowy Mother
> Spinning it from their bowels with songs of amorous delight
> (E134; *M*34, 26–28)

Like the Fates spinning threads that control men's existence, the Emanation here enacts one of the fundamental female functions according to tormented male fantasy. In this deadly web, the evil mother denies the desire of the male, whether infant or adult, and constricts his basic life forces. The aggression at the heart of this destructive image is vividly reflected in the portrait of the grim sisters weaving the Woof of Death that concludes Book the First:

> But Enitharmon and her Daughters took the pleasant charge.
> To give them to their lovely heavens till the Great Judgment Day
> Such is their lovely charge. But Rahab & Tirzah pervert
> Their mild influences, therefore the Seven Eyes of God walk round
> The Three Heavens of Ulro, where Tirzah & her Sisters
> Weave the black Woof of Death upon Entuthon Benython
> In the Vale of Surrey where Horeb terminates in Rephaim
> The stamping feet of Zelophehads Daughters are coverd with Human gore
> Upon the treddles of the Loom, they sing to the winged shuttle
> (E128; *M*29, 51–59)

The psychological ingredients of the sequence are revealed in the juxtaposition of Enitharmon and her daughters, and the Seven Eyes of God, with the bloody horror of Milton's sixfold Emanation. The benign women performing soothing duties are overwhelmed by the violent energy of the daughters of Zelophehad, while the masculine presence in the splintered form of the father, the Seven Eyes of God,[6] is likewise unable to undermine their power. The son's fury against the unnurturing mother, converted to this aggressive portrait of her, is stronger than his struggling faith in both the benevolent mother figure, Enitharmon, and his own masculine being, realized through the father.

A further example of the evil mother's destructiveness lies in the depiction of Tirzah, as Natural Religion, controlling and destroying all of the living fibers of man, while Albion, embalmed within her bosom, is condemned to unending sleep. The final horror is her sadistic manipulation of the essence of male being: "She ties the knot of milky seed into two lovely Heavens, / Two yet but one: each in the other sweet reflected!" (E113; *M*19, 60–20, 1). Her grim authority here is supported by Urizen, the oppressive father; we note, however, that the fundamental cruel impulse emanates from the mother.

The Shadowy Female, who in Blake's scheme is the material world, represents another method by which a feminine force erodes male power. She acts not through cruelty but by means of an enervating misery. Milton's descent to earth is greeted with lamentation by the Shadowy Female, ostensibly because he promises to overthrow her influence. She sets out to create his Selfhood, so that the power he has in the world of the living will be an evil one:

> I will lament over Milton in the lamentations of the afflicted
> My Garments shall be woven of sighs & heart broken lamentations
> The misery of unhappy Families shall be drawn out into its border
> Wrought with the needle with dire sufferings poverty pain & woe
> Along the rocky island & thence throughout the whole Earth
> There shall be the sick Father & his starving Family! (E111; *M*18, 5–10)

Her mode of aggression is the female one of wailing, yet male suffering and misery are projected as elements that loosen the bonds of society. The inner nature of this social affliction is, however, revealed as the deadly religious law of Rahab and Tirzah. The Shadowy Female states her intention of putting on a human form to oppose Milton, meaning that she will be clothed in the cruelty of holiness and the anguished guilt it imposes upon men. In these sequences, we encounter some of the fundamental layers of aggression in Blake's images of stony patriarchal law and the texture of social anguish. Within this scheme, the Shadowy Female is the containing element, able to manipulate the parameters of Milton's existence, although finally in vain.

The levels of women's dominance over each aspect of man's existence is shown plainly in the experience of Orc, a figure of the rebellious son. He is tormented by the sensual delights of Oothoon and Leutha who have an internal connection with Jerusalem and Babylon:

> So spoke Orc when Oothoon & Leutha hoverd over his Couch
> Of fire in interchange of Beauty & Perfection in the darkness
> Opening interiorly into Jerusalem & Babylon shining glorious
> In the Shadowy Females bosom. Jealous her darkness grew:
> Howlings filld all the desolate places in accusations of Sin
> In Female beauty shining in the unformd void & Orc in vain
> Stretch'd out his hands of fire, & wooed: they triumph in his pain.
> (E112; *M*18, 41–45)

The true nature of female seductiveness is analyzed. Orc is the victim of the two opposing aspects of woman: the spiritual, or religious, ideal of Jerusalem and Babylon, and the rooted material element of life, the Shadowy Female herself. Man's desire is thwarted by moral precept and by the condition of nature. He is helpless in every part of his being.

Woman's seductiveness is a further category of destructive female power in *Milton* and is shown to have fundamental connections with man's split existence. Leutha, the bride of Satan, is a figure of the woman who entices men through her erotic attractions. When she speaks before the assembly of Eternals to confess her sin she stands "glowing with varying colours immortal, heart-piercing/ And lovely: & her moth-like elegance shone over the Assembly" (E106; *M*11, 32–33). Her seductive charms harden into a more menacing form as she recounts how she had felt "a Dragon-form forth issue from my limbs." From within her delightful softness, she is revealed as a phallic woman. This same transition from moth to dragon is found in some of the illustrations of women in the manuscript of *Vala*. In *Milton*, Leutha is associated with the relationship of Hayley–Satan and Blake–Palambron, as the woman who bonds the unspoken homosexual desire between two men. She lulls Satan's "masculine perceptions" in order to allow his "feminine," homoerotic love to flow towards Palambron. Leutha is then brought to Palambron's bed where "in dreams" she gives birth to Death, together with Rahab, Tirzah, and her sisters (E107; *M*13, 38–44), in other words, the fearsome sixfold Emanation. The fantasy of a union with the bride of a delusive weak father is radically linked with the guilt of forbidden incest, and thus with the emotional state of destructive anger that produces the split image of the malevolent mother. We note that in this covert coupling of Palambron and Leutha it is Oothoon, the liberated woman of *Visions of the Daughters of Albion*, who keeps watch for them. Her association with a guilty and pain-bearing love makes her own link with freedom and her willingness to provide her consort with additional female loves seem problematic. The fantasy of male erotic indulgence is distorted by guilt in the relationship of Palambron and Leutha; the presence of Oothoon provides a context of unrestricted liberty within which it can at least take place.

Alongside this array of menacing and subversive female figures in *Milton*, we find in the poem the distinct presence of benevolent and nurturing women, the Daughters of Beulah. Blake first addresses them in the invocation in plate 2 as Muses who, in a vividly physical sense, will provide him with the power to recount Milton's epic journey: "descending down the Nerves of my right arm / From out the Portals of my Brain." The Daughters of Beulah are associated with night, repose, and "mild moony lustre." They are on hand to provide peace and nurture for males suffering hardship and tribulation. When Milton, on the verge of Beulah, enters into his shadow and appears to the Immortals to be sleeping on a couch of gold, the Immortals send forth their Emanations:

> Like Females of sweet beauty, to guard round him & to feed
> His lips with food of Eden in his cold and dim repose!
> But to himself he seemed a wanderer lost in dreary night. (E109; *M*15, 14–16)

The women provide solace, yet the episode includes elements that are less than ideal. Milton appears to be in repose, but his most conscious state is one of dark disorientation; he is within his shadow, in turn associated with the Polypus, each of which is linked with death and the erosion of being. Loving female protectiveness is here inseparable from a condition of feeble masculine dependence. The strange juxtaposition recalls Blake's comments about the Felpham period and his life with Hayley, who helped to protect Blake in a "mild and pleasant slumber" while, at the same time, Blake was passing through "a Hell of terrors & horrors . . . in a Divided Existence" (E758). Hayley had provided a state of dependence that was nurturing, yet contained within it the range of fear and anger associated with the parent figures.

The female capacity for protectiveness is given a special application in the work of creative reconstruction undertaken by the Sons of Los. It is part of Los's task to expand inward every unit of time and space in the fallen world to form an eternity within. The sweetly supportive Daughters of Beulah are present within each moment and in the divisions between the moments:

> And every Moment has a Couch of gold for soft repose,
> (A Moment equals a pulsation of the artery)
> And between every two Moments stands a Daughter of Beulah
> To feed the Sleepers on their Couches with maternal care. (E126; *M*28, 46–49)

The implication of this is, as Webster observes, that maternal support must be present always as the substructure of man's existence.[7] We still notice, however, the ambivalence of the image, since the males remain in a passive, unconscious state within the maternal aura. Los–Blake strives continually to create an inner world that is an assertion of the existence of the self in the face of disintegrating external reality. This process of disintegration is manifest in the succession of distinct units of time and space, separate objects surrounded by emptiness. The emptiness signifies a disjunction between son and mother, or the loss of the good object. The breach is symbolically healed by the ideal presence of the mother, but a full, inner male self has yet to be realized. One of the functions of the Daughters of Beulah is to set up a protective defense against the threats of Satan, the weak father: "These lovely Females form sweet night and silence and secret / Obscurities to hide from Satan's Watch-Fiends" (E119; *M*23, 39–40). Their benign darkness is a bulwark against damage that may be done to the son by the feebleness and immobilization of creativity that Hayley represents.

The fullest portrait of the loving and supportive Daughters of Beulah is found in the evocation of Beulah at the beginning of Book the Second, at the point in the poem when Ololon enters it before descending to the place of earthly existence. Beulah is a realm of harmony where "Contrarieties are equally True." Its chief features are its pleasant darkness and "moony shades & hills." The central evocation of the spirit of Beulah conveys an image of the bliss of infant-mother symbiosis:

> But Beulah to its Inhabitants appears within each district
> As the beloved infant in his mothers bosom round incircled
> With arms of love & pity & sweet compassion. But to
> The Sons of Eden the moony habitations of Beulah,
> Are from Great Eternity a mild & pleasant Rest. (E129; *M*30, 10–14)

Beulah is an essential stage in the re-creation of the split and ravaged image of the mother. It is a place where the male reposes in a nurturing female aura, and "Where no dispute can come." However, its satisfactions are limited. The most desirable state is one where the male is active and potent, caught up in the eternal warring of intellect.[8] When this state is achieved at the end of *Milton*, Ololon plays the role of compliant support of a male who has realized the full strength of his masculinity and has overcome the menace of female power.

The ultimate female image in the poem is that of Ololon, the restored Emanation of Milton. She is closely associated with the Daughters of Beulah but goes beyond them in being a truly liberating and enabling force. Her positive quality proceeds from the fact that she is a woman rendered harmless to men. In place of the range of malevolent mothers found in Milton's debased Emanation, we have a submissive and innocent twelve-year-old virgin, who can appeal sensuously to men without threatening them. Los–Blake finally feels the affirmation of masculine strength in a spirit of unity when woman can be seen in this light, but only after undergoing many phases of struggle. Those struggles involve Blake's encounters with a series of masculine imagos: Hayley, the disappointing father who stirred up profound levels of suffering in Blake; Milton, the ideal poet set up to replace Hayley, who must, however, be purified before he can be the strong father; Los, Blake's fulfilled creative self; and Urizen, the harsh father who must be re-formed through the representative agency of Milton.

Blake's association with Hayley stirred up in him profound conflicts surrounding the father-son relationship. Hayley had the capacity to reproduce for him the father's promise of self-confidence, and the bitterness when that promise is not fulfilled. The relationship of Palambron and Satan is, therefore, the ground, or base, of the conflict and resolution of the other male relationships. The emotional context of the struggle and the accession to male strength is clarified by a short poem, "With happiness stretchd across the hills,"[9] which Blake transcribed in a letter written from Felpham to Thomas Butts on November 22, 1802. The letter was the second written on that day, the first being the one in which he tells Butts, after a long silence, that he has suffered through a period of darkness and depression related to his work and to public acceptance of him as an artist.

This short and informal poem, although far less subtle and complex than *Milton*, was written in the context of the same bitter personal episodes, and while Blake was probably beginning to work them through in the epic version. The context of the poem is that Blake was walking from Felpham to Lavant to meet his sister on her arrival by coach from London to stay with the Blakes. There were tensions between Blake's sister and his wife[10], which possibly introduced anxiety into the anticipation of her visit. It is significant that the path to Lavant, which Blake was treading, was in an actual sense the road to London, significant to him because it meant the road away from Hayley's influence and back to artistic independence and self-fulfillment. Upon this meaningful, actual path, Blake encounters the three dead male members of his family, his father and his brothers Robert and John:

> With my Father hovering upon the wind
> And my Brother Robert just behind
> And my Brother John the evil one
> In a black cloud making his mone
> Tho dead they appear upon my path
> Notwithstanding my terrible wrath
> They beg they intreat they drop their tears
> Filld full of hopes filld full of fears . . . (E721)

The figures of the dead are literally obstacles in Blake's path and at first appear sinister, with the numinous presence of the father in the wind and John's baleful black cloud. In his "terrible wrath," however, Blake has immovable power and transforms them into weak suppliants. As Blake exerts the strength of his aggression over his father and brothers, the obstacle in his way is reduced to a sequence of weaker forms. First of all, Blake faces a thistle that he kicks and uproots, whereupon it becomes an old man lying and writhing faintly in his path. Blake strikes with his foot this feeble form of a defeated father, an act that brings about an immediate transformation. Los appears to him in the sun and descends to him.

Blake concludes his defiance with a complaint about the harsh practical conditions of his life. With this total release of rage, and Blake's sense of union with the creative strength of Los, a shock wave runs through the universe. Blake feels confirmed in masculine strength and can now move forward strongly and freely with his father and brothers:

> Los flamd in my path & the Sun was hot
> With the bows of my Mind and the Arrows of Thought
> My bowstring fierce with Ardour breathes
> My arrows glow in their golden sheaves
> My brothers & father march before
> The heavens drop with human gore (E722)

The images of intense heat and of keen arrows, of men marching together and of blood that drops from the sky to mark the triumph of their unison, all point to specific qualities in this heightened moment of fulfillment. Blake experiences a sense of omnipotence and phallic strength within the bond of brotherhood. There is an emphasis upon elemental maleness in the arrows, at source a symbol of sexual potency, which is realized at the social level in the fantasy of men marching together and the accoutrements of archery. It is through his artistic prowess that Blake will display his masculine strength; the power of the arrows of his mind has been confirmed by Los.

We find in this poem, in a relatively simple form, the underlying pattern of feelings relating to masculine relationships and, by extension, images of women in *Milton*. In "With happiness stretchd across the hills," there appears to be anxiety on the part of the son towards an overpowering father and the brothers who, perhaps even more strongly because they are dead, appear to be surrogates of the father. This anxiety is linked to career, practical life, and position in the world because in traditional society the child derives from the father the ego strength which makes it possible to effectively take on the life of action within society. Beneath the anxiety is a deep-seated rage at the personal impotence that the emotional situation produces. What makes possible the transforming fantasy in the poem is the conversion of the image of the powerful father—the godlike voice in the cloud—into two debased images of the father that can easily be destroyed: the thistle and the weak old man. These two ludicrous phallic forms are a fantasy of a weak father deprived of his threatening aspects. The sadistic fury with which the thistle and the vulnerable old man are attacked releases the deeply buried anger, usually completely imperceptible behind the mild Palambron-like exterior and to Palambron himself. The act brings about a heightened sense of liberation, making possible both the union with Los, a projection of the creative strength derived from the ideal father, and the experience of brotherhood, itself strongly marked by sadism.

In *Milton*, where the same emotional patterns are being resolved, the masculine relationships are, however, more complicated. There are two negative and threatening father figures, Hayley–Satan and Urizen, and one positive and ideal father figure, Milton. Los is the creative power of Blake himself, realized when the threatening father has been rendered harmless and the ideal father assimilated.

Throughout much of the poem, a necessary conflict is waged between Urizen and Milton, the two aspects of the father. In their encounter in the streams of Arnon, Urizen pours "icy fluid" upon Milton's brain while Milton takes red clay and works at molding and remaking Urizen's ravaged and depleted form:

> But Milton took the red clay of Succoth, moulding it with care
> Between his palms: and filling up the furrows of many years
> Beginning at the feet of Urizen, and on the bones
> Creating new flesh on the Demon cold, and building him,
> As with new clay a Human form in the valley of Beth Peor. (E112; *M*19, 10–14)

This is a fundamental act of reparation, reflecting the experience of the child who wishes to restore to life and love the parent who has in fantasy been destroyed by aggressive hatred.[11] Milton replicates the most elemental creative act in working clay with the hands in order to restore flesh to the bare bones. Withered by the child's anger, Urizen is a cold skeleton deprived of vitality. Since making reparation is the wellspring of creativity, this sequence is essential to the affirmation of creative power in the union with Milton and Los elsewhere in the poem. It is a task associated with Milton because he is the strong ideal father. As so often in Blake, however, we notice how powerful the negative forces are, and how tough the resistance to reconciliation. At the end of the poem, in plate 40, when Ololon has descended and is united with Milton, she says that she sees him still striving with Urizen. Moments of resolution are vulnerable and may always be eroded by the lingering conflicts.

The poet's attainment of artistic power in *Milton* is far more stable and far-reaching than it is in "With happiness stretchd across the hills." A major reason for this difference is that there is an element of reparation and love for the father figure in *Milton*, whereas in the short poem we have only destructive aggression. The descent of Los and the assimilation of his creative power has the same function in each work but is given extended meaning in *Milton*, largely through the presence of Milton himself in the poem. In the epic, it is not only Los, the son's creative power, but Milton, the strong poetic father, who descends to Blake with cataclysmic force.

As a preliminary to the re-enactment of the descent of Los in the poem sent to Butts, Milton descends to Blake, first of all through the device of entering his foot. The episode follows the commencement of Milton's revitalization of Urizen, and a mood of despair on the part of Los that the work of the imagination will not be achieved. When Milton enters Blake's foot, the spirit of dark dejection is lifted:

> And all this Vegetable World appeard on my left Foot,
> As a bright sandal formd immortal of precious stones & gold:
> I stooped down & bound it on to walk forward thro' Eternity.
>
> (E115; *M*21, 12–14)

With a surge of confidence and release, Blake is able to walk forward to accomplish his creative ends. Elsewhere, before the redemptive act, the left foot is associated with earthbound darkness: now, after the act of penetration, it is encased in the bright sandal of a vision. There are pronounced phallic elements in this episode that suggest its significance. The foot itself, the act of penetration, and the visionary sandal upon the now strong, penetrated foot, have phallic associations. Plate 32 (see figure 2), the large illustration that concludes Book the First, depicts the moment of Milton's descent and has a frankly erotic feeling. It shows Blake standing flung backwards in ecstacy, his penis erect, as the brilliant flaming star of Milton descends into his foot. A black cloud trails behind the figure, extending from his left heel and billowing above his head from the top of three steps. A mirror image of this illustration appears as plate 37, this time, according to the name engraved at the top of the plate, showing the poet's brother Robert.[12]

The moment of artistic empowerment is fundamentally a sexual empowerment. Ernst Kris notes that obstacles to creativity or inspiration in

Figure 2. *Milton*, 32. Department of Prints and Drawings. Courtesy, the Trustees of the British Museum.

males can be associated with a homosexual fantasy related to the father.[13] Here, faith in creativity is restored by a fantasy of a sexual, and therefore homosexual, union with an ideal father. Until that moment, the son's creative strength is overwhelmed by oedipal fear and anger. Webster's interpretation of the scene is that it represents homosexual penetration by the poetic father, which makes possible the gift of vision.[14]

The sandal encrusted with gold and jewels recalls the jewels associated with the fruit of the Tree of Mystery in Night the Eighth of *The Four Zoas*[15] which stand for the jealous son's attainment of knowledge of the parents' sexuality. The fruits of the Tree of Knowledge have been converted from the warm, living state to cold, inanimate jewels, a possession clutched jealously as a reflection of the real experience.

Following upon Milton's descent to Blake, Los descends to him in a fashion that parallels the act in "With happiness stretchd across the hills." He stands behind him as a sun; when Blake turns around in terror, Los binds on his, Blake's, sandals in Udan-Adan, the place of formlessness, thus giving him the means to make his way out of a state of annihilation to proceed into positive activity. Blake experiences this new sense of creative power as a rapturous moment of union with the spirit of imagination:

> And I became One Man with him arising in my strength:
> Twas too late now to recede. Los had enterd into my soul:
> His terrors now posses'd me whole! I arose in fury & strength.
> (E117; *M*22, 12–14)

The act is reduplicated, carried out first by Milton and then by Los, and indeed repeated in various ways elsewhere in the poem, to emphasize the importance of this wondrous event and to convince Blake and his readers that it has truly taken place. The repetition also reveals the psychological mechanism whereby the attainment of imaginative power becomes possible: the forces that work against the possibility of reparation are overwhelming; therefore, the act of reparation is at first incomplete. Finally, when the mother imago has been rendered harmless, the destroyed father and the ideal poetic father are fused, leading to the son's incorporation of ego-strength.

The climactic enactment of the descent of Milton occurs in Book the Second, in association with the whole redemptive experience that includes the descent of Ololon, his Emanation. Since it is the event of a moment that has reverberations in eternity, the descent to Felpham is described three times. Milton is an enormous, overpowering form reaching from the sky. He contains within himself all forms of darkness and chaos, the Synagogues of Satan and the pagan gods of whom Milton had written, but as he compresses these within himself, he is a form of majesty and beauty. Satan, Milton's Spectre and representative of false art, feels his being crumble as he sees this form of Milton descend:

> And Milton collecting all his fibres into impregnable strength
> Descended down a Paved work of all kinds of precious stones
> Out from the eastern sky; descending down into my Cottage
> Garden: clothed in black, severe & silent he descended. (E138; *M*38, 5–8)

Since Milton is clothed and retains something of his puritan repression, this moment of fusion is not complete. The interplay between positive and negative forces, between confidence that the ideal enabling father will prevail and despair that the false destructive father will, after all, hold sway, continues. The familiar Blakean pattern is displayed: moments of participation in the ideal are rapturous but tenuous, while negative forces are ever threatening to encroach upon the ideal, even when the plot seems to have told us, perhaps repeatedly, that evil has been overthrown. Thus, Milton at this point announces to Satan that he will come to earth to bring self-annihilation, whereupon Satan, apparently already removed as a threat to Blake's creative freedom, replies with an even stronger statement of his divine omnipotence, commanding all living things to worship him. This absolute statement of supremacy is suddenly interrupted and therefore overwhelmed by an intensified version of the descent of Milton:

> Suddenly around Milton on my Path, the Starry Seven
> Burnd terrible! my Path became a solid fire, as bright
> As the clear Sun & Milton silent came down on my Path. (E140; *M*39, 3–5)

The images of energy concentrated in light and burning here relate it closely to the earlier moment of Los's descent; at this instant the strength of the ideal father that imparts creative confidence is integrated with the spirit of imagination. In unity, their existence is less vulnerable, and Blake incorporates both.

It is usual to place Ololon at the center of the active redemptive forces in *Milton*, as a mild female figure whose descent to earth brings healing peace and harmony.[16] A study of the position of women in Blake's art must, therefore, look carefully at this interpretation. Ololon's descent into Blake's garden at Felpham in Book the Second is interwoven with the descent of Milton, and their union is the culmination of the poem. I shall suggest, however, that her function is subordinate and contained within the male brotherhood ideal, and that in the ideal state she assumes the passive female role.

Images of male fusion and the strength that this imparts are a dominant motif of *Milton*, in both the text and the illustrations: they are a statement of the poem's fundamental emotional impetus.[17] In addition to Blake's various moments of rapturous union with Los and Milton, described in detail in the text of the poem, the illustrations, which are an integral part of the poem, make manifest the theme of the celebration of masculine strength. A striking quality of *Milton* is that it has a number of full-plate illustrations, the majority of them of male figures, in addition to the smaller designs interwoven with the words of the poem.

Plate 1 announces the theme of the work by showing, from behind, the virile naked form of Milton about to break through a barrier of billowing vapor with his outstretched right hand. Plate 10 shows Rintrah and Palambron, the angry and the mild aspects of Blake, naked figures looking at Satan as the Selfhood, a heroic male surrounded by flames. Plate 16 is the figure of Milton inspired, casting off his clothes as he advances, radiant with light from his halo and from the rays of a setting sun behind him. The complementary plates, 32, of William as Milton's star enters his left foot, and 37, of Robert in the mirror image position, have already been mentioned, and consolidate the theme of eroticized masculine strength in brotherhood.

Plates 45 and 47 crystallize the ideal of male bonding in homosexual terms.[18] Plate 47 (see figure 3), illustrating the descent of Los to Blake in a flaming sun, described verbally in plate 22, is the more explicit. It shows a kneeling Blake leaning backwards to unite with Los, the heroic form of male beauty, in fellatio. In later versions of the poem, Blake moved this plate from its original place alongside the narrative description of the event to the last full-page illustration near the end of "Book the Second," in order to stress its importance and to highlight the function of Los–Blake, the creator, which the entire action of the poem has made possible.[19] Plate 45 (see figure 4) shows Milton and Urizen after their struggle on the Arnon. The feeble Urizen kneels before the radiant form of Milton, the position of his head and the association with plate 47 again suggesting an act of oral-genital union.[20] Here, it is the ideal father of the imagination who possesses the strength, and the figure of paternal authority has been reduced to a weak old man, like the debased father in "With happiness stretchd across the hills." Far from striking the old man sadistically, however, in *Milton* the son who has incorporated the power of the ideal father—Milton who is now Blake—imparts his own vigor to him in forgiveness and reparation, betokening the liberation from aggression that makes for true creativity. In plate 47, the illustration that states the emotional center of the poem, Blake incorporates the seed of Los to become the artist who can leave the false father and poet Hayley to advance in his world.

We have observed the strength of the malevolent images of femininity in *Milton*. These are found not only in the tormenting form of the fragmented Emanation but also at the heart of the Selfhood, overtly a masculine principle, which Milton must destroy in order to redeem his Emanation. The meaning of the Selfhood is described in detail near the end of the poem when Milton and Blake are standing within Satan's universe at the moment before Milton finally obliterates it. It is a place of horror, ruin, and darkness dominated by law and fear. What Milton will bring in its place is individual freedom, "fearless majesty annihilating self" (E139; 38, 41). The Selfhood is not "selfishness" but is a false chaotic self, dominated by Urizenic rationalism and located outside of the bounds of the individual, unlike the true self that Milton will restore, which is located within.[21] As often in Blake, what is projected outside of the person brings overwhelming fear as it divides and multiplies beyond his control. Within Milton's satanic Selfhood, Blake discovers a destructive female principle, "Mystery Babylon," with her poisoned cup and scarlet veil, "woven in pestilence and war." The loss of the strong ideal father is intimately associated with the power of the malevolent mother.

The threatening female presence deep within the Selfhood is found again and again. Descending through chaos in Milton's track, Ololon sees in Ulro a state of frozen existence where the Fountains of Death and Hell undermine the principle of brotherhood, and the female members of the splintered Emanation weave the Woof of Death (E135; *M*35, 1–9). When in plate 40 she is united with Milton, she realizes what he has suffered—the

Figure 3. *Milton*, 47. Department of Prints and Drawings. Courtesy, the Trustees of the British Museum.

Figure 4. *Milton*, 45. Department of Prints and Drawings. Courtesy, the Trustees of the British Museum.

struggle with Urizen, the conflict of the Zoas, and Natural Religion—and in pity and shame assumes responsibility for all of them on behalf of women (E141; *M*40, 4–16). At this moment, the last vestige of female power flares up in the form of a vast image, spread across the sky, of Rahab as Moral Virtue, to be given its ultimate death blow by the injunction of Milton "in terrible majesty" to Ololon: "Obey thou the Words of the Inspired Man" (*M*40, 29). The repressive and forbidding influence of women within law and the injunction against incest erodes masculine power at the source. Empowered now by the male strength of Los and Milton, Blake as the Inspired Man has broken free from her and relegated woman to a passive position in subservience to him.

In plate 33, the Songs of Beulah, the Divine Voice laments the cruel jealousy of women that has cut off male loves and predicts the positive effects that Milton will have when he descends to "Redeem the Female Shade from Death Eternal:"

> When the Sixfold Female percieves that Milton annihilates
> Himself: that seeing all his loves by her cut off: he leaves
> Her also: intirely abstracting himself from Female loves
> She shall relent in fear of death: She shall begin to give
> Her maidens to her husband: delighting in his delight
> And then & then alone begins the happy Female joy
> As it is done in Beulah . . . (E133; *M*33, 14–20)

As the withholding of female love is the source of the deepest evil, so what is required of the redeemed female is a selfless generosity to the male, not only in giving herself to him but also in indulging all of his sensual needs so that she will bring him other women for his pleasure. As at the end of *Visions of the Daughters of Albion*, the act of liberation turns out to be liberation on behalf of men.[22] At this fundamental level of existence, women are ideally subservient to men. Such a fantasy of male gratification is found elsewhere in Blake, but nowhere does he project a state of equal sexual liberation for women.

Ololon is first mentioned at the instant in the poem when Milton enters Blake's foot, the initial act of penetration that foreshadows the possibility of the total incorporation of male strength. In this momentary relaxation of the forces of repression, the possibility of the assimilation of a good and nurturing female image to complete the state of imaginative power presents itself as a possibility. Ololon is envisaged first of all as a river:

> There is in Eden a sweet River, of mild & liquid pearl,
> Namd Ololon; on whose mild banks dwelt those who Milton drove
> Down into Ulro . . . (E115; *M*21, 15–17)

Ololon in this unresolved state is an undifferentiated body of soothing fluid, related to the infant's blissful symbiosis with the mother in the oceanic phase of life. The "liquid pearl" of her river refers at the same time to the semen of the homoerotic act that has just introduced her spirit into the poem. We have here the basic structure of the recurrent motif of *Milton*: triumphant male union supported by a nurturing and acquiescent female presence. Associated though she is with the jealous forces that oppress Milton, Ololon promises the erosion of that oppression.

The desent of Ololon, from fearsome sixfold oppressor to single mild consort, is made through the track already formed by Milton. In order to enter the visionary world of Los's Golgonooza from Ulro, she must first pass through the Polypus, a deadly formless shape that is the negative counterpart of the oceanic state of the river Ololon in Eden. When the saving Ololon passes through the Polypus, thus releasing man into creativity, she ceases to be "they" and becomes instead one female in the garden of Blake's Felpham cottage. She takes the form of "a Virgin of twelve years," a prepubescent maiden who awaits the fulfillment of male desire.[23] In this incarnation, she is compliant and nonthreatening to men.

The climax of the poem, which causes Blake, like Paul of Tarsus, to fall in sublime terror upon his path, is the conclusive descent of Ololon. She has reunited with Milton, she has revealed herself as a nubile maiden, and her splintered sixfold being has finally fled to nothingness. She now comes to Blake in her full power:

> Then as a Moony Ark Ololon descended to Felphams Vale
> In clouds of blood, in streams of gore, with dreadful thunderings
> Into the Fires of Intellect that rejoic'd in Felphams Vale
> Around the Starry Eight: with one accord the Starry Eight became
> One Man Jesus the Saviour. wonderful! round his limbs
> The Clouds of Ololon folded as a Garment dipped in blood
> (E143; *M*42, 7–12)

In this ultimate vision, the essential elements of earlier revelations are gathered together. The blood that flows from the sky surrounding Ololon recalls the warrior brotherhood of "With happiness stretchd across the hills" who march together with their weapons as "The heavens drop with human gore." The subjection of the female principle consolidates masculine power. The heroic male state of aggressive war is restored as the sphere of activity of the inspired poet: "the Wars of Man which in Great Eternity / Appear around, in the External Spheres of Visionary Life" (E134–35; *M*50–51). The bloody clouds of Ololon are themselves a "Garment of War" that clothes the strong male. The Starry Eight, the Seven Eyes of God with the addition of Milton, are merged and unified with the ultimate benign masculine figure, that of Christ. The son, who picks himself up from the path to go forward into the world in the supreme confidence of his inspiration, has incorporated positive images of both father and mother. The figure of Christ was associated earlier with Ololon in Eden, when the Divine Family united with her and "Jesus the Saviour appeard coming in the Clouds of Ololon!" (E116; 21, 60). This portrayal of Christ recalls also the first of the vision poems that Blake transcribed for Thomas Butts in a letter from Felpham. The first poem appears in a letter dated October 2, 1800, a few weeks after the Blakes had arrived at Felpham, when Blake was full of optimism about the benefits of his filial association with Hayley. Blake describes the experience of sitting on the beach and gazing into the sun. His surroundings are transformed into particles or jewels of light, in each of which is a man. The figures coalesce into one masculine figure bathed in light, who enfolds Blake like a loving father embracing a child (E712–13). The oppressive Urizen–Jehovah has disappeared to give way to Christ, a figure of the son who is integrated with the father and therefore has neutralized the aggression directed towards the father. In the emotional pairing of Ololon and Christ in *Milton*, we have a benign version of the parent figures who have been forgiven and lovingly re-created. The son can realize in freedom his full creative powers.

More than any other of Blake's longer poems, *Milton* mediates between the internal world and the external world. The dark, splintering interior visions are finally resolved in a unity with "the other," as the benign maternal figure fills up the empty spaces between discrete moments of fragmented time and passively enables the son to realize an active male existence.

The place of contact is the garden of Blake's cottage at Felpham. Most specifically, it is the paved garden path onto which both Milton and Ololon descend, and where Blake falls for a moment of ecstasy. Milton descends "down a Paved work of all kinds of precious stones" (E138; *M*38, 6) which is linked with "the paved terraces" of Satan's bosom at the dark moment of private anguish when Satan–Hayley accuses the subservient Palambron–Blake of ingratitude:

> Thus Satan rag'd amidst the Assembly! and his bosom grew
> Opake against the Divine Vision: the paved terraces of
> His bosom inwards shone with fires, but the stones becoming opake!
> (E103; *M*9, 30–32)

The oppressive paved terraces of Satan, charged with the aggression of fire and darkness, become at the point of contact with the external world an open path of bright stones.[24] The path leads out of the enclosed internal state into an exterior world that has become vividly real. It is associated with the path to Lavant, and to London, where, in "With happiness stretchd across the hills," Blake's progress was initially impeded until he attained the strength to walk on with assurance into the world of action.

In *Milton*, this supremely joyful moment is marked by the vivid coming to life of the lark and the thyme, the symbols in the poem of artistic inspiration. When the lark and thyme are mentioned earlier in the poem they belong to a more enclosed and schematic world. Both are found in Golgonooza, near the eastern gate of the city. The thyme, Los's messenger to Eden, is a small root in the darkness of Ulro that covers the Rock of Odours with its purple flowers (E136; *M*35, 54–57). The lark, who is Los's messenger through the twenty-seven churches, has his nest at this crystal gate (*M*35, 58–63). On the rock is a fountain beside which Ololon sits, and it is from here that she makes her saving descent to earth. The crystal gate has the function of a repressive barrier that must be broken before liberation can be attained,[25] while the fountain is the life flow of the good mother, which can dissolve the hard crystal of moral prohibition.

When, with the ultimate descent of Ololon, Blake has assimilatd the nurturing female, he enters the world of nature and sensory integration. At the conclusion of the poem, the lark and the thyme are no longer signifiers within a claustrophobic schema but belong freely within experience, appealing vividly to the global senses:

> Immediately the Lark mounted with a loud trill from Felphams Vale
> And the Wild Thyme from Wimbletons green & impurpled Hills.
> (E143; *M*42, 29–30)

The poem ends with a movement forward to social action, "the Great Harvest & Vintage of the Nations" (E144; *M*43). Blake, accompanied by his wife, that is Los and Enitharmon, will now return to London to bring about reform and renewal.

This experience of joy at entering into a realm beyond the self is first intimated earlier in Book the Second, following the positive evocation of mother-infant union and Ololon's descent to Beulah. There is an animated and sensuous description of birds singing, followed by a passage describing flowers which exudes open and uninhibited female sexuality:

> first the Wild Thyme
> And Meadow-sweet downy & soft waving among the reeds.
> Light springing on the air lead the sweet Dance: they wake
> The Honeysuckle sleeping on the Oak: the flaunting beauty
> Revels along upon the wind; the White-thorn lovely May
> Opens her many lovely eyes: listening the Rose still sleeps
> None dare to wake her. soon she bursts her crimson curtaind bed
> And comes forth in the majesty of beauty. (E131; *M*31, 51–58)

After his earliest works, such descriptions of nature are rare in Blake. He disliked Wordsworth's treatment of nature, insisting that true vision must be *within*, and despised landscape painting. This exuberant embrace of nature, seen in certain phases of *Milton*, which is clearly linked with a realization of the image of the good mother, testifies that the bounded self of the inner imagination has established a link with the outer world of real objects. As the fear and anger associated with the menacing maternal image are weakened by the positive and loving female presence, the son establishes harmony with an expanded world of feeling.

CHAPTER 7

The Triumph of Masculinity in *The Plumed Serpent*

The central theme of both *The Plumed Serpent* and *Milton* is the son's assimilation of strength from an ideal father, and his struggle to establish ascendancy over a powerful female. The context of the motif is a fantasy of the male usurpation of the fundamental female elements of blood and water. For Lawrence and for Blake, these works marked an important stage in establishing masculine identity. There are several striking resemblances between Lawrence's novel and Blake's poem.

In *The Plumed Serpent*, too, a fundamental theme and interest is a bond of brotherhood between strong men under a leader who has the power to transform society. The association of Ramon–Quetzalcoatl and Cipriano–Huitzilopochtli is an absolute that must be accepted by Kate, and which is a higher good than established political and religious modes in Mexico. The ideal is pure maleness, stressing the strength and beauty of men who operate in a world beyond that of women. Kate, the woman who must be convinced and won over, gradually discovers this supremacy of masculinity when she leaves Mexico City to live closer to deep natural forces in Sayula. On this journey, she enters a new world.[1] As she and Villiers are being rowed along a river approaching a lake on the way to Orilla, Kate has her first encounter with the Men of Quetzalcoatl when she sees a group of men bathing "whose wet skins flashed with the beautiful brown-rose colour and glitter of the naked natives . . ." (90). One of them, "smooth and wet and of a lovely colour, with the rich smoothed-muscled physique of the Indians," comes to speak to her as she sits in the boat, telling her that she must make a tribute to Quetzalcoatl if she goes on the lake. Kate knows that she has entered a sphere of experience that surpasses the tired superficiality of the jaded contemporary world: "She sensed a certain delicate, tender mystery in the river, in the naked man of the water, in the boatman, and she could not bear to have it subjected to the tough American flippancy" (93). It is a sphere where male beauty and strength are paramount.

The ideal beauty of the male body, as in *Milton*, is a theme that runs through *The Plumed Serpent*. Ramon, the living Quetzalcoatl, is an aristocrat among men, whose heroic physique is perfect. While distinguished from his followers when he is wearing ceremonial robes, he normally dresses in clothes that are a finer version of the peon costume, to make it clear that the source of his power lies deep within the special nature of Mexico and its ordinary men:

> He was dressed in white, dazzling, in the costume of the *peones*, the white blouse jacket and the white, wide pantaloon trousers. But the white was linen, slightly starched, and brilliant, almost unnatural in its whiteness. From under his blouse, in front, hung the ends of a narrow woolen sash, white, with blue and black bars, and a fringe of scarlet. And on his naked feet were the plaited huaraches, of blue and black strips of leather, with thick, red-dyed soles. His loose trousers were bound round the ankles with blue, red and black woolen braids. (*PS* 167)

Descriptions of the imposing presence of Ramon recur throughout the novel, charcteristically giving such details of his dress and the significance of the colors that he wears, or portraying him naked to the waist with sensuous cream-brown skin.

Although *The Plumed Serpent* apparently begins with a revulsion from blood and violence, the higher reaches of masculinity in the novel are often associated with exquisite violence detached from moral censure. In the relentlessly bloody sequence in "The Attack on Jamiltepec," when Kate assists Ramon in killing his attackers, Ramon is glorified as the consummate wielder of weapons: "And even as he leaped, Ramon shot the knife, that was all bright red as a cardinal bird. It flew red like a bird, and the drops of Ramon's handful of blood flew with it, splashing even Kate, who kept her revolver ready, watching near the stairway" (296). The gratuitous excess of blood here, which flies through the air and splashes Kate, is extrinsic to the narrative. It is stressed as a symbol of the male's confirmation of power, into which the female must be initiated as a true believer. We note furthermore that this is not a feeble woman but one who has killed a man and still bears a gun. The woman's lingering phallic power is subsumed in the male's act of violence. The similarity drawn between the knife and the red bird relies upon the phallic association of the bird, resembling the phallic connotation of the lark in *Milton*.[2] The episode culminates with Ramon plunging his victim's own knife into his throat, an act that raises him to a mystical plane of existence: "His brow was like a boy's, very pure and primitive, and the eyes underneath had a certain primitive gleaming look of virginity" (296). He than notices that his right hand is colored bright red with blood, and the transformation to ideal masculinity is complete: "He was like a pristine being, remote in consciousness, and with far, remote sex" (297). Like Blake marching with the brotherhood bearing weapons of war in "With happiness stretchd across the hills," Ramon experiences a supreme moment of elation in phallic strength. The presence of blood in both episodes is important not so much for narrative vividness as to signify aggressive domination of the female.

Cipriano, too, is a figure of ideal masculine beauty, with a self-sufficiency remote from women. He is small and birdlike, characteristically associated with red, the color of blood and aggression:

> But the wind suddenly got under Cipriano's blanket, and lifted it straight up in the air, then dropped it in a scarlet flare over his head. Kate watched his deep, strong Indian chest lift as his arms quickly fought to free his head. How dark he was, and how primitively physical, beautiful and deep-breasted, with soft, full flesh! But all, as it were, for himself. Nothing that came forth from him to meet with one outside. All oblivious of the outside, all for himself. (*PS* 201)

This powerful male must be seen and admired by Kate, the strong woman who will ultimately submit her strength to his. Lawrence dwells frequently upon Cipriano's heroic beauty, emphasizing a virility that is reflected also in the images and illustrations of Blake's *Milton*. Cipriano has "that strange archaic fulness of physique, with the full chest and the full, yet beautiful buttocks of men on old Green coins" (423). Cipriano, "the red Huitzilopochtli, of the knife" (366) is a more overtly phallic figure than Ramon, being directly linked with violence and weapons. He is Ramon's general, a Zapotec who is in his element chasing rebels and who leads his men with discipline and keen organization. His dances are "the shield and spear dance, the knife dance, the dance of ambush and the surprise dance" (364). In these dances, he surpasses everyone in his skill: "He could swerve along the ground with bent, naked back, as invisible as a lynx, circling round his opponent, his feet beating and his suave body subtly lilting to the drum. Then in a flash he was in the air, his spear pointing down at the collar-bone of his enemy and gliding over his shoulder, as the opponent swerved under, and the war-yell resounded" (365).

The central confirmation of male violence in *The Plumed Serpent* is the ceremonial killing of Ramon's attackers by Cipriano in front of the church in the "Huitzilopochtli's Night" chapter. The executions are carried out with absolute ruthlessness. At Cipriano–Huitzilopochtli's command, guards break the necks of the two main transgressors, and lay their twitching bodies on the ground (378). Cipriano himself stabs the other prisoners "to the heart, with three swift, heavy stabs" (380). The bodies are then taken into the church and men follow them to attend ceremonies from which the women are excluded. Before the altar of Huitzilopochtli, Cipriano dips his hand into a bowl of blood and raises his wet red fist. All the men present then do the same. The act recalls the earlier episode in which Ramon was initiated into full masculinity after he had fought off his attackers, and signifies that the bond of brotherhood is sealed in bloody aggression.

Kate is deeply shocked by the executions, and her wavering resolution to stay on the continent where the male is supreme is shaken. At the same time, she is spellbound by this savagery, and admires the beauty of alien masculine toughness: "And deep in her soul came a revulsion against this manifestation of pure will. It was fascinating also. There was something dark and lustrous and fascinating to her in Cipriano, and in Ramon. The black, relentless power, even passion of the will in men! The strange, sombre, lustrous beauty of it! She knew herself under the spell" (387). The woman is excluded from the supreme male experience which she judges superficially according to conventional morality. Yet Kate, the powerful woman who must be convinced of men's superior strength, cannot help responding to the vibrations from the darkly masculine mode of being that underlies the social and weakly feminine context of her judgment.

Another strong parallel between *Milton* and *The Plumed Serpent* is their ambivalent gender symbolism associated with water. Lawrence is very specific about the masculine quality of certain bodies of water, a quality that is defined by elemental Mexican manhood. When, in "To Stay or Not to Stay," Kate is deliberating about whether her future lies in Mexico, the issue essentially rests with whether she can accept Mexican men, the peons who truly characterize the country. For Kate, an emblem of this spirit of the land is the nakedly phallic pulque plant, from whose juice the evil-smelling native drink is made: "But out of the Mexican soil a bunch of black-tarnished swords bursts up, and a great unfolded bud of the once-flowering monster begins to thrust at the sky. They cut the great phallic bud and crush out the sperm-like juice for the pulque. *Agua miel! Pulque!"* *(75)* This sense of the elementally male character of Mexico stays with Kate as she makes her journey to Sayula, where she will gradually learn that she has a deep need to serve the strength of the male.

We have noted that on the first stage of the journey from Ixtlahuacan to Orilla, by river, Kate becomes aware that she is entering the male sphere of Quetzalcoatl. Even before she and Villiers engage a boatman and set out from Ixtlahuacan, a strange new quality becomes apparent as she notices that the water that bubbles up in the basins in the plaza is "milky-looking," "milky-dim" (88). This element becomes more specific when the crippled boatman, who impresses Kate with his beauty and strength, rows them upon the "flimsy, soft sperm-like water" (89). The mystical sense intensifies as they pass out into "the wide white light of the lake." Here, too, the mysterious quality of the water is masculine: "He pulled rhythmically through the frail-rippling, sperm-like water, with a sense of peace" (93).

What is truly striking about the image of spermlike water is that a large body of water such as a lake is more fundamentally a feminine image, linked with the "oceanic phase" of early infant-mother symbiosis. Certainly, the reference to "the wide white light of the lake" contains that fundamental experience. The feminine entity is transformed into a masculine one because the son must assert independence from the encompassing mother, and specifically he must assert his maleness to mark himself off as a distinct being. He does this partly through affirming the maleness, or the paternal element, within the enveloping state of narcissism. This spermlike water recalls the sequence in Blake's *Milton* where the saving female, Ololon, is characterized as a sweet river that derives a spermlike quality of pearl from the immediate juxtaposition of phallic union between son and ideal father. In *The Plumed Serpent*, the references become more specifically phallic when the water is thought of as the "lymphatic milk of fishes" (97) or "fish-milk water" (105). Again, this fundamentally feminine element is converted into an image of male strength.

A third significant resemblance between these two works by Blake and Lawrence is the manner in which a powerful female figure is rendered harmless. In *Milton*, the final transformation of the menacing sixfold Ololon is to a twelve-year-old virgin who has lost her power over the male since she is neither maternal nor sexual. Similarly, in *The Plumed Serpent*, the threateningly independent modern woman, Kate Leslie, is at certain moments converted into a child or a virgin who has accepted the superior power of men. During the early phase of her stay at Sayula, when she is learning to recognize the special qualities of the Mexican landscape and Mexican manhood, Kate is persuaded to dance at night in the plaza with an unnamed man, joining in the group of strangely abstract and impersonal dancers. Her partner's quintessential maleness dissolves the layers of social accretion that make her a self-sufficient contemporary woman: "His hand, warm and dark and savagely suave, loosely, almost with indifference, and yet with the soft barbaric nearness held her fingers, and he led her to the circle. She dropped her head, and longed to be able to veil her face. In her white dress and green straw hat, she felt a virgin again, a young virgin. This was the quality these men had been able to give back to her" (*PS* 130). The parallel with Blake is striking: a means of affirming masculinity is to see the female as a virgin who belongs passively within a male scheme of things.

Kate undergoes a similar and more far-reaching change at the ceremony when she becomes Malintzi, the goddess and bride of the living Huitzilopochtli. Significantly, she makes her decision to accept Cipriano's offer to become Malintzi after the bloody execution of Ramon's attackers. She has recoiled in horror from relentless male brutality, yet through her horror passes into a more fundamental state in which she accepts unyielding maleness. Kate sits in the church with Cipriano beneath the idol of Huitzilopochtli: "feeling his dark hand softly holding her own, with the soft, deep Indian heat, she felt her own childhood coming back on her. The years seemed to be reeling away in great circles, falling away from her" (393). Whereas Ololon became a twelve-year-old virgin, Kate becomes fourteen: "She was perhaps fourteen years old, and he was fifteen. And he was the young Huitzilopochtli, and she was the bride Malintzi, the bride-girl"

(393–94). Cipriano too is reduced in age, but is no less strong and virile for this transformation.

A further close parallel between *Milton* and *The Plumed Serpent* is the symbolic function of the star in both works. In Blake's poem, Milton is represented as a star in order to symbolize his cometlike descent from the heavens and also the strengthening power which union with him brings. In plates 32 and 37, respectively, he descends into the foot of first William and then Robert Blake, in images that denote virile self-realization. The star suggests a fulfilled, single, and triumphant male sense of self, achieved through fusion with an ideal. In *The Plumed Serpent*, the star image again denotes a triumphant fusion.

The Morning Star is the symbol of Quetzalcoatl and therefore draws together the men of Mexico in their essential male nature. As the leader and unifying spirit of men, Ramon however has a special relationship to the star. As he says in the hymn that he intones in "The Opening of the Church":

> I am the Son of the Morning Star, and child of the deeps.
> No man knows my Father, and I know Him not.
> My Father is deep within the deeps, whence He sent me forth. (*PS* 339)

Ramon is in touch with the source of male strength, and other men experience the fullness of virility through association with him. His function in the novel resembles that of Milton in Blake's poem, in that he contains the strength of the ideal father and imparts that strength to others. To be male is to be part of a living brotherhood and, within that brotherhood, to have a distinct identity.

In this hymn, Ramon goes on to define gender roles: "For man is the Morning Star. / And woman is the Star of Evening." Here and elsewhere in the novel, this does not, of course, mean equality of status. We have only to consider the postures of the men and women in the church as they listen to Ramon to see this clearly: "So that around the low dark shrubs of the crouching women stood a forest of erect, upthrusting men, powerful and tense with inexplicable passion. It was a forest of dark wrists and hands up-pressing . . ." (339). The ideal is the passivity and subjection of women. Ramon explained the meaning of the star earlier when he performed the marriage ceremony of Kate and Cipriano. "Remember," he says, "the marriage is the meeting-ground, and the meeting-ground is the star" (331). The star may be a meeting ground between two people, or between more than two people in a variety of social relationships, but always means fusion. Men are incomplete without women as women are incomplete without men; yet since women are subservient to men, the principal mode of fusion is between men or with men.

The symbolism of the star in *The Plumed Serpent* differs from Lawrence's "stellar equilibrium" in *Women in Love*, where the ideal is precisely for the man and the woman *not* to be fused: rather they should remain in balanced, interconnected, but separate existence.[3] In his Mexican novel, Lawrence has moved to a new configuration of relationships, one where the male has established a fantasy of a personal strength, delineated in a distinct shining star, as a result of union with an ideal masculinity. Like Blake, he deals with the threat of the female by reducing her to a state where she exists united with him in a subservient position.

While Kate is mulling over what the bloody executions have revealed to her about men, and is moving towards the decision to become the mystical bride of Huitzilopochtli, she gains insight into some truths about identity and fusion. Herself a separate, independent modern woman, she is a "little star," limited and insignificant. Her life will gain profound meaning if she unites herself with Cipriano–Huitzilopochtli: "Don Ramon's Morning Star, was something that sprung between him and her and hung shining, the strange third thing that was both of them and neither of them, between his night and her day" (389). The "strange third thing" between Kate and Cipriano is the presence of Ramon, a figure of the son who has integrated the ideal father. The Morning Star, Kate realizes, allows the self to penetrate the other in a new fusion founded upon masculine ego strength: "Was it true, that the gate was the Morning Star, the only entrance to the Innermost? And the Morning Star rises between the two, and between the many, but never from one alone" (390). That word "Innermost" suggests a taboo surrounding powerful desire that is broken down here because the father's strength and dominance have been incorporated. The three-part relationship is oedipal in character. The ideal father permits union with the mother to Cipriano, a fragmentary and phallic aspect of the son. The experience is seen from Kate's, the woman's, point of view rather than from Cipriano's, which would have appeared more logical; throughout the novel, the main impetus of the action is to convince her of the truth of male experience.

We must ask what Kate's function in the novel is, and why she is treated by Lawrence as she is. It is certainly noteworthy that in this novel about male power, the central character and the responsive center of the narrative events should be a woman. At the simplest biographical level, Kate is close to Frieda, and to Lawrence himself, who was approaching his fortieth birthday—Kate's age—when he was writing the final draft of the novel. Kate reflects in her experiences some of the travels and the reactions of Lawrence and Frieda, notably her disgust at the bullfight in chapter 1.[4] However, this level of Kate's significance is relatively superficial. Her function in the novel is to be changed from the strong-willed, independent, contemporary woman, in this respect reflecting Frieda as well as others, into a self-effacing, passive, and supportive wife. Although Kate gives up a great deal of her own will, she wavers in her resolve to commit herself entirely to Cipriano and Mexico, and the transformation is never quite complete. Readers usually find the end of the novel ambivalent. The effect is similar to that which we find in Blake's *Milton*, although less extreme. The image of the threatening strong woman is very persistent and tends to overwhelm the compliant and nurturing female image. Therefore, the moments of female subjection to the male are always in danger of being eroded.

Kate can be placed as the type of Lawrencean woman who is dissatisfied with debased contemporary society, a society represented for Lawrence by his Bloomsbury-related associates in London during the war years. He frequently excoriates what he sees as the values of that society, for instance, in his portrait of Rico and his friends in *St. Mawr*, and increasingly does so through a female protagonist. Having been rejected as a friend and prophet by Bertrand Russell, Middleton Murry, and others,[5] Lawrence finds it important to justify himself to a woman and then, upon that justification, to found his more far-reaching philosophy of masculine superiority.

Kate comes to Mexico feeling that her former life has ended: "Over in England, in Ireland, in Europe, she had heard the *consummatum est* of her own spirit. It was finished, in a kind of death agony" (50). Through her contact with the spermlike waters of Sayula, where the life principle is male, she gradually becomes aware of a new way of life, where she feels in contact with fundamental forces as yet unimagined: "She felt she could cry aloud, for the unknown gods to put the magic back into her life, and to save her from the dry-rot of the world's sterility" (103).

Kate can be associated with several other women in Lawrence's fiction during this phase of his life: Lou of *St. Mawr*, the woman in "The Woman Who Rode Away," and Ethel Cane of "None of That."[6] What these women have in common is a disillusionment with the values of modern Western society, which causes them to retreat to masculine domination in a primitive culture. The significance of Lawrence's treatment of Kate Leslie emerges more sharply if we consider her in relation to these other women. In each case, he subjects the woman to absolute male power. In the extreme instance of Lou, the woman becomes a virgin,[7] eternally nonmenacing and awaiting the perfect masculine domination adumbrated in Lewis and in the virile horse. Of all these women, it is Lou over whom Lawrence achieves the most perfect control, although he does not actualize her condition, since he cannot conceive of a male with the capacity for maintaining this control. The two women in "The Woman Who Rode Away" and "None of That" are controlled through extreme male aggression, in the first case through sacrificial death in an icy cave,[8] and in the second, through death following brutal gang rape. These two stories are fantasies of the destruction of the threatening woman, which do not allow a living solution. We understand why Lawrence removes himself from the horror of the events of "None of That" by using the device of two levels of narration.

"The Princess" is an incomplete version of the motif. Dollie Urquhart is raped by Romero in a dark place among the remote mountains, again a base, natural setting where man is supreme: "The strange squalor of the primitive forest pervaded the place, the squalor of animals and their droppings, the squalor of the wild."[9] In a sense, however, she triumphs over him since she survives him, marries, and remains in control of her fey life.

The Plumed Serpent is Lawrence's most subtle and complete attempt to deal with the fear of female ascendancy in a manner that retains contact with real life. Kate becomes a nonthreatening virgin at times but is not, like Lou, committed to a static existence. She is subjected to man's power but is never the object of extreme hatred and humiliation like the two women who die in a parody of sex as male aggression against females. By the same token, she is never permanently submissive. As we have seen, the menacing female may always return through her refusal of subjection to men.

A clue to the true nature of Kate's experience is given us in the use of the bullfight motif in *The Plumed Serpent* and in the story "None of That," with implications in both works that are more similar than might at first appear. The first chapter of the novel records Kate's revulsion against bullfighting, reflecting the responses of Lawrence and Frieda when they, too, went to a bullfight in Mexico City, on Easter Sunday 1923. Kate feels a sense of oppression as soon as she enters the amphitheater where the spectacle is to take place: "Now Kate knew she was in a trap—a big concrete beetle-trap" (8). She feels loathing for the ordinary Mexican people who surround her, and despises her American companions on account of their thirst for mere sensation. She is nauseated by the sight of two feeble old horses being gored and disemboweled by the bull, and leaves the amphitheater abruptly.[10] This seems to be a straightforward account of justifiable disgust. We should remind ourselves, however, that there are other scenes of bloody violence in the novel that Kate comes to find acceptable, in the chapters entitled "The Attack on Jamiltepec" and "Huitzilopochtli's Night." We should also recall that Ethel Cane in "None of That" went to a bullfight in Mexico, was initially disgusted and contemptuous, but stayed to fall fatally in love with Cuesta the bullfighter, who handles the bulls with such consummate skill: "'He had the most curious charm, quick and unexpected like play, you know, like leopard kittens, or slow sometimes, like tiny little bears. And yet the perfect cruelty. It was the joy in cruelty! She hated the blood and messiness and dead animals. Ethel hated all that.'"[11] Like all the women who watch Cuesta, Ethel, who lives by the imagination and has resisted the advances of a great number of urbane and sophisticated men, becomes totally infatuated with this man who treats the bulls as a proud macho man treats women: "'I think it must have been a long time, before the bull was killed. He killed him at last, as a man takes his mistress at last because he is almost tired of playing with her. But he liked to kill his own bull'" (713). Since Ethel is brought to submit to the ultimate masculinity not in spite of but *through* her distaste for blood and cruelty, might we not find that Kate, too, begins her initiation into the masculine principle of life with her disgusted immersion in blood and "bursten bowels"?

One of the dominant elements in the description of the bullfighting episode is revulsion against the sight and smell of the horses' bowels. The bull "smelled blood and bowels" (15). Kate is sickened by "a smell of blood, a nauseous whiff of bursten bowels" (16). The second horse lies on the ground, "a huge heap of bowels coming out. And a nauseous stench" (18). As Kate departs, her final thought about the crowd is "They might as well sit and enjoy somebody else's diarrhoea" (19). We recall the focus on the bowels, together with the stress upon darkness and dissolution, that took on a preeminent place in Lawrence's thinking at the time when he was completing the final version of *The Rainbow* and that is first fully manifested in *Women in Love*. Cornelia Nixon has given a subtle and perceptive study of this phenomenon, linking it to the many pressures that beset Lawrence during the war years.[12] She relates this set of attitudes to the need to stress male supremacy that developed at the same phase of Lawrence's life[13] and notes that in *Women in Love,* the blood tends to be associated with the female, and the "darker" elements of the bowels and the intestines with the male.[14]

The heightened stress upon the bowels in the opening chapter of *The Plumed Serpent* can be read as a form of male aggression against women and, specifically, given the violence of the setting, as a release of anal aggression against the controlling mother. The violence emanates from strong repression that is here broken down, preparing the way for the male's domination of the mother. Significant images that echo other passages in Lawrence are found in the description of Kate's initial sensations upon entering the amphitheater: she and her companions "emerged out of a tunnel in the hollow of the concrete-and-iron amphitheatre." Kate feels contempt for a "gutter-lout" who looks at their tickets and indicates their seats: "Now Kate knew she was in a trap—a big concrete beetle-trap" (8). The "tunnel" and "hollow" references suggest that the bullring has affinities with the claustrophobic womb-tomb; the "beetle-trap" is again a claustrophobic enclosing space and is also an example of Lawrence's images of destructive anger against other human beings, seen as insects or rats, here occasioned by the ticket attendant. Those images of disgusting, swarming creatures are a displacement of destructive feelings directed against the mother and forming a defense against fear of annihilation.[15] In *The Plumed Serpent*, the value of darkness, the dark gods, and the truth beyond consciousness, which are a statement of the value of the father and therefore of the son's masculinity, are asserted. In the bloody, fecal violence of the opening chapter, the mother, who will be forced to occupy a place in a world conditioned by the son's male power, is subjected to the violence of the rending of the taboo.

This first chapter of the novel also contains some telling ambiguity of gender roles. The bull, we learn from "None of That" and from the Spanish ethic of bullfighting, has a feminine quality that makes sweet the matador's conquest of the victim. Clearly, part of that femininity lies in the bull's horns, which enable the bull to be seen as a fearsome phallic woman. At the same time, the bull is devalued in Kate's eyes as she realizes that he is foolish and stupid; this undercuts her previous feelings about bulls, "fear tempered with reverence of the great Mithraic beast" (17). The bull's stupidity lies in the fact that he will not run directly at the man, whereas, Kate is told, a cow will run directly at the toreador rather than at the cloak. The female element is therefore revealed as the more menacing.

The horses in the episode are also devalued. Instead of a St. Mawr, the proud virile beast who stands for indomitable maleness, we have the feeble old horses riden by the picadors, horses that easily fall victim to the bull. There is at the immediate level, then, an aura of male shame about this episode viewed through the eyes of a strong proud woman. The humbling and subjection of this woman are, however, prefigured in fantasy. She is made to watch the nauseating sight of two horses being gored in turn by a bull in a manner that echoes the male sexual brutality that is directed in actuality against the two women in "The Woman Who Rode Away" and "None of That." In the first instance, Kate sees "a bull whose shoulder trickled blood goring his horns up and down inside the belly of a prostrate and feebly plunging old horse"(16). The second episode is no less sickening: "Down went the horse, collapsing in front, but his rear was still heaved up, with the bull's horn working vigorously up and down inside him, while he lay on his neck all twisted. And a huge heap of bowels coming out. And a nauseous stench." (18) In each of these descriptions, a hideous parody of sexual aggression against a woman is clearly apparent. This ultimate act of humiliation of women corresponds with the gang rape of Ethel Cane and the symbolic rape of "The Woman Who Rode Away," who will be struck with knives as she lies within the hollow cave. The juxtaposition of stinking disembowelment and phallic savagery leads us to the source of aggression in anal repression that crushes male development.

Having passed through this initiation, Kate has been prepared gradually to accept the apparently alien spirit of Mexico. It is a land of death, a land without hope, and one where the people with black centerless eyes live in the reality of dark unconsciousness: "Uncreated, half-created, such a people was at the mercy of old black influences that lay in a sediment at the bottom of them. . . . when anything shook them at the depths, the black clouds would arise, and they were gone again in the old grisly passions of death, blood-lust, incarnate hate" (135). They are associated with the reptilean level of existence. Kate finds Mexico actively repellent. As she says to Cipriano when she refuses an offer of marriage: "'You see, Mexico is *really* a bit horrible to me. And the black eyes of the people *really* make my heart contract, and my flesh shrink. There's a bit of horror in it. And I don't want horror in my soul'" (235). She struggles against the prospect of marriage to Cipriano since it means the loss of her past and her subjection to the dark and alien male powers: "Ah, how could she marry Cipriano, and give her body to this death? Take the weight of this darkness on her breast, the heaviness of this strange gloom. Die before dying, and pass away whilst still beneath the sun?" (246). Yet it is essential to Lawrence's purpose that Kate should accept the darkness and death that mean the supremacy of the male principle and the revolt of the male against female dominance and repression. Men's spoiling and desecration of female pride is often expressed through the image of blood associated with flowers: "And on the bright sunshine was a dark steam of angry, impotent blood, and the flowers seemed to have their roots in spilt blood" (50). Through horror, loathing, and resistance Kate is finally brought to her compliant and almost passive position at the end of the novel.

The universal, polarized images of woman are clearly seen in Kate. To Owen, she looks like "an Ossianic goddess, a certain feminine strength and softness glowing in the very material of her dress" (60). Cipriano is drawn by a mystical quality in her: "He was in the presence of the goddess, white-handed, mysterious, gleaming with a moon-like power and the intense potency of grief" (71). She has for him "the same spell that the absurd little figures of the doll Madonnas had cast over him as a boy. She was the mystery, and he the adorer, under the semi-ecstatic spell of the mystery" (81–82). However, despite the attraction she exerts over him, he maintains his male independence: "But once he rose from his knees, he knelt in the same strutting conceit of himself as before he knelt: with all his adoration in his pocket again" (82). In this aspect, Kate is a "good mother" whose nurturing love needs to be introjected: her association with the male gods, as Malintzi, is essential to the total peace and harmony of the male alliance. Both Ramon and Cipriano recognize the special quality in her that needs to be incorporated. Whereas Carlota is a destructive madonna who like the earlier Magna Mater undermines masculinity, Kate promises a benign maternal strength that is a necessary foundation for male action.[16]

Kate is seen as the malevolent "bad mother" when she threatens to withhold herself from the men, or to abandon Mexcio and what it stands for. Like Blake, Lawrence finds most threatening the woman who maintains her own independence: "when she spread the wings of her own ego, and sent forth her own spirit, the world could look very wonderful to her, when she was alone. But after a while, the wonder faded, and a sort of jealous emptiness set in" (439). What this horror of female aloneness leads to is a "cat and mouse" playing with men, devouring them to "voluptuously fill the belly of her own ego" (438). In the final chapter, when Kate stands poised in making a choice between the life that she has with Cipriano and returning for a while to her family in Europe, she is in danger of becoming a counterpart of the witchlike Rachel Witt, one of those middle-aged women who have become "real grimalkins, greyish, avid, and horrifying, prowling around looking for prey that becomes scarcer and scarcer. As human beings they went to pieces. And they remained these grey-ribbed grimalkins, dressed in elegant clothes, the grimalkin howl even passing into their smart chatter" (438). But the end of the novel seems to imply that the bad mother will be cast out and that the nurture and support of the good mother will be fully introjected into the life of Ramon and Cipriano.

Kate is necessary to the political leader and his general because she is bound up with them in a fundamental familial relationship. The image of a postrevolutionary Mexico restored to the old gods reflects an ideal state of being[17] in which father, son, and mother dwell in a tension that reproduces the oedipal moment when the son both possesses the mother and incorporates the father's strength.

We notice that despite the actual pairing of Kate, the significant female, with Cipriano, it is Ramon who is the strong, ideal leader, and in important ways her relationship with Ramon is more fundamental than her relationship with Cipriano. Cipriano derives his strength and divinity from Ramon; it is at the instigation of Ramon that he actually marries Kate; and the ideal sexual partnership of Kate and Cipriano is modeled upon that of Ramon and Teresa. A marriage between Kate and Ramon seems not to be considered possible, and yet he appears to be her ultimate mate. In a real sense, she sustains Ramon's life. She saves his life by shooting one of his attackers. When, at the end of the novel, she speaks to Ramon about her plan to return to Ireland, he seems momentarily close to death through the effort of maintaining his new social organization: "his face seemed to go grey and peaked, as a dead man's, only his eyes watched her blackly, like a ghost's" (428). At first she feels unable to help him, then "he only gazed with those fixed, blank eyes. A sudden deep stillness came over her: a sense of power in herself." She realizes that "She was a woman. He was a man, and–and–and therefore not quite real. Not true to life." She lays her hand "compassionately" upon his, whereupon he is "stung" back to consciousness by her "motherly" touch (428). The vulnerability of the male ego even, or especially, behind the elevated grandeur of Ramon, and its true dependence upon the strong mother, is revealed.[18] The statement that to be a man is to be not quite real is made very hesitantly, but it is made, nevertheless, and is substantiated by Ramon's ghostly state. Male fear is concealed within the exaggerated splendor of the leader of men, an image that is a defense against the overwhelming female.

The emotional connection between Ramon and Kate is partly defined by references to the bowels. Carlota, the cold and destructive wife-mother, injures Ramon within his fundamental being: "She seemed to have the power still to lacerate him, inside his bowels. Not in his mind or spirit, but in his old emotional, passional self: right in the middle of his belly, to tear him and make him feel he bled inwardly" (206). Carlota must be opposed and cast out because she erodes the dark basis of the male ego. The hope is that Kate, who had failed to give her whole being to Joachim, her previous husband, will now give reliable support to Ramon. In the ambivalence of her commitment to the male, she reflects the reality of man's wavering confidence in woman; she is capable, however, of bringing a precious quality of maternal sustenance to the anguished son:

> "Man is a column of blood, with a voice in it," he said. "and when the voice is still, and he is only a column of blood, he is better."
>
> She went away to her room sadly, hearing the sound of infinite exhaustion in his voice. As if he had a hole, a wound in the middle of him. She could almost feel it, in her own bowels. (*PS* 407)

Kate is aware again of the hollowness or ghostliness in the male imago, but imparts strength through her sympathy, which is felt at an elemental level.[19] Since she provides this positive support for male power and creativity, she enables Ramon to continue in existence. The image of the "column of blood," alluded to here so wearily by Ramon, is a phallic reference that testifies to the effort required to maintain even an impersonal male existence. When the voice is not required, the male approximates more to the silent, female mode of existence and rests in its own being.

Although the shadowy Teresa, who submits her entire soul to Ramon, is ostensibly presented as the ideal of womanhood, we notice that she is considered by the men to be less essential to the brotherhood than is Kate herself. The transformation of Kate into the goddess Malintzi is an urgent matter; whereas, there are no immediate plans for Teresa to become a goddess. With her thin, snakelike form, Teresa has been subsumed into the male. While she presents no threat to men, she lacks Kate's female sensuousness, which is dangerous but absolutely necessary to them.

As Cipriano is ultimately dependent upon Ramon for his power, by the same token, Kate's true relationship is with Ramon, the man alongside whom she fights and whose life she saves. She is aware of important distinctions between the functions that the two men have for her: "'Ah!' said Kate to herself. 'I'm glad Cipriano is a soldier, and doesn't get wounds in his *soul*.' At the same time, she knew that without Ramon, Cipriano was just an instrument, and not ultimately interesting to her" (408).

What then is the psychological significance of the relationship between the three key characters in *The Plumed Serpent*? This is the crucial issue in the novel, and several accounts have been given. David Cavitch says that Ramon is Kate's ideal son, replacing Joachim who had died because he had usurped her first husband, a father figure;[20] Judith Ruderman considers that Ramon and Cipriano have a strong father-son relationship, from which they wish to exclude Kate, the powerful mother;[21] Daniel Dervin states that Lawrence himself is reflected in each of the characters, "as ego ideal in Don Ramon, as phallic-sadistic son in Cipriano, and as a fusion with Frieda in Kate Leslie."[22] These definitions of the psychological dynamics of the novel all seem incomplete. While Cavitch is right in seeing Ramon as a son figure, this is only one aspect of his function. To corroborate her view, Ruderman notes the interesting connection in name between Cyprian, Ramon's biological son, and Cipriano; however, I do not agree with her that Kate is excluded from the male circle, since it appears that women always remain essential to Lawrence's scheme. Dervin seems closest to the truth, yet it cannot be accurate to say that Lawrence actually *is* each of these characters; rather, the two men are each an aspect of his psyche, while Kate represents some of the complex of feelings toward women, which were partly crystallized for Lawrence in Frieda.

Cipriano is most clearly a son figure, and a son engaged in the thick of conflict with father and mother for his phallic independence. He is associated with knives, birds, reptiles, and sheer love of the life of a fighter: "I am the red Huitzilopochtli, of the knife" (366). He reveals obsessive anal patterns in his passion for cleanliness, neatness, and industry among his soldiers (364). His quality of self-containment, or of being closed off from others, denotes a desperate need to maintain the boundaries of his ego from being overwhelmed: "How dark he was, and how primitively physical, beautiful and deep-breasted, with soft, full flesh! But all, as it were, for himself. Nothing that came forth from him to meet with one outside. All oblivious of the outside, all for himself" (201). The tenuousness and vulnerability of this self-image of the phallic male is shown in the fact that he is not the final and constant love object of the desired mother.

An important contrast is made between the physique of Ramon and Cipriano, Ramon being the larger and more heroic figure, and Cipriano a type of the small, dark Lawrencean man. Although he lacks obvious male strength, however, Cipriano has the keen physical quality that comes from the primitiveness of his pure Indian blood, and is said to have the "second strength," a power that comes from behind the sun: "'I am of the red Huitzilopochtli and the power from behind the sun'" (365). This special quality is to be the essence of fire itself, which corresponds with the phallic in Cipriano's nature: "And Cipriano the master of fire. The living Huitzilopochtli, he had called himself. The living firemaster. The god in the flame;

the salamander" (320). The sun itself, as in Blake, is the father's strength, or the ego ideal. Since Ramon stands in a fatherly relation to Cipriano, is the father and leader of his people, and is obviously the "first" strength of the sun itself, it is Ramon who is the actual sun and the ego ideal. Cipriano–Huitzilopochtli's color is the red of fire and the sun, and Ramon–Quetzalcoatl's color is the blue of cool, reflected light because the envious son, Cipriano, has in fantasy abrogated to himself the father's phallic strength, but remains nevertheless secondary to the father and is not the true "sun"[23]. Kate is made to recognize the dual presence of these male entities when she first arrives at Sayula, the place where she will succumb to masculine dominance: "Concrete, jarring, exasperating reality had melted away, and a soft world of potency stood in its place, the velvety dark flux from the earth, the delicate yet supreme life-breath in the inner air. Behind the fierce sun the dark eyes of a deeper sun were watching, and between the bluish ribs of the mountains a powerful heart was secretly beating, the heart of the earth" (109). Here the true sun and stronger power lie behind the more obvious sun, associated beyond the phallic with the male darkness of the bowels and the depths of the earth. It is Ramon who belongs more clearly in this sphere of existence.

Ramon has qualities of both a father and a son, reflected in his relationships with Kate and Cipriano. As a father, he embodies a fantasy of an integrated ego ideal, who has the attributes of the grandiose self of the early phase of narcissism.[24] He is the potent divine leader, taking his strength from an ideal father bonded with the mother. The strength that Ramon, as son, has assimilated is that of a father who cannot be seen as a phallic being because he has been shamed and castrated by the mother, and he is therefore associated with dark and fundamental anal forces rather than with the phallic. His phallic aspect, as Quetzalcoatl, is the regressive and mystical serpent, a creature of the darkness of the earth.

Since Ramon's assimilation of the ideal father's strength is incomplete and unstable, we find another, split-off aspect of the son in Cipriano. The heroic transformation of the dark qualities in Ramon conceal an aggression that is apparent in Cipriano. Cipriano is not a complete figure, since he is self-enclosed, dependent for his significance upon the father, and is the agent of a "second strength" that still has its actual source in Ramon. As a son, Cipriano derives his phallic power from Ramon, but since the phallic is not manifest in Ramon, the phallic in Cipriano lacks substance and confidence and, for that reason, seems overstressed and exaggerated. The relationship between the two is expressed by the emblem of Quetzalcoatl, in which the eternal, mystical serpent with its tail in its mouth, corresponding to Ramon, surrounds the eagle, or the birdlike Cipriano (118).

The tenuousness of Ramon's, and therefore of Cipriano's, ego strength, is shown in a curious sequence in the novel that also illustrates the complexities of the interplay between the two male characters and Kate, as a mother figure of shifting perspectives. The events of the chapter entitled "The First Waters" follow upon "Lords of the Night and Day," where Ramon has been singing some of the hymns of Quetzalcoatl with a small group of male followers at his hacienda. Still naked to the waist from the ceremonies, Ramon comes to join Kate, Carlota, and Cipriano, who has just arrived and in contrast to Ramon is dressed in his military uniform. The two men embrace in a manner that accentuates the father-son relationship: "The two men embraced, breast to breast, and for a moment Cipriano laid his little blackish hands on the naked shoulders of the bigger man, and for a moment was perfectly still on his breast" (181–82). Cipriano receives the sanction for his actions from the protection of the strong father who still has about him the divine aura of Quetzalcoatl. Cipriano's childlike dependence is further stated as he gazes into Ramon's face "with black, wondering, childlike, searching eyes, as if he, Cipriano, were searching for *himself* in Ramon's face"(182, emphasis added). Cipriano is indeed searching for himself, since without Ramon he has no existence. The two men then stand side by side looking out over the lake, the symbol of feminine power abrogated by the male. Kate looks at the "soft, cream-brown skin" of Ramon's back, shudders at his pure sensuality and then: "In spite of herself, she could not help imagining a knife stuck between those pure, male shoulders. If only to break the arrogance of their remoteness" (182). Kate's imagined attack upon Ramon, the essence of male strength and pride, is a revelation of fundamental aggression on the part of an evil, phallic mother.[25] With her castrating weapon, she threatens both the ideal of the father and also the son, Cipriano, standing by his side, who cannot assimilate that ideal. The image is an inversion of a deeper aggression on the part of the son, who attacks in anger the sensuous wholeness of the mother and in his consequent fear of annihilation feels threatened in his male being. Upon experiencing this ultimate fantasy of aggression, Kate feels shame and wishes to withdraw inwardly into "the soft, untrespassing self, to whom nakedness is neither shame nor excitement, but clothed like a flower in its own deep, soft consciousness" (183). Again, Kate's response reflects in inverted form the response of the aggressive son, who in fear of self-destruction retreats into a protective, isolated self.

Ramon is manifestly a father figure in the novel, as the leader of his men and in his relationship to Cipriano. In the passage just described, when Cipriano lays his head upon his breast, Ramon appears as a loving parent who even has maternal characteristics. This quality is further emphasized later in the same chapter. Ramon has just heard with approval that Cipriano has suggested marriage to Kate, and smiles down at her with "a shadow of curious knowledge on his face"; then, as he folds his arms over his breast, "the cream-brown flesh, like opium, lifted the bosses of his breast, full and smooth" (187). The three discuss the subject of peace, which Ramon considers irrelevant as a social objective. Kate then becomes aware of Ramon's fatherliness: "There was a certain vulnerable kindliness about him, which made her wonder, startled, if she had ever realised what real fatherliness meant. The mystery, the nobility, the inaccessibility, and the vulnerable compassion of man in his separate fatherhood" (187–88). At the same time, she knows that Ramon is more beautiful to her than any white man, that her contact with him is "more precious than any contact she had known," and that Cipriano by comparison is "incomplete" (188).

Within the context of these various juxtaposed themes, Ramon's fatherliness has usurped the tenderness of the mother and, in a sense, absorbed her. He offers the child mystery and separateness, which is the sensuous self-absorption of narcissism. He condones by implication the lack of peace or state of strife, corresponding to Blake's contraries, which the oedipal child must feel in interrelationships with the parents. Ramon is shown as an ideal *parent*, ideal because he is the masculine model that the son desires, and because he has projected onto him the best qualities of the mother. He therefore allows a narcissism in which the mother is less powerful, so that the son can absorb a masculine imago. It is notable that, in this sequence, Ramon approves the marriage of Kate and Cipriano, but that Kate, here as elsewhere, feels that her fundamental bond is with Ramon, and that Cipriano is unsatisfactory or incomplete. If we see this from the point of view of the son who cannot totally assimilate the ideal father, we note that Cipriano, having first overcome paternal sanction against union with the mother, is then once more excluded from the parents' relationship. Kate herself, the mother who is made to witness and approve this and so much of the action of the novel, accepts her ideal union with Ramon, the aspect of the son who has attained the father's power by negating her own. Since the assimilation of the ego ideal by the son is never, however, complete, the two aspects of the son remain fragmented.

Towards the end of the novel, Kate makes her peace with two symbols of masculinity, the serpent and the bull. Watching a snake enter the darkness of a hole at the bottom of a wall, she accepts its way of life and its own place in creation: "She felt a certain reconciliation between herself and it" (425). A little later, in the final chapter, Kate watches men trying to load a cow and a bull into the hold of a ship. The cow enters easily enough, but the bull is resistant. This creature, who was shown as stupid and undignified in the bullfighting sequence at the beginning of the novel, as well as less effective in combat than the cow, is now reinstated as an emblem of male pride, and even assimilates some of the indomitable aspects of the serpent: "He stood huge and silvery, dappled like the sky, with black snake-markings down his haunches" (432). Eventually, and when he himself wills it, he descends like the serpent into the lower darkness. Kate indicates in these two episodes that she has learned to accept male power and the wonderful alien male place of darkness. Although the final ambivalence of the ending remains, we are prepared to believe that the strong woman has learned to subject herself to masculine dominance.

CHAPTER 8

Conclusion: Pastoral Reconciliation in Blake's Illustrations to *Virgil* and *Job*, and in Lawrence's *Lady Chatterley's Lover*

Artistic creation does not remove the causes of personal difficulties, nor does the artist's coming to terms with aspects of the self through producing a work of art destroy the sources of inspiration. The deepest psychological patterns probably do not change throughout a person's life. Nevertheless, we find in both Blake and Lawrence a more balanced image of masculinity and a more positive feeling towards women in their later lives. In some of Blake's engravings of the 1820s, the woodcut illustrations he made for Thornton's edition of *Virgil* in 1820–21, and the etched version of the *Illustrations to the Book of Job* of 1826, he achieves a notable sense of poise and tranquility. Lawrence's final novel, *Lady Chatterley's Lover*, published in 1928, two years before his death, has often been attacked as a sexist work. It also, however, celebrates a tender and harmonious relationship between a man and a woman, and has lost much of the strident masculinity of the leadership period.

The last years of Blake's life, from about 1818 until his death in 1827, were softened by his association with a group of young artists, including John Linnell and Samuel Palmer. These young men admired and supported Blake, and stood to him somewhat in the relationship of affectionate sons to father. During this final and relatively serene period, he produced supreme works in the visual arts that are more publicly accessible than much of his engraved poetry. The designs for *Virgil* and the *Book of Job* will be discussed here because they suggest a loosening of tensions surrounding the themes of women and masculinity. Blake's late works also included the unfinished series of Dante watercolors, an oeuvre of vaster proportions that cannot be summed up in a simple fashion.

The illustrations to Thornton's *Virgil* are unusual in Blake's work in that they are woodcuts, a medium that he used rarely. They depict episodes in Ambrose Philips's imitation of Virgil's first Eclogue, in which Colinet, a young shepherd, bemoans his sad condition to Thenot, an old shepherd. After describing his sufferings to Thenot, Colinet is consoled. Most strikingly, he commits himself to the service and protection of Menalcas, the lord of the region. He then joins in the cheerful activities of pastoral life. Blake's exquisite woodcuts are on a minute scale, but are full of sensitive details and evocations of the natural scene. Samuel Palmer was deeply impressed by their "mystic and dreamy glimmer," and was inspired by them in his own visionary paintings of the Shoreham period.[1]

In the woodcuts, Blake deals with landscape and detailed aspects of the natural scene to an uncharacteristic degree. As we have noted, he tended to despise landscape and to distrust pure nature. In these designs, nature is freed from some of the traditional emblematic quality that it often has in Blake.[2] As David Bindman says, there is "a sense of harmony between man and nature" here.[3] One design, plate VI, is a study of landscape devoid of human figures. This reflects a more open acceptance of a bond with nature, linked to the infantile bond with the mother, that appears only fitfully in much of Blake's work, although it is an urgent theme of much Romantic art.

Another motif in these illustrations seems to indicate some resolution of earlier conflicts. In the frontispiece (see figure 5), which shows the forlorn Colinet leaning against a tree, we notice that his musical instruments, his shepherd's pipe and reeds, are hanging on the trunk. In the penultimate woodcut (see figure 6, no. 5), when he has accepted his lot and the advice of Thenot, we see him joyfully returning homeward with another young shepherd singing and playing the instruments he has now taken down from the tree. The state reflected in the first illustration is the son's sense of parental oppression extended to his expressive life and his phallic identity.[4] The instruments, symbolizing his artistic and sexual vigor, hang helpless and impotent upon the tree of parental authority and prohibiton. Through recounting his tribulations to a father figure and embracing the authority of the lord Menalcas, he is able to accept the father's values and to form a loving relationship with him. Thence, he is released into a state of personal wholeness and creativity.

The *Illustrations to the Book of Job* were published in 1826, the year before Blake's death. They are engraved versions, with some variations, of a series of paintings originally made between 1805 and 1810[5] for Thomas Butts. It is often agreed that the illustrations mark a kind of culmination of Blake's composite art: the technical quality of the engravings is very fine, while Blake unites the visual images with the text, extracts from *Job*, in a strikingly balanced fashion.[6] Whereas in the engravings of the poetry the verbal element is often dominant, here the visual image is central, but harmonized beautifully with the text.

One of the significant motifs of the *Virgil* designs appears again in the *Job* illustrations. In plate I, "Job and his Family" (see figure 7), we see Job and his wife sitting beneath a tree while their sons and daughters surround them kneeling, all in postures of pious prayer. The parents have books open on their laps to symbolize the repressive power of the fixed word of the law. The overshadowing tree of oedipal prohibition substantiates the import of the design. As in the *Virgil* frontispiece, musical instruments hang in the tree, implying again that creativity and desire have been thwarted on account of the parents' moral injunction.

In Blake's version of *Job*, the patriarch has transgressed in thus imposing his deadening rule upon his family. The final plate, XXI, "Job and his Wife Restored to Prosperity" (see figure 8), displays the transformation in the family brought about by Job's attainment of wisdom through suffering. Parents and children are again beneath the sheltering tree but now stand, joyfully making music together. The tomes of repressive law have disappeared. In Blake's epic poems, such moments of triumphant liberation often appear fleeting and short-lived. The final plates of *Job* evince the tranquil quality of having achieved a lasting state of resolution.

In the *Job* illustrations, we find also a serene and positive feeling towards women. Marion Milner has noted that Job comes to accept the female, after having initially repudiated her. By this, Milner means most specifically that Job accepts the functioning of the female within himself.[7] She bases her observation upon the Kleinian notion of the re-creation of "both the destroyed self and the destroyed loved object in the aesthetic experience of art."[8] Thus, she comments that in plate XIV, "The Creation," or "When the Morning Stars Sang Together," the moon goddess is given equal prominence with the sun god.[9] The most important portrayal of this harmonious

To face page 13.

ILLUSTRATIONS

OF

IMITATION OF ECLOGUE I.

FRONTISPIECE.

THENOT AND COLINET.

The Illustrations of this English Pastoral are by the famous BLAKE, the illustrator of *Young's* Night Thoughts, and *Blair's* Grave; who designed and engraved them himself. This is mentioned, as they display less of art than genius, and are much admired by some eminent painters.

Figure 5. Thornton's *Virgil*, Frontispiece. Department of Printing and Graphic Arts, The Houghton Library, Harvard University.

Figure 6. Thornton's *Virgil*, XIV-XVII. Department of Printing and Graphic Arts, The Houghton Library, Harvard University.

Figure 7. Job, I. Gift of Miss Ellen Bullard. Courtesy, Museum of Fine Arts, Boston.

Figure 8. Job, XXI. Gift of Miss Ellen Bullard. Courtesy, Museum of Fine Arts, Boston.

Figure 9. Job, XX. Gift of Miss Ellen Bullard. Courtesy, Museum of Fine Arts, Boston.

re-integration of the female is found in Plate XX, "Job and his Daughters" (see figure 9), where we see Job sitting with his three daughters, wrapped in mutual affection. With outstretched arms, Job points out to them depictions of some of the painful events of his past life. The treatment of the three women contrasts sharply with what we have often found in the poetry, where a group of three females, for instance, the Daughters of Urizen or the threefold maiden of "The Crystal Cabinet," is likely to be sinister. Here, Job's previous anguish is subsumed into a stable and loving affiliation. We are reminded, by contrast, of Milton's stern relationship with his three daughters.[10] The most remarkable change from earlier attitudes is found in one of the extracts from the biblical Book of Job (42:15) that Blake selected as part of the engraved text: "& their Father gave them Inheritance among their Brethren," referring to the three women. In *Milton* and elsewhere, Blake named the splintering multiple image of menacing females the Daughters of Zelophehad, sisters who in the Book of Numbers had earned from Moses the right to inherit property. The extension of the prerogative of inheritance to women specifically seems to erode the supremacy of males; therefore, it is selected as a key threatening element in women. In this portrayal of Job and his daughters, Blake accepts the social position and influence of women, and affirms a loving and necessary bond with them.[11]

Lady Chatterley's Lover, too, reflects a more positive feeling towards women. The novel was written shortly after Lawrence's last visit to Eastwood and to the countryside of his childhood in September 1926, and is a powerful response to that visit.[12] The ambivalence he felt is reflected in his comment that in Eastwood he felt "at once a devouring nostalgia and an infinite repulsion."[13] The emotional conflicts surrounding the place and the relationships associated with it remained with him throughout his life. Lawrence's restless wanderings around the world from the time of his elopement with Frieda have been seen as an attempt to escape from the clutching power of his mother and his motherland. *Lady Chatterley's Lover* is, in some ways, an act of reconciliation with both mother and country.

The principal male figure of the novel is the gamekeeper, Parkin in the second version, *John Thomas and Lady Jane*, and Mellors in the third version, *Lady Chatterley's Lover*, usually considered definitive. The two characterizations are somewhat different: Parkin is more tender and vulnerable, Mellors more aggressively masculine.[14] Parkin–Mellors is a developed and triumphant form of Annable, the gamekeeper in *The White Peacock*. These figures in Lawrence's first and last novels have in common their occupation, something of their personal history, and their views about women and about society. Although Annable is a vibrant presence in the novel, he cannot be allowed a full existence or given open acknowledgment as Cyril's strong father. Mellors, however, is the protagonist of the novel. He is more than a father figure: he is an ideal father whose strength the son has incorporated.

We can argue that the transformation in the presentation of the gamekeeper springs from changes within Lawrence himself. The dead biological father and the evanescent ideal father of *The White Peacock* are related to the weak and shamed Walter Morel of *Sons and Lovers*; after the period when he wrote *Sons and Lovers*, Lawrence came to be reconciled in spirit with his own father, to the detriment of his loyalty to his mother.[15] He was thus able to maintain a more positive sense of his masculine power, which, however, showed itself during the leadership period as an exaggerated maleness and a need to dominate women. In *Lady Chatterley's Lover*, both of these tendencies are softened: Mellors, although sexist, is not associated with physical violence of the order that we find in *The Plumed Serpent* and "The Woman Who Rode Away." Admittedly, misogyny and bullying remain concealed in the very sexual ethos of the novel,[16] yet there is a positive and tender feeling towards woman here that was absent from the preceding phase.[17]

The insubstantial shadow that lies behind the overassertive masculinity of Mellors is Clifford Chatterley, impotent, intellectual, abstracted from concrete life. He is the male figure, like Gerald or Urizen, who is a projection of the fear of castration and insubstantiality.[18] Although he has a key function in the novel, he is always mastered by the colorful vigor of Mellors. Lawrence overcomes lingering anxiety about male weakness as he establishes faith in male pride.

The energy and spontaneity of the novel come from the breakdown of oedipal fears[19] through a sustained fantasy of masculine strength. This is partly reflected in the emotionally charged function of flowers in the narrative. We have noted in Lawrence's earlier fiction the symbolic force of various kinds of white flowers: the snowdrops, expressive of an unnamed yearning, in the woods where Cyril and his friends first encounter Annable; the lilies reeling in the moonlight when Mrs. Morel, pregnant with Paul, is confirmed in her terrible female power; and Miriam's sacramental white rosebush, which expresses her sublimation of sexuality. All of these flowers evoke the mother's prohibition of the son's oedipal desires, transformed into a mystical taboo. Lawrence's descriptions of nature, and especially of flowers, are always vitally animated. Yet beyond this, in the early fiction, there is a particular intensity in the evocations of flowers matched, in *The White Peacock*, by the interest in birds and birds' eggs. These reflect strong feelings surrounding parent relationships.

In *Lady Chatterley's Lover*, this passionate focus upon flowers, and also birds, returns, now with a striking exuberance and sense of liberation. The narrative is alive with spring flowers and blossom, culminating in the scene where Connie and Mellors in jubilant tenderness adorn each other's bodies with flowers. Lawrence wrote the novel after his final return to Eastwood, and in many ways he re-creates the specific social reality of that visit. Yet we note that, although it was in September 1926 that he had been in the Midlands, it is the flowers of spring and early summer that he brings to life in the novel. The return to his childhood home rekindled deep memories of the landscape that was bound up with his fundamental emotional life. These memories are now integrated into a feeling of peace and reconciliation as he assumes the strength of the father and feels liberated from the fierce white purity of the mother's taboo.

We observe, too, that the pheasants that Mellors cares for are part of the fabric of the love relationship, as a measure of the nurturing gentleness of the man and the tender maternal aspect of the woman. In *The White Peacock*, the imagery of families of wild creatures evoked violence on the part of mothers towards the young, and established fathers as the more tender parents. In this final novel, Mellors retains a supreme nurturing capacity. Connie, delighting in the mother pheasants and their chicks, and in her own pregnancy, is a mother figure restored to the gentle maternal function. In her subservience to the phallic strength of the incorporated ideal father, she has become a nonthreatening, loving figure.

Lady Chatterley's Lover was one of Lawrence's last works, the lonely and courageous statement of a dying man. Blake's illustrations to *Virgil* and the *Book of Job* were produced in a period of relative contentment. The circumstances behind these works are very different. We can say, however, that the two men struggled with immense personal conflicts, and by means of artistic creation and reparation arrived at some measure of balance and harmony. Each forged an image of masculine strength and thus was able to go some way to restoring the loving good mother.

The images of women and men depicted in Blake and Lawrence make a powerful impression upon their readers because each was able to get very close to the elemental sources of love and hate. If we reach some comprehension of the forces that lie behind their themes and narratives—male envy of the female reproductive capacity and fear of the dominant mother—we may gain a deeper insight into the dynamics of personal and social relationships.

Notes

Preface

1. Storch, "Blake and Women: 'Nature's Cruel Holiness,'" *American Imago* 38 (1981) 221–46, rpt. in Layton and Shapiro, eds., *Narcissism and the Text* (New York: New York Univ. Press, 1986), 97–115.
2. Storch, "The 'Spectrous Fiend' Cast Out: Blake's Crisis at Felpham," *MLQ* 44 (1983):115–35.
3. Majdiak & Wilkie, "Blake and Freud: Poetry and Depth Psychology," in *Journal of Aesthetic Education* 6 (1972), 87–98.
4. George, *Blake and Freud* (Ithaca & London: Cornell Univ. Press, 1980).
5. Webster, *Blake's Prophetic Psychology* (Athens: Univ. of Georgia Press, 1983).
6. I do not include Jungian studies, e.g., Christine Gallant's *Blake's Assimilation of Chaos* (Princeton, N.J.: Princeton Univ. Press, 1978), since the Jungian notion of universal symbolism differs greatly from Freudian analysis of the individual.
7. Webster, "Blake, Women, and Sexuality," in *Critical Paths: Blake and the Argument of Method*, ed. Dan Miller, Mark Bracher, and Donald Ault (Durham, N.C.: Duke Univ. Press, 1987), 204–24.
8. Webster, *Prophetic Psychology*, 3.
9. Webster, "Blake, Women, and Sexuality," 210, 217.
10. Weiss, *Oedipus in Nottingham* (Seattle: Univ. of Washington Press, 1962).
11. Howe, *The Art of the Self in D. H. Lawrence* (Athens: Ohio Univ. Press, 1977).
12. Ibid., 11.
13. Ruderman, *D. H. Lawrence and the Devouring Mother* (Durham, N.C.: Duke Univ. Press, 1984).
14. Nixon, *Lawrence's Leadership Politics and the Turn Against Women* (Berkeley, Los Angeles & London: Univ. of California Press, 1986).
15. Dervin, *A "Strange Sapience": The Creative Imagination of D. H. Lawrence* (Amherst, Mass.: Univ. of Massachusetts Press, 1984).

Chapter 1

1. See ch. 5, *Sexual Politics* (Garden City, N.Y.: Doubleday, 1970). I concur with Peter Balbert, *D.H. Lawrence & the Phallic Imagination* (New York: St. Martin's Press, 1989), e.g., 4–7, in his view that some feminist responses to Lawrence, notably Millet's, oversimplify and misunderstand him. However, I cannot agree with Balbert that we should accept the *fantasies* of masculinity that we find in Lawrence's fiction.

2. Hilary Simpson in *D.H. Lawrence and Feminism* (DeKalb: Northern Illinois Univ. Press, 1982) traces the development of Lawrence's attitudes towards women, from early sympathy to later animosity, relating it to manifestations of growing antifeminism in his contemporary society; Cornelia Nixon, in *Lawrence's Leadership Politics*, examines the deep changes in Lawrence's feelings about women and politics that came about during the war years.

3. Susan Fox in "The Female as Metaphor in Blake's Poetry," *Critical Inquiry* 3 (1977), 507–19, notes an antipathy toward women in Blake's work in the Lambeth poems following *Visions of the Daughters of Albion*; in *Poetic Form in Blake's Milton* (Princeton, N.J.: Princeton Univ. Press, 1976), 212–22 she argues that in *Milton* females are either weak or pernicious. Diana Hume George, *Blake and Freud*, 185–207, observes that in the epics Blake equated woman with nature and in that respect detested her, although George does not regard this as a fundamental antagonism against women. See also my "Blake and Women: 'Nature's Cruel Holiness,'" where I suggest that beneath Blake's sympathetic critique of women's social condition lies antagonism against females. Webster, in *Prophetic Psychology* & "Blake, Women and Sexuality," e.g., 219–20, asserts that Blake's oedipal guilt and anxiety led him to produce very negative images of women in the later epics.

4. Simpson, e.g., in ch. 3, "Lawrence, Feminism and the War," *Lawrence and Feminism*.

5. Paul Delany's *D.H. Lawrence's Nightmare: The Writer and his Circle in the Years of the Great War* (New York: Basic Books, 1978) is also an invaluable study of this period of Lawrence's life and of the profound changes that took place in him.

6. Nixon's central thesis is that Lawrence, while rewriting *Women in Love*, changed from benign phallic imagery to a dark imagery associated with the bowels and with male domination of women, e.g., 81–86, 123–29.

7. Gilbert & Gubar, *No Man's Land: The Place of the Woman Writer in the Twentieth Century*, vol. 1: *The War of the Words* (New Haven & London: Yale Univ. Press, 1987), e.g., 28–62.

8. Mark Schorer, *William Blake: the Politics of Vision* (1946; rpt. New York: Vintage Books, 1959), 139–46; David V. Erdman, *Blake: Prophet Against Empire*, rev. ed. (Garden City, N.Y.: Doubleday, 1969), 152–162.

9. It is generally assumed that *Visions of the Daughters of Albion* displays a

view of women's social position that is identical with Mary Wollstonecraft's. However, Susan Fox in "The Female as Metaphor," 512–13, points out that Blake presents Oothoon as a woman without will and power, not Wollstonecraft's ideal: Brenda Webster, *Prophetic Psychology*, 107–8, notes that the ideal of the poem is male sexual pleasure, whereas Wollstonecraft seeks to replace woman's role as a sex object.

10. In relation to Blake, note Gilbert and Gubar's point that one male response to women's greater social power might be to expect increased eroticism from women, *No Man's Land*, 47–48.

11. Nancy Chodorow, *The Reproduction of Mothering: Psychoanalysis and the Sociology of Gender* (Berkeley, Los Angeles & London: Univ. of California Press, 1978), 173–77.

12. Heinz Kohut, *The Analysis of the Self* (New York: International Universities Press, 1971), 145–47. Melanie Klein attributes this overvaluation of masculinity in part to overcompensation for the anxieties relating to the womb and the father's penis experienced by the boy during the feminity phase, *Love, Guilt and Reparation & Other Works, 1921–45* (New York: Delacorte Press/Seymour Lawrence, 1975), 190–91.

13. Howard R. Wolf, "British Fathers and Sons, 1773–1913: From Filial Submissiveness to Creativity," *Psychoanalytic Review* 52 (1965), 53–70, defines a period in which the rebellion of sons—e.g., John Stuart Mill, Samuel Butler, Lawrence, Freud himself, and, we may add, Blake—against fathers, is a dominant theme. In accordance with the views of Chodorow, we may determine that this development had as much to do with the emotional dominance of mothers as with the new independence of sons.

14. See Gilbert and Gubar's discussion of this movement, led in Britain by such figures as Ezra Pound, T.E. Hulme, and T.S. Eliot, 21–22, 153–55. Note also the contempt for the female, seen as indefinite and murky, in fascist imagery, presented in Klaus Theweleit's *Male Fantasies*, vol. 1, *Women, Floods, Bodies, History* (Minneapolis: Univ. of Minnesota Press, 1987), e.g., in ch. 1. Nixon, 5–9, argues that the cult of masculinity tended to be antifeminine only in male artists who were also politically authoritarian.

15. A. Walton Litz, in "Lawrence, Pound, and Early Modernism" (*D.H. Lawrence: A Centenary Consideration*, ed. Peter Balbert and Philip L. Marcus [Ithaca & London: Cornell Univ. Press, 1985], 15–28), discusses imagist elements, recognized by Pound, in Lawrence's early writings.

16. See Jack Lindsay, "The Impact of Modernism on Lawrence," in *Paintings of D.H. Lawrence*, ed. Mervyn Levy (London: Cory, Adams & Mackay, 1964), 35–53.

17. Frederick J. Hoffman in "Lawrence's Quarrel With Freud, ch. 6 of *Freudianism and the Literary Mind* (1945; rpt. New York: Grove Press, 1959), observes, e.g., 152–54, that the real influence of Freudian theory upon Lawrence was quite superficial. Lawrence has often been studied from a psychoanalytic perspective,

for instance by Daniel Weiss in *Oedipus in Nottingham*. Daniel Dervin's *A "Strange Sapience"* is an object-relations analysis.

18. Diana Hume George in *Blake and Freud* claims that Blake's work anticipated Freud's, e.g., 17; Brenda Webster considers that, while Blake was "profoundly in touch with the unconscious," 8, meaning the general unconscious, the content of his art in some sense reflects his own individual psyche.

19. Melanie Klein, *Love, Guilt and Reparation*, 287–88, 377; Hanna Segal, *Introduction to the Work of Melanie Klein*, 2nd ed. (New York: Basic Books, 1974), 35–36, 82–83.

20. Melanie Klein, *Envy and Gratitude & Other Works, 1946–63* (New York: Delacorte Press/Seymour Lawrence, 1975), 249–54; *Love, Guilt and Reparation*, 290–91; Segal, 26–30, 77–8.

21. Freud and Klein commented on the "sacred and profane" images of women in art and society. See *Love, Guilt and Reparation*, 394–95.

22. One important exposition of what is meant by the two positions is in the 1935 paper, "A Contribution to the Psychogenesis of Manic-Depressive States," *Love, Guilt and Reparation*, 262–89.

23. Segal, *Introduction* 75–76.

24. Melanie Klein and Joan Riviere, *Love, Hate and Reparation* (1937; rpt. New York: W.W. Norton, 1964), 107–10; cf. Simon Stuart, *New Phoenix Wings: Reparation in Literature* (London: Routledge & Kegan Paul, 1979), 53–95.

25. Klein, *Love, Guilt and Reparation*, 186–89; *Envy and Gratitude*, 196–98; Segal, 103–16.

26. Klein, *Love, Guilt and Reparation*, 189–192; *Envy and Gratitude*, 306. For a study of theories of the "femininity complex" in men in a range of analysts, see Daniel S. Jaffe, "The Masculine Envy of Woman's Procreative Function," *Journal of the American Psychoanalytic Association* 16 (1968), 521–48.

27. Klein, *Love, Guilt and Reparation*, 190–91.

28. Juliet Mitchell, *Psychoanalysis and Feminism: Freud, Reich, Laing and Women* (New York: Vintage Books,1975) 227–31.

29. David Punter in "Blake, Trauma and the Female," *New Literary History* 15 (1984), 486–88, discusses male malaise about economic and social changes in the late eighteenth century that affected the family and the position of women. It seems that, except for the lower stratum of the working class, this would lead to a stronger valuation of women at the center of the home.

30. In her study of the complexity of male-female relationships in Lawrence, "Love and Power: a Reconsideration of Sexual Politics in D. H. Lawrence," *Modern Fiction Studies* 21 (1975), Lydia Blanchard notes that in the early novels Lawrence reveals relationships through conflict, and that this conflict is a direct result of the effects of industrialization, e.g. 433 and 443.

31. G. E. Bentley, Jr., in *Blake Records* (Oxford: Clarendon Press, 1969) gathers together the early biographical records of Blake. Aileen Ward, for example in

"Canterbury Revisited: The Blake-Cromek Controversy," *Blake: An Illustrated Quarterly* 22 (1988): 80–92, has reconstructed the social and psychological reality of parts of Blake's life, with important implications for the study of his work.

32. Bentley, *Blake Records*, 7–8.

33. Michael Ballin, "D. H. Lawrence's Esotericism: D. H. Lawrence and William Blake in *Women in Love*" in *D. H. Lawrence's Women in Love: Contexts and Criticism*, ed. Michael Ballin (Waterloo, Ont.: Wilfred Laurier University [no date]) 77, notes similarities in the religious background of the two artists.

34. Moore, Harry T., *The Priest of Love: A Life of D. H. Lawrence*, rev. ed. (New York: Farrar, Straus & Giroux, 1974), 8–10.

35. Donald Davie in *A Gathered Church: The Literature of the English Dissenting Interest, 1700–1930* (New York: Oxford Univ. Press, 1978), 7, comments that Lawrence's criticisms of Bloomsbury display "the dissenting conscience at odds with the Evangelical conscience."

36. Eli Zaretsky, *Capitalism, the Family and Personal Life* (New York: Harper Colophon, 1976), 34.

37. E. P. Thompson, *The Making of the English Working Class* (1963; rpt. Harmondsworth, Middlesex: Penguin Books, 1968), 405–6.

38. Bentley, *Blake Records*, 7, 519.

39. His former friend John Middleton Murry's enthusiastic study, *William Blake* (London: Johathan Cape), did not appear until 1933.

40. An affinity between Blake and Lawrence has often been noted, if not extensively studied. See, for instance, F.R. Leavis, *For Continuity* (Cambridge: Minority Press, 1933), 111; Constantine N. Stavrou, "William Blake and D.H. Lawrence," *University of Kansas City Review* 22 (1956), 235–40; Michael G. Ballin, "D. H. Lawrence and William Blake: A Comparative and Critical Study" (Diss., Univ. of Toronto, 1972); Myra Glazer, "Why the Sons of God Want the Daughters of Men: On William Blake and D. H. Lawrence," in *William Blake and the Moderns*, ed. Robert J. Bertolf & Annette S. Levitt (Albany: State Univ. of New York Press, 1982), 164–85; John Colmer, "Lawrence and Blake," in *D.H. Lawrence and Tradition*, ed. Jeffrey Myers (Amherst, Mass.: Univ. of Massachusetts Press, 1985), 9–20.

41. Lawrence, *Studies in Classic American Literature*, 73; Letters, 4:556.

42. *Phoenix: The Posthumous Papers of D.H. Lawrence*, 560.

43. See Storch, "'The Very Image of Our Conceptions': Blake's Allegory and the Role of the Creative Poet," *Bulletin of Research in the Humanities* 83 (1980), 262–79.

44. Yeats noted that in the prophetic books, the surface is perpetually dissolving to reveal another below it; qtd. by Colin Clarke, *River of Dissolution: D. H. Lawrence & English Romanticism* (London: Routledge & Kegan Paul, 1969), 29n, in distinguishing Blake from the other Romantic poets.

45. Aldous Huxley, *Point Counter Point* (New York: Harper & Row, 1928), 103.

46. Chambers, "The Collected Letters of Jessie Chambers," *D.H. Lawrence Review* 12 (Spring-Summer 1979), 92. In this letter of January 14, 1935, she refers to a study by Delavenay finally published as *D.H. Lawrence and Edward Carpenter* (New York: Taplinger, 1971); see e.g., 184, 187.

47. *Phoenix*, 570.

48. Emile Delavenay in *D.H. Lawrence: The Man and His Work, The Formative Years, 1885–1919* (Carbondale: Southern Illinois Univ. Press, 1972) notes Lawrence's allusion to Blakean concepts in "The Crown," e.g., 327–30.

49. See for example Lawrence, *Reflections on the Death of a Porcupine*, 253–62.

50. *Kangaroo*, 128.

51. Howe, *Art of the Self*, 93, comments that Kangaroo is a destructive oedipal mother; Ruderman, *Devouring Mother*, 112, sees him as a mother figure with a benign and a malevolent aspect.

52. Jessie Chambers, *D. H. Lawrence: A Personal Record by E.T.*, 2nd ed., ed. J. D. Chambers (1935; rpt. London: Frank Cass & Co. Ltd., 1965), 62–63.

53. Ibid., 102.

54. Ibid., 81.

55. Vivian de Sola Pinto, "William Blake and D.H. Lawrence," in *Essays Presented to S. Foster Damon*, ed. Alvin H. Rosenfeld (Providence, R.I.: Brown University Press, 1969), 98–102; Michael Ballin, *Lawrence's Women in Love*, 76.

56. Ballin, "Lawrence and Blake," 5. Glazer also comments on the centrality of the body and sexuality in the work of both artists, 166–67.

57. *Phoenix*, 179.

58. Cf. Gilbert & Gubar, *No Man's Land*, 47–48.

59. See, e.g., Irene Tayler, "The Woman Scaly," *Bulletin of the Mid West Modern Language Association* 6 (1973), 74–87.

60. Lawrence, *The Plumed Serpent*, 422.

61. *Complete Poems* I, 40.

62. Ballin, *Lawrence's Women in Love*, 75, notes the similarity of the treatment of pity in Blake and Lawrence.

Chapter 2

1. Alexander Gilchrist, Blake's first biographer, speaks for an earlier age's response to the newness and originality of this vision of childhood when he refers to Blake's "chameleon sympathy with childlike feelings," *Life of William Blake* (London & Cambridge: Macmillan & Co., 1863), 1: 72; E.D. Hirsch, Jr., *Innocence and Experience: An Introduction to Blake* (New Haven & London: Yale Univ. Press, 1964), 21, notes the uniqueness of the *Songs of Innocence* as "religious poems for children and adults."

2. Since Blake's own day, many readers have focused on the *Songs* and ignored the rest of Blake. This is an unbalanced view of him, but we note that

the material of the *Songs* communicates itself easily, while in later works Blake's imagery increasingly becomes "private."

3. Klein, *Love, Guilt and Reparation*, 384, 349; Segal, 27, 82.

4. Segal, *Introduction to Klein*, 26.

5. George has analyzed the poem as an expression of oedipal feelings and frustrations, *Blake and Freud*, 89–90; Webster discusses it in *Prophetic Psychology*, 148–49, as Blake's "most direct statement" of oedipal rage and trauma.

6. See Marion Milner, *The Hands of the Living God: An Account of a Psychoanalytic Treatment* (New York: International Universities Press, 1969), 382–84.

7. Klein, *Envy and Gratitude*, 50; *Love, Guilt and Reparation*, 155; Segal, 103–4.

8. Klein, *Love, Guilt and Reparation*, 187–88; *Envy and Gratitude*, 135.

9. See my earlier comments on the Cynic's "Song," "Blake and Women," 230–32. Webster discusses the "Song" in *Prophetic Psychology*, 14–15, and comments that in it Blake illustrates "the formation of a vicious psychological cycle."

10. Klein, *Love, Guilt and Reparation*, 187.

11. See Klein & Riviere, *Love, Hate, and Reparation*, 109.

12. These poems do, of course, reflect acute social observations. But the very repetitiousness of the parent-child patterns suggest also a less deliberate source, cf. Webster, *Prophetic Psychology*, 4–8.

13. Klein, *Envy and Gratitude*, 68; *Love, Guilt and Reparation*, 375, 411; Segal, 5.

14. Fox, in both *Blake's Milton*, 509, and "the Female as Metaphor," 202, curiously says of this sequence that the boy lost by his father is found by his mother. It seems clear, however, that the boy is led back to the suffering mother by an idealized father.

15. Compare Lacan's equation of the father with the symbolic order of language; the silence of the father here, therefore, points to a lack of masculine ego strength.

16. Klein, e.g., *Envy and Gratitude*, 64, 216.

17. George discusses the poem, *Blake and Freud*, 106–8, as the imposition of the severity of the superego upon the narcissistic child.

18. Another possible but more remote subject of the verb is "all" (1.12) the gathered congregation. The merging of people, priest, and parents reflects the impregnable social system by which the boy is circumscribed.

19. Gary A. Wiener in "Lawrence's 'Little Girl Lost,'" *The D.H. Lawrence Review* 19 (1987), 243–53, draws a parallel between "The Little Girl Lost" and Lawrence's *The Lost Girl*, in that both females go south to a more sensually fulfilling life. This is a striking analogy, but it does not extend to the fact that Blake's lost girl sleeps throughout most of the pair of poems, and it does not explain the changing aspect of the parents.

20. Hirsch suggests that she may be dead, and that the lioness's removal of her dress symbolizes the soul's separation from the body after death, 224–25.

21. Consider the figure of the maid–governess–nurse as seductress and intruder

into the family circle, e.g., Jane Gallop, *The Daughter's Seduction: Feminism and Psychoanalysis* (Ithaca, N.Y.: Cornell Univ. Press, 1982), 143–46.

Chapter 3

1. Since Millett's attack, there has been a tendency to regard Lawrence as an antifeminist pure and simple, but there are some notable studies in which the complexity of Lawrence's emotional response to women is acknowledged. Charles Rossman in "'You are the Call and I am the Answer': *D. H. Lawrence Review* 8 (1975), 255–324, gives a balanced account of the subtlety of Lawrence's fictional treatment of women. Martin Green, *The von Richthofen Sisters: The Triumphant and the Tragic Modes of Love* (New York: Basic Books, 1974), 78–88, makes plain Lawrence's affinity with a matriarchal ordering of life. Carol Dix in *D. H. Lawrence and Women* (Totowa, N.J.: Rowman & Littlefield, 1980) describes Lawrence's sympathetic understanding of women, and his faith in the male-female relationship. Hilary Simpson relates Lawrence's increasing antifeminism to a hardening of antifeminist attitudes in external society. Judith Ruderman in *The Devouring Mother* links Lawrence's leadership ideal to a wish to withdraw from dependence on women.

2. Many critics pay little attention to the novel, regarding it as an immature failure. Michael Squires, however, in ch. 8 of *The Pastoral Novel: Studies in George Eliot, Thomas Hardy, and D. H. Lawrence* (Charlottesville: Univ. Press of Virginia, 1974) shows that it has positive value when read as a novel with roots in the pastoral tradition. Robert E. Gajdusek, "A Reading of The White Peacock," in *A D. H. Lawrence Miscellany*, ed. Harry T. Moore (Carbondale: Southern Illinois Univ. Press, 1959), 189, states that *The White Peacock* is closer to the truth of Lawrence's early emotional life than *Sons and Lovers*.

3. This phenomenon was noted when the novel first appeared, by an anonymous reviewer in the *Daily News* in Feb. 1911; see *D. H. Lawrence: The Critical Heritage*, ed. R.P. Draper (New York: Barnes & Noble, 1970), 41.

4. Klein, *Love, Guilt and Reparation*, 154–55; *Envy and Gratitude*, 280–81; Klein & Riviere, *Love, Hate, and Reparation*, 109–10. See also Freud's discussion of a masochistic fantasy in the 1919 paper, "A Child is Being Beaten."

5. Chodorow, *Reproduction of Mothering*, 173–77, 188–89; Kohut, *Analysis of the Self*, 145–47.

6. Lawrence's views about both feminist women and militant miners later became explicitly hostile. Here the hostility is embedded in a genuinely sympathetic attitude.

7. Lawrence, *Sons and Lovers* (Harmondsworth, Middlesex: Penguin Books, 1976), 285.

8. Lawrence, e.g., in Act II of *A Collier's Friday Night* in *The Complete Plays*, 499-500.

9. See Vladimir Propp, *Morphologie du Conte*, trans. Marguerite Derrida (Paris: Editions du Seuil, 1965), 106–7.

10. Howe, *Art of the Self*, 6.

11. The association between flowers and female sexuality is a central motif in Lawrence. See, for instance, Mark Spilka, *The Love Ethic of D. H. Lawrence* (Bloomington & London: Indiana Univ. Press, 1955), 43–59.

12. This episode has often been discussed: Faith Pullin, "Lawrence's Treatment of Women in *Sons and Lovers*," in *Lawrence and Women*, ed. Anne Smith (New York: Barnes & Noble Books, 1978), 56, recognizes it as the most "overtly misogynistic statement" in Lawrence's early work; Graham Hough, *The Dark Sun* (1956: rpt. New York: Octagon Books, 1973), 31, sees it as a representation of the "unanchored, unsatisfied, unliving woman" in Lawrence's fiction; Kristin Morrison, "Lawrence, Beardsley, Wilde: The White Peacock and Sexual Ambiguity," *Western Humanities Review* 30 (1976), 241–48, notes the ambivalent gender of the bird as used in the novel, with homosexual connotations for Cyril and Annable.

Chapter 4

1. Irene Tayler in "The Woman Scaly," 84–87, a sensitive reading of Blake, argues, however, that in the redeemed visionary state the divisions between men and women will vanish; Diana Hume George in "Is She Also the Divine Image? Feminine Form in the Art of William Blake" (*Centennial Review* 23 (1979), 129–140), and in *Blake and Freud*, while acknowledging all of the negatives in Blake's portrayal of women, contends, e.g. in *Blake and Freud*, 185–207, that Blake has a balanced and equitable view of women as social beings.

2. Susan Fox in "The Female as Metaphor" recognizes the subservient and sometimes negative function of women in Blake; Anne K. Mellor in "Blake's Portrayal of Women," *Blake: An Illustrated Quarterly* 16 (1982), 148–55, shows that Blake reflects patriarchal attitudes in his presentation of women.

3. Alicia Ostriker in "Desire Gratified and Ungratified: William Blake and Sexuality," *Blake: An Illustrated Quarterly* 16 (1982), 156–65, observes that there are four distinct attitudes toward sexuality and women in Blake, and that these indicate a true ambivalence on his part.

4. Webster, e.g., *Prophetic Psychology*, 271; "Blake, Women and Sexuality," 221–22. These roles assigned to women frequently change, proving the vanity of Blake's fantasy solution.

5. E.g., Irene Tayler in "The Woman Scaly." David Erdman in *Blake: Prophet Against Empire*, rev. ed. (Garden City, N.Y.: Anchor Books, 1969), 253–54 acknowledges the difficulties presented by "man-made allegories." Leopold Damrosch, *Symbol and Truth in Blake's Myth* (Princeton, N.J.: Princeton Univ. Press, 1980), 181–84, points out that the Emanation is "more than a metaphor," and describes it on p. 181 as "a sort of emotional storm center . . . in which some

of the most painful tensions of Blake's thought come together." Ostriker, 158–59, is one of those to make the point that the Emanations resemble the Jungian "anima." Damrosch, however, observes on p. 182 that Blake's women do not have the complementary "animus."

6. See David Erdman's editorial comment relating to p. 55 of the *Vala* manuscript, E833.

7. George in *Blake and Freud,* 189, suggests that Blake later attempted to soften and extend the limiting meaning of the Emanations, e.g., in *J*90, 1–2.

8. Klein, *Love, Guilt and Reparation*, 189–90, describes the "femininity phase" in the male child, where envy of the womb leads to fantasies of giving birth. This occurs at the anal-sadistic stage; the desired baby is equated with feces, and the child wishes to rob the mother.

9. Webster, in *Prophetic Psychology*, 161–64, discusses the *Book of Urizen* version as a fantasy of anal birth.

10. Webster, (ibid., 111) shows that the Shadowy Female is an object of Blake's anger both as a sexually unfaithful mother and as a depriving mother. Mellor, 148–49, also notes that Blake characteristically portrays women carrying out traditionally female tasks.

11. E.g., Klein, *Envy and Gratitide*, 144.

12. Klein, *Love, Guilt and Reparation*, 384, gives an example of an attempt to make a parent harmless by this device.

13. In Webster's discussion of this sequence, *Prophetic Psychology*, 212–14, she observes that in it there is a strong fear of being "drained" and weakened, a mother by her infant or a man sexually by a woman.

14. Jean H. Hagstrum in "Babylon Revisited, or the Story of Luvah and Vala" in *Blake's Sublime Allegory*, ed. Curran & Wittreich (Madison, Wis.,: Univ. of Wisconsin Press, 1973), 101–18, examines the relationship throughout the epics of Luvah and Vala as a study in "fallen love," and notes, 106–10, the figure of the phallic woman in Blake. However, he does not seek in Blake's own psyche a coherence for the many permutations in the figure and images.

15. Cettina Tramontano Magno and David V. Erdman, in their commentary on this page in William Blake, *The Four Zoas*, A Photographic Facsimile of the Manuscript with Commentary on the Illuminations (Lewisburg: Bucknell University Press, 1987) observe, 39, that the figures represent "four stages of metamorphoses" in the hybrid male-female form of primitive sexuality. Gallant, *Assimilation of Chaos*, 61, notes the universality of these images from a Jungian perspective; John E. Grant, "Visions in *Vala*" in Curran & Wittreich, 159–60, observes that they have parallels in the engraved works.

16. E.g., harpies, or the cannibalistic Russian witch Baba Yaga with bird features, mentioned by Propp, *Morphologie*, 106–7. Compare the castrating harpy figure in Lawrence.

17. Hagstrum, "Babylon Revisited," *Blake's Sublime Allegory*, ed. Curran & Wittreich, 101.

18. Webster, "Blake, Women and Sexuality," 210, 217.

19. Klein's central statement about envy, of the riches of the lost good object, is the "Envy and Gratitude" paper of 1957. See, e.g., *Envy and Gratitude*, 183–88.

20. Klein, *Love, Guilt and Reparation*, 220, 238.

21. Ibid., 219, 188.

22. See Freud's 1913 paper, "The Theme of the Three Caskets," *Standard Edition*, 12:291–301, where Freud interprets the motif of the three women, such as the Fates, in mythology and folklore, as a figure of death and of the inexorable control of the rhythms of nature.

23. Ibid., 294–96.

24. Mellor in "Blake's Portrayal of Women," 149–51, points out that women in Blake are depicted as engaging in the traditional female tasks.

25. Compare the image of the loaves in Lawrence's *Sons and Lovers*, 205–207, where the burning and burial of the loaves may reflect a wish both for the death of the mother and of another child.

26. It is generally acknowledged that Blake's concept of the Female Will is problematic, e.g., Erdman, *Prophet Against Empire*, 254. Recent critics tend to be divided on the issue: David Aers in "William Blake and the Dialectics of Sex" (*ELH* 44 (1977), 500–514) and "Blake: Sex, Society and Ideology"; Diana Hume George in *Blake and Freud* 190–201; and David Punter in "Blake, Trauma and the Female" (*New Literary History* 15 (1984), 475–90, see the Female Will as a defensive strategy adopted by women in a fallen world. I would agree rather with Susan Fox in "The Female as Metaphor" and Anne K. Mellor in "Blake's Portrayal of Women," who note a more fundamental antagonism towards women in Blake.

27. See ch. 1, 5–7.

28. See Storch, "Very Image of Our Conceptions," 267–70.

29. Klein, *Envy and Gratitude*, 34; Segal, 26–27.

30. Klein, e.g., *Envy and Gratitude*, 78–79.

31. Klein, *Love, Guilt and Reparation*, 250–52, 362–63.

32. Cf. Milner, *Hands of the Living God*, 382–84.

33. Compare Marguerite Beede Howe's comment, *Art of the Self*, 98, on the character of oedipal guilt feelings in Lawrence: "Repression and punishment are not associated with the stern father, but with the stern mother."

34. Klein, *Love, Guilt and Reparation*, 188–89, 214; Segal, 4.

35. Catherine Haigney in "Vala's Garden in Night the Ninth: Paradise Regained or Woman Bound," *Blake: An Illustrated Quarterly* 20 (1987), 116–24, argues also that the usual view of this scene as one of joyful innocence is erroneous; she sees the motif as a sequence of repetitive cyclic states in which the male dominates the female.

36. The cabinet and the threefold female are linked with Beulah: see, e.g., Hazard Adams, *William Blake: A Reading of the Shorter Poems* (Seattle: Univ. of Washington Press, 1963), 123–25. We note their correspondence with the weakening effect of Beulah upon the male.

37. Hazard Adams, 81–83, relates the opposing cycles of male and female development to Yeats's system, and says that it is the female's "perpetual assertion of apartness or selfhood" that keeps the cycles in motion.

38. Like the Emanations, Beulah was a later addition to *Vala*: a sense of persecution brings about a further polarized split into bad and good elements.

39. This fantasy seems to be an image of the monstrous hybrid form of the parents: Klein, *Envy and Gratitude*, 297–98; Segal, 107.

40. Erdman, *The Illuminated Blake* 378.

41. Ibid. It is often observed that Blake's ideal female figures may look male rather than female. Erdman comments that in the repainting of the faces in the E copy of plate 99 of *Jerusalem*, she appears more masculine, suggesting an allusion to the Prodigal Son motif. Mellor in "Blake's Portrayal of Women," 151–53, notes that Blake characteristically glorifies the male form and, in his visual art as well as in his poetry, subsumes the female under the male.

Chapter 5

1. Sandra Gilbert in "Potent Griselda: 'The Ladybird' and the Great Mother," in Balbert & Marcus, 130–161, gives a comprehensive study of the theme of matriarchal power in Lawrence at play in "The Ladybird" and other works; Ruderman in *Devouring Mother* investigates the male's fear of being devoured by the mother figure in Lawrence's work, and as reflected in others' comments upon him and his relationship with Frieda.

2. Simpson in *D. H. Lawrence and Feminism* gives an extensive acount of Lawrence's contact with the women's emancipation movement, especially 19–42.

3. Martin Green has shown the importance of this movement to Lawrence. He gives an account of Frieda's association with it, and Lawrence's knowledge of it through her; *Von Richthofen Sisters*, 73–85.

4. Anne Smith gives a perceptive study of the quality of Lawrence's relationships with women, especially Frieda, in "A New Adam and a New Eve—Lawrence and Women: A Biographical Overview," in *Lawrence and Women*, ed. Smith, 9–48.

5. Howe, *Art of the Self*, e.g., 18. The other pole of the emotional state is "engulfment." Howe also uses Erikson's parallel notion of the desire for merger & the fear of losing autonomy, 39. Gavriel Ben-Ephraim in *The Moon's Dominion: Narrative Dichotomy and Female Dominance in Lawrence's Earlier Novels* (Teaneck, N.J., London & Toronto: Assoc. Univ. Presses, 1981), argues that males in Lawrence feel overwhelmed by female power, which they both resist and wish to be absorbed by, e.g., 44, 223.

6. Dix, in *D. H. Lawrence and Women*, stresses Lawrence's sensitivity towards women and feminist concerns, e.g., 22–23.

7. Spilka, *Love Ethic*, 60–63, contends that the Freudian pattern is merely superimposed upon the narrative, and that the deeper emotional interest is the dualistic conflict between man and woman, which in turn is the true theme of the subsequent novels.

8. Hoffman notes in *Freudianism and the Literary Mind*, e.g. 151-55, that the influence of Freud upon *Sons and Lovers* was rather superficial, despite the response of his contemporaries.

9. E.g., in "Mourning and Melancholia," 1917.

10. This sequence in the novel vividly recalls a Kleinian play situation in which a child's behavior towards representative small figures yields up deep analytic meaning. It has been discussed several times. Grover Smith, Jr., in "The Doll-Burners: D. H. Lawrence and Louisa Alcott," *MLQ* 19 (1958), 28–32, points out the similarity between this episode and one in Alcott's *Little Men*, which Lawrence may have read, where a group of children burn a doll called Annabella in an act of sacrifice. Smith relates Paul's destruction of Arabella to rebellion against his mother and to the sexual "sacrifice" of Miriam. I would argue that whether or not Lawrence knew Alcott's version, the power of his own scene of doll-burning comes from personal sources. Daniel Dervin examines the incident at length in a Winnicottian study in "Play, Creativity and Matricide: The Implications of Lawrence's 'Smashed Doll' Episode," *Mosaic* 14 (1981), 81–94. He convincingly links the destruction of the doll with the child Paul's creation of a new and more assertive self.

11. In the 1927 paper "Criminal Tendencies in Normal Children," *Love, Guilt and Reparation*, 175, Klein describes a fantasy of two brothers acting as accomplices to kill and eat the mother.

12. Mark Spilka remarks that Paul suffers not from an oedipus complex but from a lack of male identity: "The *Sons and Lovers* Manuscript," in *D. H. Lawrence*, ed. Balbert and Marcus, 39–40. Faith Pullin comments in "Lawrence's Treatment of Women in *Sons and Lovers*," in *Lawrence and Women*, ed. Smith, 52, that the "true love" in the novel is that between Paul and his father.

13. I am grateful to Nora Foster Stovel for first pointing out to me this correspondence.

14. A loaf in a child's fantasy can also stand for a baby, i.e., here a hated rival. Bill Veeder, of the University of Chicago, and others have suggested that the word "swathed" reflects the meaning of the cognate "swaddled," therefore strengthening the sense of the baby as victim. I prefer to read "swathed" as "bandaged", conveying the notion of a mutilation that is covered up.

15. Lawrence, *Collier's Friday Night*, *Plays*, 508. The play was written between 1906 and 1909, and was never produced in Lawrence's lifetime.

16. Louis L. Martz in "Portrait of Miriam: A Study in the Design of *Sons*

and Lovers," *Imagined Worlds: Essays on Some English Novels and Novelists in Honour of John Butt*, ed. Maynard Mack and Ian Gregor (London: Methuen & Co. Ltd., 1968), 351, describes the narrative technique that Lawrence adopts in the novel in order to manage "the deep autobiographical problems that underlie the book," whereby Paul's point of view is set against both the action and the portrait of Miriam.

17. For a detailed discussion of the development from the concerns and imagery of *The Rainbow* to those of *Women in Love*, see Mark Kinkead-Weekes, "The Marble and the Statue, *Imagined Worlds*, ed. Mack and Gregor, 371–418; and "Eros and Metaphor: Sexual Relationship in the Fiction of Lawrence," *Lawrence and Women*, ed. Smith, 113; and also Nixon, *Lawrence's Politics*, e.g., 113–130.

18. See my discussion of the Female Will in Lawrence and Blake in ch. 1, 5–7.

19. However, Daniel Schneider in *D. H. Lawrence: The Artist as Psychologist* (Lawrence, Kansas: Univ. Press of Kansas, 1984), 59-67, gives a very coherent account of the schema, with the "spontaneous will" as the organizing principle.

20. Freud, notably in "Mourning and Melancholia," 1917.

21. Lawrence, *Psychoanalysis and the Unconscious* in *Fantasia of the Unconscious*, 229.

22. Lawrence, "Education of the People," in *Reflections on the Death of a Porcupine*, ed. Herbert, 126.

23. Lawrence, *Fantasia*, 109.

24. Howe, *Art of the Self*, 45–46, refers to the paradox of the womb in Lawrence, since it both gives birth to the self and threatens to annihilate it.

25. The meaning of Ursula's encounter with the horses, which causes her miscarriage, resists easy definition. The animals are often taken to symbolize a vital power which she must encounter in order to be born into a new self: Mark Kinkead-Weekes, "The Marble and the Statue," 409–10; Julian Moynahan, *The Deed of Life: the Novels and Tales of D. H. Lawrence* (Princeton, N.J.: Princeton Univ. Press, 1963), 66–69. Nixon, *Lawrence's Politics*, 91–100, sees the horses as female and associated with the mysteries of pregnancy and birth which link both women and men, e.g., Tom Brangwen, with universal forces.

26. Howe, *Art of the Self*, 48, states that Ursula is a vampire who sucks out Skrebensky's soul, and that through this act Lawrence exorcises the deadened social self and the dependent self.

27. Compare a version of the beaked phallic woman in Blake, in the sketches on p. 26 of the *Vala* manuscript, fig. 1.

28. Ben-Ephraim, *Moon's Dominion*, 209, describes this episode as a rejection of Hermione's culture and an escape into an "organic and flowering element."

29. Ballin, "Lawrence's *Women in Love*," 75, notes the similarity between Lawrence's negative treatment of feminine pity and Blake's.

30. This central Lawrencean symbol is often discussed: Kinkead-Weekes, "Eros and Metaphor," 111–12, considers that the reunified rose-form of the moon is

a marriage of opposites that leads beyond destruction to a mature vision of sex; Ben-Ephraim, *Moon's Dominion*, 222–25, sees the moon here, as throughout his study, as a dominant female principle against whom male aggression is fruitless.

31. Nixon, *Lawrence's Politics*, e.g., 122–130, 149–52. Her major thesis is that this dark sensuality is linked with suppressed homosexuality and right-wing politics.

32. Howe, *Art of the Self*, 65.

33. The attitude towards women in *St. Mawr* is shifting and difficult to define, and it has sometimes been read as a feminist work, e.g., Julian Moynahan, "Lawrence, Woman, and the Celtic Fringe," in *Lawrence and Women*, ed. A. Smith, 132–34. I would agree rather with Ruderman when she says in *Devouring Mother*, 139–41, that in the novel the weak male is despised, while Lou is left alone at the end to await the arrival of the "serpent-bird," the "long-deposed father."

Chapter 6

1. See my more extensive discussion of the effect of the relationship with Hayley in "The Spectrous Fiend Cast Out," 115–135.

2. Fox, *Blake's Milton*, 214, notes that in the poem females are "either passive or pernicious;" John Howard, *Blake's Milton: A Study in the Selfhood* (Cranbury, N.J. and London: Assoc. Univ. Presses, 1976), 174, finds that, apart from Satan and Urizen, the "principle factors of evil are female in *Milton*."

3. Webster, *Prophetic Psychology*, 256.

4. Ibid., 250-71; "Blake, Women and Sexuality," 221–23. Webster maintains that Blake's aggressive obsessions remain despite the positive feeling of the conclusions of *Milton* & *Jerusalem*. She is, of course, correct. I suggest, however, that the *fantasy* of male strength and of the benign female is in itself a kind of resolution, even though a fantasy. Furthermore, we find evidence in the three long epics of true *reparation*, which makes for a more positive permanent state.

5. See for example, Northrop Frye, *Fearful Symmetry* (1947; rpt. Boston: Beacon Press, 1962), 351–52; Fox, *Blake's Milton*, 66–67, 77.

6. Cf. Webster, *Prophetic Psychology*, 255. Damrosch, *Symbol and Truth*, 255, finds that the Seven Eyes are "rather abstract, and never fully dramatized."

7. Webster, *Prophetic Psychology*, 265–66.

8. Fox comments, *Blake's Milton*, 214, that Blake "does not say that all females are weak, but he does imply that all weakness is female." Of the attributes of Beulah specifically she goes on to say, "when you enter Beulah from Eden you are female; when, restored and strong, you return to mental strife, you are male."

9. See my more complete discussion of this poem in "The 'Spectrous Fiend' Cast Out," 126–132.

10. This is a traditional assumption, based in part upon l.49 of this poem, "Must my Wife live in my Sisters bane."

11. See Segal, *Introduction to Klein*, 75, 92-93; Klein & Riviere, *Love, Hate, and Reparation*, 107–10; Stuart, *New Phoenix Wings*, 53–95.

12. Erdman, *Illuminated Blake*, 253.

13. Kris, *Psychoanalytic Explorations in Art* (London: George Allen & Unwin, 1959) 298–301.

14. Webster, *Prophetic Psychology*, 259.

15. See my discussion in ch. 4, 74–75.

16. W. J. T. Mitchell, "Blake's Radical Comedy," *Blake's Sublime Allegory*, ed. Curran and Wittreich, 293 & 300, refers to the redemptive effects of the female imagination; Howard, *Blake's Milton*, 252–54, sees her as "revealed religion," "divine revelation," and "eternal truth," while still subservient to Milton.

17. W. J. T. Mitchell, "Style and Iconography in the Illustrations of Blake's *Milton*," *Blake Studies* 6 (1973), 64, notes, that *Milton* is "primarily a poem about a brotherhood of prophets."

18. See my discussion of the themes of male bonding and homoeroticism in these two illustrations in "The 'Spectrous Fiend' Cast Out," 133–34.

19. Erdman points this out in his commentary, *Illuminated Blake*, 263.

20. W. J. T. Mitchell, "Style and Iconography," 66–68, notes the homoerotic implications in the conjunctions of the pairs of figures in these two plates. In Webster's discussion of these illustrations, *Prophetic Psychology*, 261–62, she asserts that the homosexuality overlays a deeper fantasy of idealized union, and cites clinical examples from Heinz Kohut in which males revive "infantile omnipotence" as a result of sexual merger.

21. Cf. Ronald L. Grimes, "Time and Space in Blake's Major Prophecies," *Blake's Sublime Allegory*, ed. Curran and Wittreich, 76–77.

22. Erdman, E50; *VDA*7, 23–26. Webster also notes the parallel between these two sequences in *Prophetic Psychology*, 267, and in "Blake, Women and Sexuality," 221.

23. Irene Tayler in "Say first! What Mov'd Blake?", *Blake's Sublime Allegory*, ed. Curran and Wittreich, 233–58, argues that this maiden is Blake's revised version of the Lady in *Comus*, whom Milton erroneously presents as a cold virgin (254–58).

24. These precious stones are associated with the jewels of the Tree of Knowledge, signifying sexual truth, and with the jewels on Blake's sandal after Los's penetration of his left foot.

25. Webster recalls in *Prophetic Psychology*, 267, the traditional symbolism of the lark as a phallus, and sees the episode of the lark's song as the omnipotent infant basking in the parents' admiration.

Chapter 7

1. The mythic significance of this pattern in the novel has been noted: Jascha Kessler, "Descent in Darkness: The Myth of the Plumed Serpent," in *A D. H.*

Lawrence Miscellany, ed. Harry Moore, 239–61; John B. Vickery, *Myths and Texts: Strategies of Incorporation and Displacement* (Baton Rouge & London: Louisiana State Univ. Press, 1983), 102–31.

2. Webster, *Prophetic Psychology*, 257.

3. Howe, *Art of the Self*, 116–18, discusses the star image in the two novels, suggesting that the motif is similar in the two cases, and that in both central relationships the women, Ursula and Kate, are subjected to the man. As I have argued, however, the emotional configuration is quite distinct in the two representations, and the need to subject the woman in *The Plumed Serpent*, almost achieved in fantasy, is of a different order.

4. For studies of Lawrence's travels in Mexico and the correspondences between his own experience and those recounted in the novel, see L. D. Clark, *The Dark Night of the Body: D. H. Lawrence's The Plumed Serpent* (Austin: Univ. of Texas Press, 1964); and Charles Rossman, "D. H. Lawrence and Mexico," in *D. H. Lawrence*, ed. Balbert and Marcus, 180–209.

5. See Delany's account of the bitterness of Lawrence's life from 1915 to 1918, following the philistine rejection of *The Rainbow* and including the erosion of his friendship with Russell and Murry, in *D. H. Lawrence's Nightmare*. Others, notably Simpson and Nixon, have seen this painful period of Lawrence's life as the source of his exaggerated philosophy of masculinity.

6. Ross Parmenter discusses the relationship between these works and *The Plumed Serpent* in *Lawrence in Oaxaca: A Quest for the Novelist in Mexico*, (Salt Lake City: Peregrine Smith Books, 1984), 223–28. "None of That," although it has obvious affinities with the novel, is less often discussed in association with it.

7. Dervin, *A "Strange Sapience,"* 138, refers to Lou as an "eternal virgin" who is the chaste mother reborn.

8. Howe notes in *Art of the Self*, 112, that the protagonist of "The Woman Who Rode Away" is sacrificed so that the men "might win away her mana."

9. Lawrence, *St. Mawr and Other Stories*, 184.

10. Charles Rossman, "Lawrence and Mexico" in *D. H. Lawrence*, ed. Balbert and Marcus, 193, comments that the bullfight, to which Kate and Lawrence reacted with disgust, is "a synecdoche for the whole of Mexico City and, indeed, for all of postrevolutionary Mexico that tries to modernize itself."

11. Lawrence, *The Complete Short Stories*, 3:712.

12. Nixon, *Lawrence's Politics*, see especially 45–51, 61–63, 81–85.

13. Ibid., 136–37, 229–34.

14. Ibid., 62–63.

15. We note that the expression of a positive masculinity can often contain an element of these apparently disgusting creatures, such as the ratlike appearance of certain men, e.g., Lewis of *St. Mawr*, and note, too, that darkness and the earth are generally associated with acclaimed values. Dervin, in *A "Strange Sapience,"*

sees these images as "projections of unacceptable drives and wishes, which block a line of sexual development," 173, and says that the dark gods replace the protective "feminine skein around the self," 172.

16. Ruderman in her perceptive reading of *The Plumed Serpent* in "Rekindling the Father Spark: Lawrence's Ideal of Leadership, "*D. H. Lawrence Review*, 13 (1980), 248–50, discusses the madonna image in the novel, equating Kate with Carlota. I suggest however that there is a difference in attitude towards the two women, since Kate's benign power can be subsumed into the male scheme.

17. Dervin, *A "Strange Sapience,"* 33, refers to the ideal society in the novel as a kind of family romance fulfillment, and as a blueprint for Rananim, Lawrence's vision of the perfect community.

18. Howe states in *Art of the Self*, 131, that Ramon is actually dying. However, this does not seem to be supported by the rest of the narrative.

19. In *Lady Chatterley's Lover*, where an ideal relationship is projected, loving sympathy is expressed through the traditional expression of sympathy felt reciprocally in the bowels.

20. Cavitch, *D. H. Lawrence and the New World* (New York: Oxford Univ. Press, 1969), 188.

21. Ruderman, "Rekindling the 'Father-Spark,'" *D. H. Lawrence Review*, 251–53.

22. Dervin, *A "Strange Sapience,"* 160.

23. Cf. Blake's figure of red Orc, who is an embodiment of fire and energy, yet is ultimately evanescent and insubstantial.

24. Kohut, *Analysis of the Self*, 106–8, discusses the manner in which the child attempts to save primary narcissism by concentrating perfection and power upon the self, here called the grandiose self.

25. Ibid., 146. Kohut, states that "behind the imagery concerning the relationship of a boy's grandiose self with a depreciated father . . . lies regularly the deeper imago of the dangerous, powerful rival-parent, and, as stated before, the defensive oedipal narcissism is principally maintained to buttress the denial of castration anxiety."

Chapter 8

1. Martin Butlin, *William Blake* (London: Tate Gallery, 1978), 138; David Bindman, *Blake as an Artist* (Oxford: Phaidon, 1977), 205.

2. Cf. Jean Hagstrum, *William Blake: Poet and Painter* (Chicago & London: University of Chicago Press, 1964), 51–57.

3. Bindman, *Blake as Artist*, 205. He believes, however, that Palmer misconstrued the spiritual significance of landscape in Blake.

4. Ibid., 204. Bindman notes that Blake is "particularly sensitive to the implications of artistic crisis in Colinet's melancholy."

5. Ibid., 208.

6. E.g., Bindman, *Blake as Artist*, 212, Butlin, *Blake*, 98. Blunt, *Art of Blake*, 85–86, states that the designs have a quality of "universality" because they no longer seem eccentric.

7. Milner in "Psychoanalyis and Art," *Psychoanalysis and Contemporary Thought*," ed. John D. Sutherland (London: Hogarth Press, 1958), 86–87, 94–95.

8. Ibid., 94.

9. Ibid., 86–87.

10. Bo Lindberg, *William Blake's Illustrations to The Book of Job* (Abo, Finland: Abo Akademi, 1973), 343; and Damrosch, *Symbol and Truth*, 334, refer to the apocryphal "Testament of Job," known to Blake, in which, like Milton, Job dictated his work to his daughters.

11. Lindberg, *Illustrations to Job*, 343, notes that in the "Testament of Job" the stories and the musical instruments themselves are the inheritance that Job gives to his daughters.

12. Derek Britton, *Lady Chatterley: The Making of the Novel* (London: Unwin Hyman, 1988), gives a detailed account of that final visit to England and of its bearing upon the novel. In *The Creation of Lady Chatterley's Lover* (Baltimore & London: Johns Hopkins University Press: 1983), Michael Squires studies closely the successive stages of Lawrence's work on the manuscript.

13. Lawrence, "Return to Bestwood," *Phoenix II*, 257.

14. Britton, *Lady Chatterley*, 49–51, suggests that Parkin reflects Lawrence's awareness of his own feminine aspect, but that the rage occasioned by his increasing bad health made him turn away from self-knowledge towards the compensatory maleness of Mellors.

15. See for instance Edward Nehls, ed., *D. H. Lawrence: A Composite Biography* (Madison: Univ. of Wisconsin Press, 1957–59), 2:126.

16. As commentators have often observed, e.g., Ruderman, *Devouring Mother*, 164.

17. Lawrence's restoration of tender and loving feelings to sex has had a profound effect on many readers, e.g., Squires, *Creation of Lady Chatterley*, 15–16.

18. Ibid., 58ff. Britton, *Lady Chatterley*, 56, notes Frieda's comment that Lawrence put a great deal of himself into Clifford Chatterley, by which he believes she meant his personal experience.

19. Dervin states that in the novel a final resolution of oedipal conflicts is achieved, e.g., *A "Strange Sapience*," 35 & 146.

References

Primary Sources

WILLIAM BLAKE

The Complete Poetry and Prose of William Blake. Edited by David V. Erdman. Newly Revised Edition. Berkeley & Los Angeles: Univ. of California Press, 1982.

The Four Zoas. A Photographic Facsimile of the Manuscript with Commentary on the Illuminations by Cettina Tramontano Magno and David V. Erdman. Lewisburg: Bucknell Univ. Press; London and Toronto: Associated Univ. Presses, 1987.

The Illuminated Blake. Annotated by David V. Erdman. Garden City, N.Y.: Anchor Press, Doubleday, 1974.

D.H. LAWRENCE

The Complete Plays. New York: Viking Press, 1966.

The Complete Poems of D. H. Lawrence. Edited by Vivian de Sola Pinto and Warren Roberts. 2 vols. New York: Viking Press, 1964.

The Complete Short Stories. 3 vols. Harmondsworth, Middlesex: Penguin Books, 1976.

Fantasia of the Unconscious, & Psychoanalysis and the Unconscious. Harmondsworth, Middlesex: Penguin Books, 1977.

Kangaroo. Harmondsworth, Middlesex: Penguin Books, 1950.

Lady Chatterley's Lover. Harmondsworth, Middlesex: Penguin Books, 1960.

The Letters of D. H. Lawrence. General editor, James T. Boulton. Vols. 1–4. Cambridge & New York: Cambridge Univ. Press, 1979–1987.

Phoenix: The Posthumous Papers of D. H. Lawrence, 1936. Edited by Edward D. McDonald. Harmondsworth, Middlesex: Penguin Books, 1978.

Phoenix II: Uncollected, Unpublished, and Other Prose Works. Edited by Warren Roberts and Harry T. Moore. Harmondsworth, Middlesex: Penguin Books, 1978.

The Plumed Serpent. Edited by L. D. Clark. Cambridge & New York: Cambridge Univ. Press, 1987.

The Rainbow. Edited by Mark Kinkead-Weeks. Cambridge & New York: Cambridge Univ. Press, 1989.

Reflections on the Death of a Porcupine. Edited by Michael Herbert. Cambridge, London & New York: Cambridge University Press, 1988.

St. Mawr and Other Stories. Edited by Brian Finney. Cambridge & New York: Cambridge Univ. Press, 1983.

Sons and Lovers. Harmondsworth, Middlesex: Penguin Books, 1976.

Studies in Classic American Literature. New York: Viking Press, 1961.

The White Peacock. Edited by Andrew Robertson. Cambridge, London & New York: Cambridge Univ. Press, 1983.

Women in Love. Edited by David Farmer, Lindeth Vasey & John Worthen. Cambridge, London & New York: Cambridge Univ. Press, 1987.

Where available, the volumes of the Cambridge Edition of the Letters & Works of D. H. Lawrence, General editors James T. Boulton and Warren Roberts, have been used.

Secondary Sources

ON WILLIAM BLAKE

Adams, Hazard. *William Blake: A Reading of the Shorter Poems*. Seattle: Univ. of Washington Press, 1963.

Aers, David. "William Blake and the Dialectics of Sex." *ELH* 44(1977): 500–514.

Bentley, G. E., Jr. *Blake Records*. Oxford: Clarendon Press, 1969.

Bindman, David. *Blake as an Artist*. Oxford: Phaidon, 1977.

Blunt, Anthony. *The Art of William Blake*. New York: Columbia Univ. Press, 1959.

Butlin, Martin. *William Blake*. London: Tate Gallery, 1978.

Curran, Stuart and Joseph Anthony Wittreich, eds. *Blake's Sublime Allegory*. Madison: Univ. of Wisconsin Press, 1973.

Damrosch, Leopold, Jr. *Symbol and Truth in Blake's Myth*. Princeton, N.J.: Princeton Univ. Press, 1980.

Erdman, David V. *Blake: Prophet Against Empire*. Garden City, N.Y.: Doubleday, 1969.

Fox, Susan. "The Female as Metaphor in Blake's Poetry." *Critical Inquiry* (1977): 507–19.

———. *Poetic Form in Blake's Milton*. Princeton, N.J.: Princeton Univ. Press, 1976.

Frye, Northrop. *Fearful Symmetry*. 1947. Rpt. Boston: Beacon Press, 1962.

Gallant, Christine. *Blake's Assimilation of Chaos*. Princeton, N.J.: Princeton Univ. Press, 1978.

George, Diana Hume. *Blake and Freud*. Ithaca & London: Cornell Univ. Press, 1980.

Gilchrist, Alexander. *Life of William Blake*. 2 vols. London & Cambridge: Macmillan & Co., 1863.

Grimes, Ronald L. "Time and Space in Blake's Major Prophecies." In Curran and Wittreich. 59–81.

Hagstrum, Jean H. "Babylon Revisited, or the Story of Luvah and Vala." In Curran and Wittreich. 101–18.

———. *William Blake: Poet and Painter*. Chicago & London: Univ. of Chicago Press, 1964.

Haigney, Catherine. "Vala's Garden in Night the Ninth: Paradise Regained or Woman Bound." *Blake: An Illustrated Quarterly* 20(1987): 116–24.

Hirsch, E.D., Jr. *Innocence and Experience: An Introduction to Blake*. New Haven & London: Yale Univ. Press, 1964.

Howard, John. *Blake's Milton: A Study in the Selfhood*. Cranbury, N.J. and London: Associated Univ. Presses, 1976.

Keynes, Geoffrey, ed. *The Illustrations of William Blake for Thorton's Virgil with the First Eclogue & the Imitation by Ambrose Philips*. London: Nonesuch Press, 1937.

Lindberg, Bo. *William Blake's Illustrations to The Book of Job*. Abo, Finland: Abo Akademi, 1973.

Majdiak, Daniel and Brian Wilkie. "Blake and Freud: Poetry and Depth Psychology." *Journal of Aesthetic Education* 6(1972): 87–98.

Mellor, Anne K. "Blake's Portrayal of Women." *Blake: An Illustrated Quarterly* 16(1982): 148–55.

Milner, Marion. "Psycho-Analysis and Art." In *Psychoanalysis and Contemporary Thought*. Edited by John D. Sutherland. London: Hogarth Press, 1958. 77–101.

Mitchell, W. J. T. "Blake's Radical Comedy: Dramatic Structure as meaning in *Milton*." In Curran and Wittreich. 281–307.

———. "Style and Iconography in the Illustrations of Blake's *Milton*." *Blake Studies* 6 (1973): 47–71.

Murry, John Middleton. *William Blake*. London: Jonathan Cape, 1933.

Ostriker, Alicia. "Desire Gratified and Ungratified: William Blake and Sexuality." *Blake: An Illustrated Quarterly* 16(1982): 156–65.

Punter, David. "Blake, Trauma and the Female." *New Literary History* 15(1984): 475–90.

Schorer, Mark. *William Blake: The Politics of Vision*. 1946. Rpt. New York: Vintage Books, 1959.

Storch, Margaret. "Blake and Women: 'Nature's Cruel Holiness.'" *American Imago* 38(1981): 221–46.

———. "The 'Spectrous Fiend' Cast Out: Blake's Crisis at Felpham." *MLQ* 44 (1983): 115–35.

———. "The Very Image of our Conceptions: Blake's Allegory and the Role of the Creative Poet." *Bulletin of Research in the Humanities* 83(1980): 262–79.

Tayler, Irene. "The Woman Scaly." *Bulletin of the Mid West Modern Language Association* 6(1973): 74–87.

———. "Say First! What Mov'd Blake? Blake's *Comus* Designs and Milton." In Curran and Wittreich. 233–58.

Thornton, Robert John. *The Pastorals of Virgil*. 3rd ed. London, 1821.

Ward, Aileen. "Canterbury Revisited: The Blake-Cromek Controversy." *Blake: An Illustrated Quarterly* 22(1988): 80–92.

Webster, Brenda. *Blake's Prophetic Psychology*. Athens: Univ. of Georgia Press, 1983.

———. "Blake, Women, and Sexuality." In *Critical Paths: Blake and the Argument of Method*. Edited by Dan Miller, Mark Bracher, and Donald Ault. Durham & London: Duke Univ. Press, 1987. 204–24.

ON WILLIAM BLAKE AND D.H. LAWRENCE

Ballin, Michael G. "D. H. Lawrence and William Blake: A Comparative and Critical Study." Diss. Univ. of Toronto, 1972.

———. "D. H. Lawrence's Esotericism: D. H. Lawrence and William Blake in *Women in Love*." In *D. H. Lawrence's Women in Love: Contexts and Criticism*. Edited by Michael Ballin. Waterloo, Ont.: Wilfred Laurier Univ., n.d.). 70–87.

Colmer, John "Lawrence and Blake." In *D. H. Lawrence and Tradition*. Edited by Jeffrey Myers. Amherst: Univ. of Massachusetts Press, 1985. 9–20.

Glazer, Myra. "Why the Sons of God Want the Daughters of Men: On William Blake and D. H. Lawrence." In *William Blake and the Moderns*. Edited by Robert J. Bertolf and Annette S. Levitt. Albany: State Univ. of New York Press, 1982. 164–85.

Leavis, F. R. *For Continuity*. Cambridge: Minority Press, 1933.

Pinto, Vivian de Sola. "William Blake and D. H. Lawrence." In *Essays Presented to S. Foster Damon*. Edited by Alvin H. Rosenfield. Providence, R.I.: Brown Univ. Press, 1969. 84–106.

Stavrou, Constantine N. "William Blake and D. H. Lawrence." *Univ. of Kansas City Review* 22(1956): 235–40.

ON D.H. LAWRENCE

Ben-Ephraim, Gavriel. *The Moon's Dominion: Narrative Dichotomy and Female Dominance in Lawrence's Earlier Novels*. Teaneck, N.J., London & Toronto: Associated Univ. Presses, 1981.

Balbert, Peter. *D. H. Lawrence and the Phallic Imagination: Essays on Sexual Identity and Feminist Misreading*. New York: St. Martin's Press, 1989.

——— and Philip L. Marcus, eds. *D. H. Lawrence: A Centenary Consideration*. Ithaca & London: Cornell Univ. Press, 1985.

Blanchard, Lydia. "Love and Power: a Reconsideration of Sexual Politics in D. H. Lawrence." *Modern Fiction Studies* 21 (1975): 431–43.

Britton, Derek. *Lady Chatterley: The Making of the Novel*. London: Unwin Hyman, 1988.

Cavitch, David. *D. H. Lawrence and the New World*. New York: Oxford Univ. Press, 1969.

Chambers, Jessie. "The Collected Letters of Jessie Chambers." Edited by George J. Zytaruk. *The D.H. Lawrence Review* 12(1979), no. 1, 2.

———. *D. H. Lawrence: A Personal Record by E. T.* Edited by J. D. Chambers, 2nd ed. London: Frank Cass & Co. Ltd., 1965.

Clark, L. D. *The Dark Night of The Body: D. H. Lawrence's The Plumed Serpent*. Austin: Univ. of Texas Press, 1964.

Clarke, Colin. *River of Dissolution: D.H. Lawrence & English Romanticism*. London: Routledge & Kegan Paul, 1969.

Delany, Paul. *D. H. Lawrence's Nightmare: The Writer and His Circle in the Years of the Great War*. New York: Basic Books, 1978.

Dervin, Daniel. *A "Strange Sapience": The Creative Imagination of D.H. Lawrence*. Amherst: Univ. of Massachusetts Press, 1984.

———. "Play, Creativity and Matricide: The Implications of Lawrence's 'Smashed Doll' Episode." *Mosaic* 14 (1981): 81–94.

Delavenay, Emile. *D. H. Lawrence and Edward Carpenter*. New York: Taplinger, 1971.

———. *D. H. Lawrence: The Man and His Work, The Formative Years, 1885–1919*. Carbondale: Southern Illinois Univ. Press, 1972.

Dix, Carol. *D. H. Lawrence and Women*. Totowa, N.J.: Rowman & Littlefield, 1980.

Gajdusek, Robert E. "A Reading of the White Peacock." *A D. H. Lawrence Miscellany*. Edited by Harry T. Moore. Carbondale, Ill.: Southern Illinois Univ. Press, 1959. 188–203.

Gilbert, Sandra. "Potent Griselda: 'The Ladybird' and the Great Mother." In Balbert and Marcus. 130–61.

Green, Martin. *The von Richthofen Sisters: The Triumphant and the Tragic Modes of Love*. New York: Basic Books, 1974.

Hough, Graham. *The Dark Sun: A Study of D. H. Lawrence.* 1965. Rpt. New York: Octagon Books, 1973.

Howe, Marguerite Beede. *The Art of the Self in D. H. Lawrence*. Athens, Ohio: Ohio Univ. Press, 1977.

Kessler, Jascha. "Descent in Darkness: The Myth of the Plumed Serpent." In *A D. H. Lawrence Miscellany*. Edited by Harry T. Moore. Carbondale, Ill.: Southern Illinois Univ. Press, 1959. 239–61.

Kinkead-Weekes, Mark. "Eros and Metaphor: Sexual Relationship in the Fiction of Lawrence." In *Lawrence and Women*. Edited by Anne Smith. 101–21.

———. "The Marble and the Statue: The Exploratory Imagination of D. H. Lawrence." In Mack and Gregor. 371–418.

Lindsay, Jack. "The Impact of Modernism on Lawrence." In *Paintings of D. H. Lawrence.* Edited by Mervyn Levy. London: Cory, Adams & Mackay, 1964. 35–53.

Litz, A. Walton. "Lawrence, Pound, and Early Modernism." In Balbert and Marcus. 15-28.

Mack, Maynard and Ian Gregor, eds. *Imagined Worlds: Essays on Some English Novels and Novelists in Honour of John Butt*. London. Methuen & Co. Ltd., 1968.

Martz, Louis L. "Portrait of Miriam: a Study in the Design of *Sons and Lovers*." In Mack and Gregor. 343–69.

Moore, Harry T. *The Priest of Love: A Life of D. H. Lawrence*. Rev. ed. New York: Farrar, Straus & Giroux, 1974.

Morrison, Kristin. "Lawrence, Beardsley, Wilde: The White Peacock and Sexual Ambiguity." *Western Humanities Review* 30(1976): 241–48.

Moynahan, Julian. *The Deed of Life: The Novels and Tales of D. H. Lawrence*. Princeton: Princeton Univ. Press, 1963.

———. "Lawrence, Woman and the Celtic Fringe." In *Lawrence and Women*. Edited by Anne Smith. 122–35.

Nehls, Edward, ed. *D. H. Lawrence: A Composite Biography*. 3 vols. Madison: Univ. of Wisconsin Press, 1957–59.

Nixon, Cornelia. *Lawrence's Leadership Politics and the Turn Against Women*. Berkeley, Los Angeles & London: Univ. of Calif. Press, 1986.

Parmenter, Ross. *Lawrence in Oaxaca: A Quest for the Novelist in Mexico*. Salt Lake City: Peregrine Smith Books, 1984.

Pullin, Faith. "Lawrence's Treatment of Women in *Sons and Lovers*". In *Lawrence and Women*. Edited by Anne Smith. 49–74.

Rossman, Charles. "You are the Call and I am the Answer." *D. H. Lawrence Review* 8(1975): 255–324.

———. "D. H. Lawrence and Mexico." In Balbert and Marcus. 180–209.

Ruderman, Judith. *D. H. Lawrence and the Devouring Mother*. Durham, N.C.: Duke Univ. Press, 1984.

———. "Rekindling the Father Spark: Lawrence's Ideal of Leadership." *D. H. Lawrence Review* 13(1980): 248–50.

Schneider, Daniel. *D. H. Lawrence: The Artist as Psychologist.* Lawrence, Kans.: Univ. Press of Kansas, 1984.

Simpson, Hilary. *D. H. Lawrence and Feminism*. Illinois: Northern Ilinois Univ. Press, 1982.

Smith, Anne, ed. *Lawrence and Women*. New York: Barnes & Noble Books, 1978.

Smith, Grover, Jr. "The Doll-Burners: D. H. Lawrence and Louisa Alcott." *MLN* 19(1958): 28–32.

Spilka, Mark. "For Mark Schorer with Combative Love: The *Sons and Lovers* Manuscript." In Balbert and Marcus. 29–44.

———. *The Love Ethic of D. H. Lawrence*. Bloomington & London: Indiana Univ. Press, 1955.

Squires, Michael. *The Creation of Lady Chatterley's Lover.* Baltimore & London: Johns Hopkins Univ. Press, 1983.

———. *The Pastoral Novel: Studies in George Eliot, Thomas Hardy, and D. H. Lawrence.* Charlottesville: Univ. Press of Virginia, 1974.

Weiner, Gary A. "Lawrence's Little Girl Lost." *The D. H. Lawrence Review* 19 (1987): 243–53.

Weiss, Daniel. *Oedipus in Nottingham: D. H. Lawrence.* Seattle: Univ. of Washington Press, 1962.

THEORETICAL AND GENERAL REFERENCES

Chodorow, Nancy. *The Reproduction of Mothering: Psychoanalysis and the Sociology of Gender.* Berkeley, Los Angeles & London: Univ. of California Press, 1978.

Davie, Donald. *A Gathered Church: The Literature of the English Dissenting Interest, 1700–1930*. New York: Oxford Univ. Press, 1978.

Freud, Sigmund. *The Standard Edition of the Complete Psychological Works*. Trans. & ed. James Strachey et al. 24 vols. London: The Hogarth Press & The Institute of Psychoanalysis, 1953–74.

Gallop, Jane. *The Daughter's Seduction: Feminism and Psychoanalysis*. Ithaca, N.Y.: Cornell Univ. Press, 1982.

Gilbert, Sandra M. and Susan Gubar. *No Man's Land: The Place of the Woman Writer in the Twentieth Century*, Vol. 1: *The War of the Words*. New Haven & London: Yale Univ. Press, 1987.

Hoffman, Frederick J. *Freudianism and the Literary Mind*. 1945. Rpt. New York: Grove Press, 1959.

Huxley, Aldous. *Point Counter Point*. New York: Harper & Row, 1928.

Jaffe, Daniel S. "The Masculine Envy of Woman's Procreative Function." *Journal of the American Psychonanalytic Association* 16(1968): 521–48.

Klein, Melanie. *Envy and Gratitude & Other Works, 1946–63*. New York: Delacorte Press/Seymour Lawrence, 1975.

———. *Love, Guilt and Reparation & Other Works, 1921–45*. New York: Delacorte Press/Seymour Lawrence, 1975.

——— and Joan Riviere. *Love, Hate, and Reparation*. New York: W. W. Norton, 1964.

Kohut, Heinz. *The Analysis of the Self*. New York: International Universities Press, 1971.

Kris, Ernst. *Psychoanalytic Explorations in Art*. London: George Allen & Unwin, 1959.

Layton, Lynn and Barbara Ann Schapiro, eds. *Narcissism and the Text: Studies in Literature and the Psychology of Self*. New York & London: New York Univ. Press, 1986.

Millett, Kate. *Sexual Politics*. Garden City, N.Y.: Doubleday & Co., 1970.

Milner, Marion. *The Hands of the Living God: An Account of a Psychoanalytic Treatment*. New York: International Universities Press, 1969.

Mitchell, Juliet. *Psychoanalysis and Feminism: Freud, Reich, Laing and Women*. New York: Vintage Books, 1975.

Propp, Vladimir. *Morphologie du Conte*. Trans. Marguerite Derrida. Paris: Editions du Seuil, 1965.

Segal, Hanna. *Introduction to the Work of Melanie Klein*, 2nd ed. New York: Basic Books, 1974.

Stuart, Simon. *New Phoenix Wings: Reparation in Literature*. London: Routledge & Kegan Paul, 1979.

Theweleit, Klaus. *Male Fantasies*, Vol. 1. *Women, Floods, Bodies, History*. Minneapolis: Univ. of Minnesota Press, 1987.

Thompson, E. P. *The Making of the English Working Class*. Harmondsworth, Middlesex: Penguin Books, 1968.

Vickery, John B. *Myths and Texts: Strategies of Incorporation and Displacement*. Baton Rouge & London: Louisiana State Univ. Press, 1983.

Winnicott, D. W. *The Maturational Processes and the Facilitating Environment: Studies in the Theory of Emotional Development*. New York: International Universities Press, 1965.

———. *Playing and Reality*. London: Tavistock Publications, 1971.

Wolf, Howard R. "British Fathers and Sons, 1773-1913: From Filial Submissiveness to Creativity." *Psychoanalytic Review* 52(1965): 53–70.

Zaretsky, Eli. *Capitalism, The Family and Personal Life*. New York: Harper Colophon, 1976.

Index

Sons and Adversaries was designed by Dariel Mayer, composed by Lithocraft, Inc., and printed and bound by BookCrafters, Inc. The book is set in Janson and printed on 50-lb Glatfelter Natural.